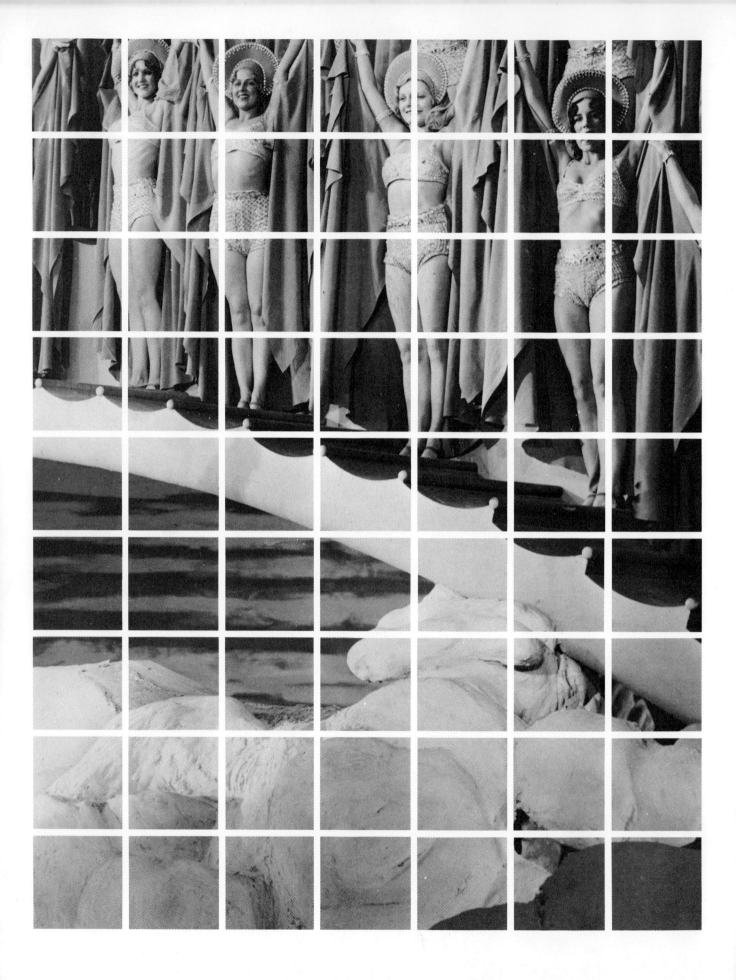

IT'S ONLY A MOVIE

By Clark McKowen

and William Sparke

Designed by Mel Byars

Prentice-Hall, Inc., Englewood Cliffs, New Jersey

C13-509208-6
P13-509190-X

Library of Congress Catalog Card Number: 70-149081
Printed in the United States of America
Current Printing (last number):
10 9 8 7 6 5 4 3 2 1

Prentice-Hall International, Inc. London
Prentice-Hall of Australia, Pty. Ltd. Sydney
Prentice-Hall of Canada, Ltd. Toronto
Prentice-Hall of India Private Limited New Delhi
Prentice-Hall of Japan, Inc. Tokyo

Credits for text and pictures are listed on page 187.

To Ruth.

1637212

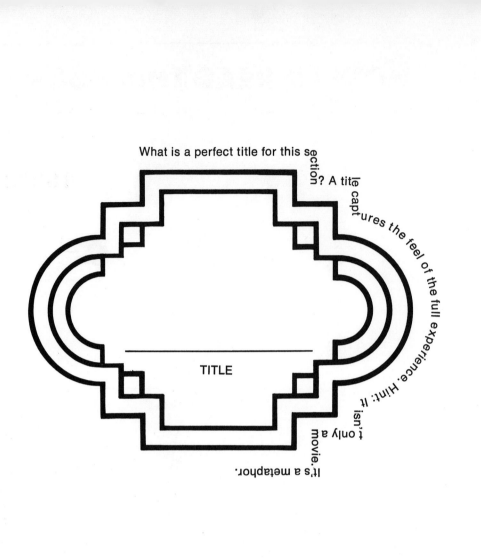

What is a perfect title for this section? A title captures the feel of the full experience. Hint: It isn't only a movie. It's a metaphor.

_____

TITLE

Explore each others' metaphors.
It isn't only a metaphor. It's an angle of vision.

AN EVENING

How much better it is to
Have seen the films only, where
The lean sergeant in the two-day
Beard says, "Let's get out of
Here!" and runs in a zig-zag
Across the field of crossfire, and,
Except for dropping into a
Pothole here and there, makes
It; where only the naive
Kid (the one who prays nights)
And the gruff-talking, soft-hearted
Bum get killed, and no
One else gets killed; where the
Generals and the folks
At home and the statesmen are
All good, and the Lord is all
Good; and, afterwards, on the summer
Evening reconnaissance, there are no
Dead in the avenues, only the traffic
Cop is armed, the sounds going
Off like bombs all around are
Shrapnel-less, and the lights that
Flicker over the city do
Not light the new objectives: the
Bright, shifting eyes behind the
Piled rubble, and the coils of
Barbed wire strung across tomorrow.

James Crenner, *The Aging Ghost.*

AT THE MOVIES

A

Q

What would you expect
from a film course?

Well, I'd like to be a little more
perceptive. I'd like to appreciate
the underlying innuendos that aren't
obvious. Sometimes I think you either
have it or you don't. I've come a
long way over the last few years simply
by going to a lot of movies and coming
home furious because I missed so much
and knew I was missing something. Now
I see the same things and enjoy them
thoroughly. I take them for granted.
I don't even say, "Ah, there's a flashback, but they're not playing flashback music." How do I know it's a
flashback without the music?

You've caught on to the
techniques of the medium.
They're part of your equipment.

Yes. For example, in *King of Hearts*
even though the situation was logically
absurd, I felt myself going with it. I
think you have to love movies so much
to begin with that you're willing to
roll with those things.

But you don't want clichés
either.

Right. You have to keep
a certain amount of skepticism—
maybe not as much as Pauline
Kael, but they do have to
convince you.

You don't want to accept second-
rate material as though it were
great.

Yes. And I guess the first thing you ought
to learn is how to get the right illusion,
right in the first few minutes of the movie.

4

HITCHCOCK

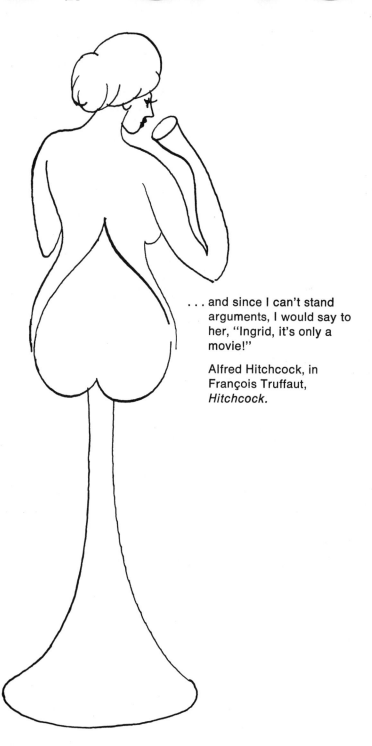

. . . and since I can't stand arguments, I would say to her, "Ingrid, it's only a movie!"

Alfred Hitchcock, in François Truffaut, *Hitchcock.*

New Math

Students finishing high school today have seen:

250	commercial films in theaters and the equivalent of
7,500	two-hour feature films on TV.
7,750	Total.
	In twelve years of schooling the time spent in class was the equivalent of
5,400	feature films, or
2,350	fewer.

Do I need any close-ups? Actually I don't: the full shot of the two bodies is expressive enough. Be content with that! Don't be so desperately anxious to cover yourself with extra positions. If this full shot doesn't hold up, what does?

Nevertheless. I decide on close-ups to avoid being stuck when editing. A big dramatic full shot and nothing to cut into? Much too difficult a scene: it's dangerous to do without close-ups.

The danger of the full shot: You are aware only of two struggling bodies. Close-ups are necessary to get at the human aspect. All convulsions of lust, aggressiveness, self-torment. Take the close-ups! If they're up to it, the two on the floor.

Vilgot Sjöman,
Evergreen Review.

After a game, experiment, puzzle, or exercise has been probed, talk about it with others. Expand viewpoints. Play with the stories, photographs, poems, bits and pieces.

This is not a book to be memorized and studied. Probe and explore. Create significance.

Engage your own power of intellect and develop your own film sense. Keep a journal as a laboratory for exploring ideas which emerge from the probing.

Determine for yourself what conclusions should be drawn from the data, if any. Develop your own point of view and your capacity to enrich your film experiences.

Have a good time. It's only a movie.

√ **A Way In** Before he directed *Citizen Kane*, Orson Welles saw *Stage Coach* 40 Times. True or False?

Step 1 or Step 40: Select a short film you have seen several times. Or experiment with some new one.

Then. Count the cuts and keep a tally. Probe with others what you noticed while counting. That's all. The rest will follow. This is the only way in. True or false? Try a TV commercial. Compare two TV shows.

Moviegoing √
Rule 1:
Don't blink.

Picasso:

I don't want people to like the film. I want them to feel it. Let 'em squirm. That way it gets them really into it. I want them physically involved, not mentally. Robert Rafelson, director of *Head* and *Five Easy Pieces.*

"One should no more try to understand

It is seven-thirty.   I'm not hungry and the cinema doesn't start until nine o'clock; what am I going to do? Jean-Paul Sartre, *Nausea,* 1938.

art than one should

Juliet of the Spirits is a bird song. *The Birds* is birdsong?

try to understand the song of a bird."

FLA CITRUS CO

TECHNIQUE

Vienna, 1832:
Simon Ritter von Stampfer
exhibits a stroboscope.
**The number of film-production
courses in the 100 largest U.S.
colleges and universities has increased since 1955 by: 25%,
50%, or 75%.**
Suspense is simply the dramatization
of a film's narrative material, or, if
you will, the most intense presentation possible of dramatic
situations. Here's a case in point:
A man leaves his home, hails a
cab and drives to the station to
catch a train. This is a normal
scene in an average picture.
Now, should that man happen
to look at his watch just
as he is getting into the cab
and exclaim, 'Good God, I shall
never make that train!' that
entire ride automatically becomes a sequence of pure suspense. Every red light, traffic
signal, shift of the gears or touch
on the brake, and every cop on
the way to the station will inten-
sify its emotional impact. The
manifest clarity and persuasive
power of the image are such
that it simply will not occur to
the viewer to reason: 'What's the
hurry? Why can't he take the
next train?' Thanks to the tension created by the frenzied
imagery on the screen, the
urgency of the action will never
be questioned.
François Truffaut, *Hitchcock.*
**As for the camera:
stop arranging the sheets
in order to conceal physical
blemishes. No affectation
with lighting, shadows, camera
angles. Let people alone. The
camera that samples naked skin.
Our old friend semi-exposure.
All that voluptuous nosing about.
The whole forest of pornographic
film clichés in which the two
holies arrange such peaceful meetings: commercialism and middle-class morality. Push it aside. Let Lena and
Börje behave naturally—that will be
quite shocking enough. Vilgot
Sjöman, *Evergreen Review.***

8

Raw Materials
by George Bluestone

Such differences as we have already noted in the two media (novels and film) become even more obvious when we examine, in more detail, the peculiar properties of each. The film is based on the optical principle known as **persistence of vision.** After exposure, the retina of the eye retains the image of a picture approximately 1/10 of a second longer than the duration of actual contact. The principle was applied in the old zoetrope, for example, where apertures were cut in a freewheeling disc. When the disc was revolved at a given speed, the light through the apertures would seem to be continuous. A series of separate images, run behind the apertures, would create the illusion of constant motion. The principle has remained the same from the flashcards of the nickelodeon to the splendor of the widescreen. In the movie theater we sit in darkness much of the time. Our eye fills in the gaps.

The silent film was made up of separate frames joined on rolls of celluloid at a standard rate of sixteen frames to the foot. In sound films, twenty-four frames or 1½ feet per second run before the lens of the standard projector. At this rate, the eye receives the illusion of normal movement. The average film runs about 80 minutes and measures about 7,200 feet in length, although historically films have varied from as little as 50 feet or less to as much as 48,000 feet or more. Full-length films are made up of 1,000 or 2,000-foot reels, so that in the latter case an average feature runs about four reels. The standard width of the film strip is 35 mm, and a substandard width of 16 mm is popular for noncommercial use. Innovations in stereoscopic films have set off further experiments with 55 and 65 mm film, which may very well render the conventional mechanics obsolete. Whatever the standards of the future, however, it is highly probable that the film's basic materials will remain more mechanically fixed than those of the more traditional arts.

Beyond these limitations, however, the camera is free to use almost endless visual variations. It is at this point that the camera, its reel of sensitized **film sprocketed in place, announces itself as an artistic instrument.** The camera can go anywhere, see anything, in the natural world. Placed in front of a church, it can effect a number of distortions without even moving. Beginning with a two-inch lens, the cameraman can shoot the church in its entirety and end with a forty-inch lens which reveals no more than a notice pinned to the door. The two-inch lens most nearly corresponds to the vision of human eyesight and may therefore be used as a norm. Lenses of less than two inches distort space by extending and exaggerating distances, as through the wrong end of a telescope; lenses of more than two inches distort space by reducing and compressing distances, as through the magnifying end. **Gauzes can be used to soften the outlines of scenes;** masks can be used to give the illusion of looking through a keyhole or a heart or a cathedral arch. Sometimes the lens is smeared to give blurred or watery effects. Even immobilized, the camera makes space pliable.

More significantly, however, the camera can move, and its mobility has enabled it to achieve unprecedented visual effects. At this point, **the film declares its historical independence from the theater.** Mobile, the camera can

Young people are not afraid to carry a running projector around, spraying the images on walls and ceilings for distortions which communicate. Anthony Schillaci.

To hear a taste. To see a smell.

Dead object.

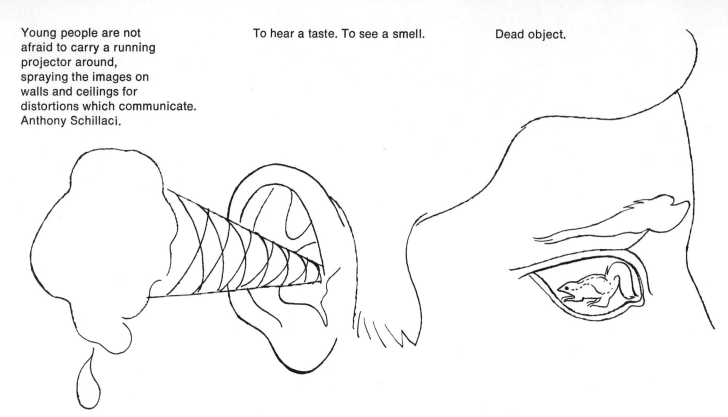

see over a hundred miles of prairie, or count the eyelashes on an actor's lids. It can whirl over ballrooms; ride on cranes up houses into windows; move on a truck alongside galloping horsemen; take nose dives on the fuselage of an airplane; pan up skyscrapers by pivoting vertically on its tripod; or, by pivoting horizontally, brood across a deserted battlefield.

Similarly, it can distort light to fit a desired mood—deepen shadows, highlight faces, amplify contrast, turn night into day or faintly defined clouds into sharp ones. John Howard Lawson emphasizes these capabilities by suggesting that "the light pattern is the key to the composition, which is never static. The composition is not merely a commentary on the action. There is a changing dynamic relationship between each person or object in the scene and the camera." Thus, when the camera swings through the window to find the sleeping man in the first shot of *Body and Soul*, "the instrument itself is acting."

Like a precocious child, however, the camera can become offensive through sheer virtuosity. Basil Wright is correct when he

says that "the good cameraman is as sparing as possible in the use of elaborate stunts." The technique of the camera has, after all, been evolved by the demands of men making films for a specific end. Consequently, "the apparatus should be subservient to the idea."

On the face of it, to be sure, the camera approximates our ordinary perceptions. "It is the normal part of our behaviour," says Ernest Lindgren, "to look one moment at one thing, and the next moment at another, according to the direction in which our attention is attracted." In order to alter our view, a mere movement of the eyes is sufficient. But sometimes we turn our head, or move it up or down. Sometimes the impulse for movement is transferred to our whole body, and, to get a particular angle of vision, we turn around or walk. Indeed, this selective and erratic manner of seeing, Lindgren argues, "is the keystone, not merely of the whole theory of film editing, but of the whole technique of filmic representation."

V. I. Pudovkin suggests the same thing in his axiom, "The lens of the camera replaces the eye of the observer." But Basil Wright,

the British photographer, points out, as Pudovkin and Lindgren ultimately do, the essentially radical departure of eye from camera:

First and foremost we must remember that the camera does not see things in the same way as the human eye. The brain behind your eye selects the points of emphasis in the scene before you. You can look at a crowd and see nothing but one umbrella, or you can look at an empty field and see millions of separate blades of grass. . . . Not so the camera. The lens soullessly records on a sensitized piece of celluloid simply the amount of light of differing values that passes through it. No amount of thinking on the part of the cameraman will achieve any other emphasis. Out of a wide landscape it will not pick out that certain tree. You, as a person, have got to interfere, to place the camera in such a way that the picture it records will somehow give the emphasis you require.

With Pudovkin's observation that the marked difference between the natural event and its appearance on the screen is exactly "what makes the film an art," we are brought to the heart of the

The instrument itself is acting.

California:
At UCLA the film
God Is Dog Spelled Backwards
shows 3,000 years of art in
three minutes. Some images last
only 1/24th of a second.

The light pattern is the key
to the continuously unfolding
composition.

creative film process. Bound by
its respect for physical reality,
but unbound by the vision of any
one spectator, the lens becomes
an ideal, unrealistic eye; unbound by natural observation,
the eye of the spectator becomes
omniscient. It took several years
for film-makers to understand
that the film's angle of vision was
non-naturalistic; that being non-
naturalistic, yet bound by optical
and mechanical laws, the film
had found its informative power.
In many early films, an immobilized camera, set at a given
distance, recorded the action before it in sequences that cor-
responded roughly to theatrical
acts. In spite of some amazing
effects in Méliès, who used
the technique, the results remained little more than animated
postcards.

Then, in the history of film technique, there came two astral
hours. In *Enoch Arden*, D. W.
Griffith outraged his superiors
by alternating a medium shot
with a close-up instead of filming
his scene continuously in the
usual manner. Griffith, in mobiliz-
ing the camera, had discovered
the principle of editing. Having
found the true nature of motion
pictures, Griffith went on to dis-

cover, through the camera, a
multitude of ways in which to
render spatial movement through
exciting visual rhythms. In a
short time, the inter-cut, the
parallel development, the extreme long shot, the fade-out,
the dissolve, the flashback, all
became common currency in
editing techniques.

Once film technicians discovered
that the strips of celluloid were
their real raw material, and once
directors interrupted the camera's naturalistic eye to join the
film in ways contrary to nature,
the mode of transition from one
shot to the next became all important. Spatial transition, the
core of editing, becomes, in
Raymond Spottiswoode's phrase,
"the grammar of the film." And
the principle is as central today
as it was in its infancy. Lindgren
gives us the main design:
The normal method of transition
from shot to shot within a scene
is by means of a cut which gives
the effect of one shot being in-
stantly replaced by the next. The
normal method of transition from
one scene to another is by means
of the mix or dissolve which is
always associated with a sense
of the passage of time or of a
break in time. A sequence is nor-

mally punctuated by a fade-in at
the beginning and a fade-out at
the end. The fade may be quick
or slow according to the emotional mood of the film at the
moment it occurs and to the degree of emphasis which the
director desires to give the pause
at that particular point.

Where Lindgren's statement has
the matter-of-factness of as-
similated transition, Pudovkin's
adumbration has the ring of a
manifesto: "I claim that every object, taken from a given viewpoint and shown on the screen
to spectators, is a dead object,
even though it has moved before
the camera. . . . Every object
must, by editing, be brought upon
the screen so that it shall
have not photographic but cinematographic essence." If by a
"dead object" in this context we
understand "dead" to mean lacking in significance with respect
to a total structure, just as a
phrase detached from a poem is
dead, then Pudovkin will not
seem to be overstating his case.
And if we remember that the
analogy to poetry is figurative
and not literal, then the domain
of the film will remain autono-
mous. In his brilliantly pioneering
work on film aesthetics, Vachel

11

Fake it.   Pretending to be Fake.   The sound of chocolate is . . .

See page 22 for an explanation of this photo.

Don Siegel.

Lindsay grasped the difference firmly: "A list of words making a poem and a set of apparently equivalent pictures forming a photo-play may have entirely different outcomes. **It may be like trying to see a perfume or listen to a taste."**

When, however, Pudovkin insists without reservation that the material of the film director consists not of real processes happening in real space and real time but merely of those pieces of celluloid on which those processes have been recorded—then aesthetic emphasis turns to distortion. So exhilarating was the discovery of the film's formative principles, that the rhythm of montage tended to obscure the photographic demands of the individual shot. It is becoming increasingly clear that in addition to its place in the sequence, the photograph must be granted its own integrity. In order for the shot to be integrated into a larger structure, the shot itself must be recognized as a copy of physical reality. The sled in *Citizen Kane* must first be recognizable as a sled before it can be contrasted to the fantastic cluster of art works upon the lawn. If the cinematic eye can link diverse spatial images, the images themselves must be meticulously arranged. Like musical notes, each image must have the proper timbre before the entire sequence can be strong. Even though the photographic image is different in quality from the object it records, Panofsky's observation that what we work with in the film is *physical reality* seems highly relevant. For although it is true that all the objects and persons in the film can be arranged in all sorts of ways, "there is no running away from them."

Arnheim, in his discussion of film metaphor, suggests the same thing. Noting that the sound-film is so sensory a medium that things which belong together abstractly and not materially cannot be shown together, he goes on to say: **"Just as a grinning death's-head does not in a film appear as a symbol but as an actual part of the human skeleton, so the connection between two objects shown on a film simultaneously never seems metaphorical but always at once real and ontological."** Like Panofsky, Arnheim is suggesting that there is a photographic literalness in the film which is inescapable and which makes metaphor impossible except in a highly restricted sense. Even Thomas Mann, who seriously misjudges the film in other respects, supports the notion that almost any story will be accepted so long as it "is set in a frame of scenic and mimic detail which is true to life and reality . . . ." Any discussion of editing, then, must remain at least peripherally aware of the shot's obligation to representational fidelity. The film's spatial freedom is always modified by realistic demands.

Rosebud

The End

THE SOUND ENVELOPE

The Adventurers was purchased by Paramount for one million dollars before Harold Robbins even wrote it.

A jazz sound track is the equivalent of piano music during silent films?

Philadelphia, U.S.A., 1861: Coleman Sellers, a machinist, patents a revolving disk with separate frames and a succession of pictures called a kinematoscope.

Decisions, decisions, decisions, decisions.

What's Up, Tiger Lily:
For about $66,000 Woody Allen bought a very bad Japanese spy thriller from Toho. He then cut out some footage, erased the Japanese talk track and dubbed in some English dialogue.

The search for "the plans" became a search for an egg salad recipe; "He who makes the best egg salad can control the world."

A full-blooded Oriental was introduced as Phil Moscowitz, who vilified his victim as "Spartan dog! Roman Swine! Spanish fly!" Someone else opined, "Two Wongs don't make a white."

Select a short film.
Run it three times.
Each time play a different record in place of the original sound track. Then run it with the original sound track. Film has only one reality? Film has four realities? Film is the sum of many realities? Film is immutable regardless of circumstance? Each time reality is the same, but emotional reaction differs?

Film is visual. True or False?
You can only see montage?
You can not hear time?

The devil made it happen:
After Roman Polanski blasted British censors for removing the devil's rape of Mia Farrow from *Rosemary's Baby* the advance sales on the continent doubled.

Mae West had full control of her movies from the start and single-handedly pulled Paramount Studios out of the jaws of bankruptcy.

"In the first scene I ever filmed I was supposed to walk into a road house owned by George Raft. The director wanted to cut the scene right after my line. I had to tell him it's what you do AFTER a funny line that helps the laugh. If you cut it, you'll kill it. Just keep the camera on me for two minutes. I'll build that laugh into a yell."

Anyone who saw that scene in *Night After Night* will remember that they did it her way. As she walked into the room shimmering like a fully trimmed Christmas tree, the checkroom girl gasped and said, "Goodness, what beautiful diamonds!" Mae gave her a quick look and replied:

"Goodness had nothin' to do with it, dearie," and ambled slowly up the stairs and into history.

Terrence O'Flaherty,
San Francisco Chronicle.

15

Earlids: Insert ear plugs. View the world for ten minutes. The world is a silent movie. Compose a sound track for reality. Sound explains and interprets reality. True or False?

Warren was in his office—a tiny pink room at the end of an empty corridor in a tiny pink stucco building that looked like a temporary wartime army hut for training-center personnel. He was sitting on top of the desk, talking animatedly on the phone to a music publisher about the score for *Bonnie and Clyde.* "Let's go with a hillbilly sound. No, I do *not* want bossa nova."
Rex Reed, *Esquire.*

Eyes, ears and lips of the world.

Identify these stars. You have two minutes.
Bonus puzzle. Complete this to save face after your disastrous performance on the above. Divide the rectangle into four equal and similarly shaped portions. Each portion must contain an eye, an ear and a mouth.

ALLOWABLE FORMS.

An episodic structure, like that of Godard's *La Chinoise*, may seem intriguing to some viewers and irritating to others; but this phenomenon is at least partly explainable by differing expectations about the "allowable" forms of film. ¶People who are reasonably willing to let poets write lyrics which are non-narrative do not always extend this privilege to film-makers, whose control of the viewer's time is absolute and literal (unless he closes his eyes).
Ernest Callenbach, *Film Quarterly.*

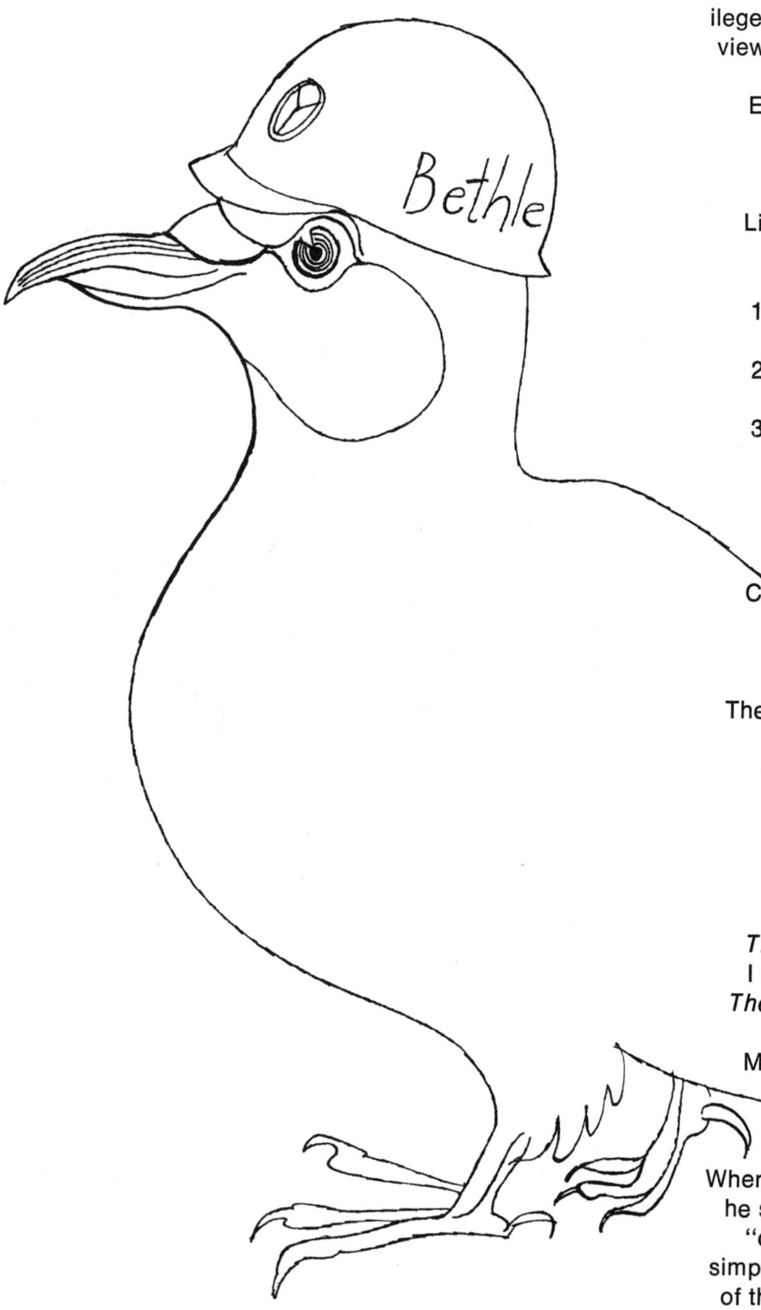

List any forms you would not allow.
Why are you so dogmatic?

1. _____

2. _____

3. _____

Censorship buffers culture-shock.

The budget for the average Japanese film is about $80,000.
Donald Richie.

How you can tell its for real:
After reading the first part of *The Autobiography of Malcolm X*, I realized that what was shown in *The Cool World* was for real and not just a movie.
Michael Muccigrosso, moviegoer.

Whenever an American moves overseas, he suffers from a condition known as "culture shock." Culture shock is simply a removal or distortion of many of the familiar cues one encounters at home and the substitution for them of other cues which are strange. A good deal of what occurs in the organization and use of space provides important leads as to the specific cues responsible for culture shock.
Edward T. Hall, *The Silent Language.*

Film
as
line,
or
f i l m
as
l a b y r i n t h ?

Film as a river of cause and effect?

Or film as
a heaped
structure
of
images,
high,
open,
POROUS
and
radioactive?

Philip Crick, *Screen Education.*

The How of It

Classify the following
as labyrinth or line.

Bonnie and Clyde
Catch 22
Shoot the Piano Player
Blow Up
The Seventh Seal
Fellini's Satyricon
Death in Venice
Mildred Pierce
Trash
Now Voyager
L'Aventurra

LINE
OR
LABYRINTH

But everything changes when you tell about
life; it's a change no one notices: the proof
is that people talk about true stories. As
if there could possibly be true stories; things
happen one way and we tell about them in the
opposite sense. You seem to start at the
beginning: "It was a fine autumn evening in
1922. I was a notary's clerk in Marommes."
And in reality you have started at the end. It
was there, invisible and present, it is the
one which gives to words the pomp
and value of a beginning . . .
Jean-Paul Sartre, *Nausea.*

France, 1839:
Louis Daguerre invents
photography.

The film budget for *The Adventurers*
was thirteen million dollars.

The bell of the Ciné-Eldorado resounded in the
clear air. This is a familiar Sunday noise,
this ringing in broad daylight. More
than a hundred people were lined up along the
green wall. They were greedily awaiting the
hour of soft shadows, of relaxation, abandon, the
hour when the screen, glowing like a white stone
under water, would speak and dream for them.
Vain desire: something would stay taut in them:
they were too afraid someone would spoil their lovely
Sunday, they would be disappointed: the film
would be ridiculous, their neighbour would be smoking
a pipe and spitting between his knees or else
Lucien would be disagreeable, he wouldn't have a
decent word to say, or else, as if on purpose,
just for today, for the one time they
went to the movies their intercostal neuralgia would
start up again. Soon, as on every Sunday, small,
mute rages would grow in the darkened hall.

Jean-Paul Sartre, *Nausea.*

Living Desert

Desert Fox

Red Desert

Desert Song

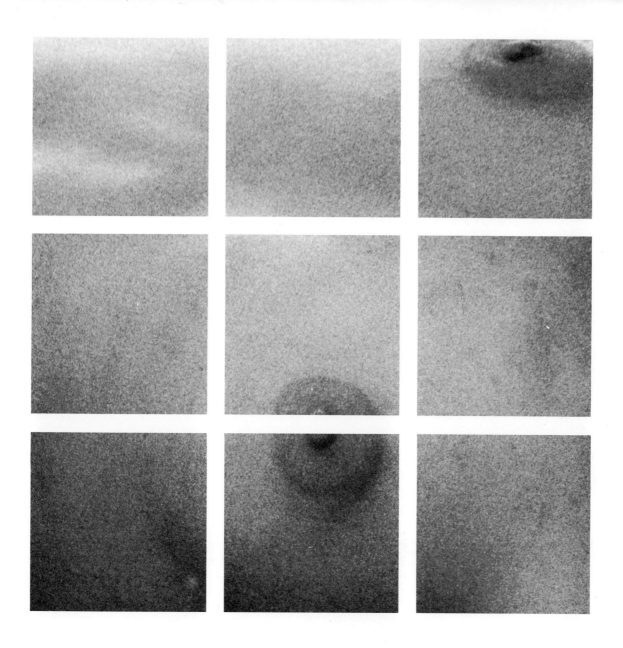

Moon full breasts

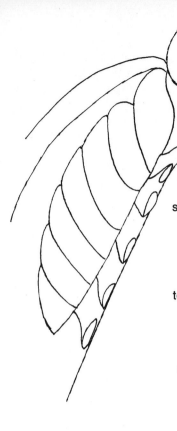

Super X

Warhol confronts us with
our own escapism and weak-
nesses of conditioning. He
shows us the underbelly of our
nostalgia; he proves that we
are not interested in reality
. . . but in its Hollywood version; by confronting us with
actual freaks who don't have
to pretend, he makes us admit
that we want to be just like
the people next door, and we
want them to be just like us.
When you're pretending you
can always stop; but when it's
for real, it's for real. To admit
that these non-actors are
more unusual, more attractive
and more gifted than "great"
stars of the past is to admit
that everything we've grown
up with is sham. That's not far
from the truth.

Gene Youngblood,
Los Angeles Free Press.

See page 12 for an
explanation of this photo.

Maybe you need a new analogy.
Movies aren't always just a story anymore.
Sometimes they're more like a party: Interesting
guests, good snippets of dialogue,
disjointed overheard phrases,
unexpected happenings, groupings that constantly
shift and alter. You are in the middle.
It flows around you.
The host never explains the party.
The host sets up the possibilities.
List your last three favorite parties
and their hosts. Why were these parties
good movies?

What the hell is going on here?
What's happening in the movies?
I go to a movie and I come out
and I don't know what happened.
Nothing adds up. Things are all
out of order. I don't know why
scenes are stuck in where they are.

Who is Jackie Curtis?

Do you know that in Thailand
they use no subtitles or dubbing?
They shut off the sound and a man
stands somewhere near the screen and
interprets all the roles, using
different voices.

François Truffaut, *Hitchcock.*

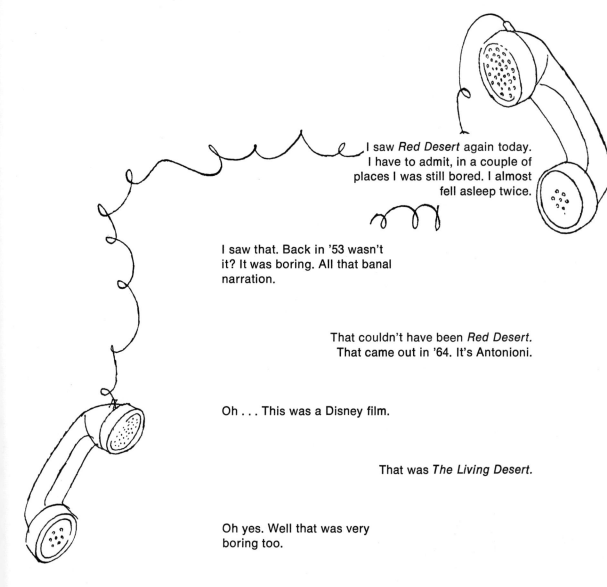

I saw *Red Desert* again today. I have to admit, in a couple of places I was still bored. I almost fell asleep twice.

I saw that. Back in '53 wasn't it? It was boring. All that banal narration.

That couldn't have been *Red Desert*. That came out in '64. It's Antonioni.

Oh . . . This was a Disney film.

That was *The Living Desert*.

Oh yes. Well that was very boring too.

Red Desert is a superior kind of boredom.

But clichés in a new context can become
unclichéd
which is to discover that they are no
longer ordinary.

Corita Kent.

CULTURE SHOCK

Q: What were some of these new techniques you discovered with *I Am Curious?*
A: One which was new to me was the interview. I approached a minister of trade. While filming him I put in a fictive situation, with me (as the interviewer) looking at Lena. This gave it another dimension. For me the important word was "play"—play with reality, don't just depict it. I discovered another new technique with Lena in a discussion with the Russian poet Yevtushenko. I interviewed him to get shots, but found the interview was no good. It didn't really boil down to the important things. So what I did was shoot three separate sequences: one of Lena, one of Yevtushenko, and one of the interpreter. In the film I combine these three—Yevtushenko's was the actual interview; the sequences with Lena and the interpreter were staged. But somehow you discover that you can work with the camera and edit and cut in a funny sort of way. I hadn't realized that before.

Vilgot Sjöman,
Evergreen Review.

Save My Seat
There is still a newer wave of films on its way from Italy. Here are some synopses, so that you can plan your weekends.

The Occurrence
Giovanna has lost her thimble. For the first two and three-quarters hours of the film, she and her friends look for it. In the final ten minutes, she is raped, and we are left with a sense of loss.

The Occurrence is the first film made by the cruel and talented Dominic Fabiani, and stars his good friend and constant companion Fabiana Dominici.

Carlo and His Brothers
Carlo and His Brothers is the odyssey of Carlo and his brothers, Niccolo, Giacomo, Ottorino, Gioacchino, Giuseppe, Vittorio, Gaetano, Ruggiero, Cesare, and Pietro, who emigrate from the suburbs of Rome to midtown Rome. In the course of the conflicts brought by the crude uprooting forced on them by the Industrial Revolution, Nicolo becomes deeply obsessed with Giulietta, who loves Ruggiero and Pietro. Gaetano marries Francesca, whose affair with Giuseppe has caused him heartlessly to leave Gina, who, in her bitterness, impulsively tells Ce-

sare that Floria has been carrying on a liaison with Goldfine.

At the big family reunion, Antonietta, unable to contain her unhappiness, reveals her pregnancy. In their grief, the brothers visit the childlike Sylvana, who for all of them has been their only contact with the soil from which they have been uprooted. They rape her, and we are left with a sense of loss.

Carlo and His Brothers is the first film from the perverse and talented Penuche Marchesi, and stars his good friend and constant companion Gérard Durain.

Mother and Daughter
Gia and Maria, mother and daughter, walk the length of wartime Italy to present their last pair of stockings to the Pope.

The stockings are lost in Torino, where they settle to look for them. After Torino is devastated by American bombs, Gia and Maria are raped by the Army, and we are left with a sense of loss.

This is the twenty-seventh film about war-torn Italy by the bitter and successful Carissimo De Vita; it stars his good friends and constant companions Lucia Vengerini and Patsy Harkness.

Mike Nichols,
The New Yorker.

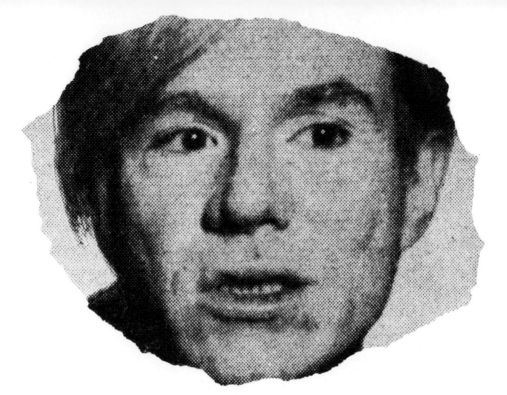

Films reflect culture.
Culture reflects films.
Why are both of these statements correct?

". . . the hollow dole of the real."

Andy's Thing
Louis B. Mayer's fondest memories were of the Andy Hardy films. "In one," he recalled, "Andy's mother was dying—and they showed him standing outside the door. Standing. I told them: Don't you know that an American boy like that will get down on his knees and pray? They listened—the biggest thing in the picture."
Time.

Yet, in Japan, devotion to the myth is extreme. Shiro Kido, the Louis B. Mayer of Shochiku, believes so strongly in the traditional family system, what he considers the "healthy family life," that he advocates it in all Shochiku productions with an almost religious fervor. The difficulty is that such an attitude no longer reflects the reality of Japanese life and that it appeals to an ever decreasing audience. Kido knows this very well and yet he is apparently willing to sacrifice commercial considera-

tions to further propagandize the system.
Anderson and Richie,
The Japanese Film.

To become aware of the possibility of the search is to be on to something. Not to be onto something is to be in despair. The movies are onto the search, but they screw it up. The search always ends in despair. They like to show a fellow coming to himself in a strange place—but what does he do? He takes up with the local librarian, sets about proving to the local children what a nice fellow he is, and settles down with a vengeance. In two weeks time he is so sunk in everydayness that he might just as well be dead.
Walker Percy, *The Moviegoer.*

Woman Shoots Andy.
San Francisco Chronicle,
June 4, 1968.
Associated Press
New York

Andy Warhol, the pop artist and underground film producer, was shot and critically wounded by a woman in his Manhattan office yesterday, police said.

One bullet also grazed an English art gallery owner, Mario

Amaya, 30, of London. He later was released from Columbus Hospital, where Warhol underwent surgery.

Police Inspector Thomas Maguire said Warhol, 36, was shot once in the upper chest with a small caliber gun.

He was in surgery two hours later and the hospital described his condition as "still very serious and critical."

Police said the woman sought admission to Warhol's office by identifying herself to a secretary as Valeria Solanis. An actress by that name appeared in the Warhol film, "I, a Man," a parody of a Swedish film about a nymphomaniac.

The woman, who walked out of the sixth floor office near Union Square, was sought by police.

Viva, an actress who has been described as Warhol's most recent "superstar," rushed to the hospital, where she told reporters she had been talking on the telephone to Warhol at the time of the shooting.

"I heard five shots and a lot of screaming," Viva said. "I heard Andy screaming. I thought it was a joke; then the phone was dropped."

ALLOWABLE FORMS.

An international, intercultural language of the eye.
Grierson.

Film has only one tense.

Rule: You have to be in love with the movies.

Filmic time
The film director has as his material the
finished recorded celluloid. . . . The elements
of reality are fixed on those pieces; by
combining them in his selected sequence according to his desire, the director builds
up his own "filmic" time and "filmic" space.

V. I. Pudovkin.

minimal art

Classify these movies by American genres. What conventions support these genres? Do the genres and conventions overlap? List the American myths revealed. List the conventions within these genres.

ASTROMYTHS

DOWNTOWN THEATERS

CREST OR 3-7373 Mkt. Opp. 6th
Continuous from 10 A.M.
"PLANET OF THE APES"
"FANTASTIC VOYAGE"

EMBASSY Market-7th HE 1-5221
Top AAA PROGRAM
TWO NEW COLOR HITS!
TERRIFIC EXCITEMENT BEGINS
WHEN THEY HIT THE BEACH!
ROBERT MITCHUM
ROBERT RYAN-PETER FALK
ATHUR KENNEDY-EARL HOLLIMAN
"BATTLE OF ANZIO"
10:19, 2:23, 6:18, 10:33
A MOST ASTONISHING JOURNEY
INTO THE UNKNOWN!
"TORTURE GARDEN"
JACK PALANCE-BEVERLY ADAMS
12:33, 4:37, 8:52

ESQUIRE Market at 5th St.
GA 1-8866
"HANG 'EM HIGH"
11:00, 2:45, 6:35, 10:25
"SCALPHUNTERS"
1:00, 4:50, 8:40

GAYETY 80 Turk St. nr. Market
OR 3-2577
"THE 7 INS"
and all new Gayety Kittens

GAY PAREE 122 6th & Mission
HE 1-5550
BABY OIL BABY in
DOING WHAT'S NATURAL

GUILD HE 1-5327. Mkt. opp. Jones
Continuous from 10 a.m.
ELVIS PRESLEY-NANCY SINATRA
"SPEEDWAY"
Lee Marvin "Point Blank"

HUB Market opp. Grant. 362-1855
Open 9 A.M. ADULTS ONLY
FIRST S.F. SHOWING!!!
IN SENSUAL SHOCKING COLOR
"SCARLET NEGLIGEE"
Co-hit "HOT BLOODED WOMAN"

PARIS Market-4th SU 1-5814
Doors Open 9:45
"LOVE IS A 4 LETTER WORD"
and all new GIRL SHOW
No one under 18 admitted!

PEERLESS 3rd Miss. DO. 2-4918
Cont. from 9:45 Daily
LOCAL GIRLS IN BLUSHING COLOR
SEE-A-RAMA

POWELL Powell & Market
SU 1-9639
"OUR MOTHER'S HOUSE"
"WORLD IN MY POCKET"

REGAL Mkt. nr. Jones. HE 1-0508
Continuous from 9 A.M.
"HONEYMOON MACHINE"
"ANY NUMBER CAN WIN"
"NO TIME TO KILL"

SCREENING ROOM 220 Jones Nr. Turk
673-3384
A YOUNG GIRL LEARNS
ALL ABOUT IT!!
AND 3 RAW, BOLD
EAGER FEATURETTES

STAGE DOOR Mason nr G'ry
YU 6-4767
"BENJAMIN" 7 & 10:25
"PRIVILEGE" 8:45 only

STRAND 1127 Market. UN 1-8234
OPEN 10 A.M. DAILY
John Wayne-Robert Mitchum
"EL DORADO"
James Mason-Maximilian Schell
"A DEADLY AFFAIR"
Bingo Game Nightly at 8:40 p.m.

DISTRICT THEATERS

ALEXANDRIA Geary & 18th
BA 1-8181
EXCLUSIVE—ZERO MOSTEL
in MEL BROOKS'
"THE PRODUCERS"
Shown at 6:30, 8:20, 10:00

AMAZON Mission-Geneva
JU 5-1174
"DEVILS BRIGADE"
"SCALPHUNTERS"

AVENUE 2650 San Bruno Ave.
584-2636
"GO WEST" The Marx Bros.
plus Organ Concert

BALBOA Balboa-38th
BA 1-8181
RAQUEL WELCH-DUDLEY MOORE
"BEDAZZLED"
Lynn Redgrave-Rita Tushingham
"SMASHING TIME"
Bedazzled 8:40, Time 7:00 & 10:30

CASTRO Castro-Market
MA 1-6120
"GREEN BERETS" at 9 p.m.
"COOL HAND LUKE" 6:50

COLISEUM Clement-9th
BA 1-8181
ROBERT MITCHUM-PETER FALK
"ANZIO" 8:40
James Coburn-Carroll O'Conner
"WATERHOLE #3" 7 & 10:40

CORONET Geary at Arguello
BA 1-8181
OSKAR WERNER-BARBARA FERRIS
"INTERLUDE"
Shown at 6:00, 8:05, 10:10

CROWN Mission nr. 22nd St.
MI 7-6995
"ANZIO"
"WATERHOLE 3"

EL REY 1970 Ocean Ave. JU 7-1000
FREE PARKING
ADULT ENTERTAINMENT
SANDY DENNIS-KEIR DULLEA
"THE FOX"
Hayley Mills-Avril Angers
"THE FAMILY WAY"
FOX 8:55, Family 7 & 10:45
Summer Kiddie Show Today
"ZEBRA, IN THE KITCHEN"
"STOP, LOOK & LAUGH"

EMPIRE W. Portal Ave at Vicente
Phone 661-5110
DEBORAH KERR-DAVID NIVEN
"PRUDENCE & the Pill"
AUDREY HEPBURN-ALBERT FINNEY
"2 FOR THE ROAD"
Pill at 8:05, Road 7 & 10:35

4 STAR Clement-23d Av. SK 2-2650
★ ★ ★ ★
DEBORAH KERR-DAVID NIVEN
"PRUDENCE & The Pill"
Richard Widmark-Henry Fonda
Inger Stevens-Harry Guardino
"DETECTIVE MADIGAN"
Pill 7 & 10:35, Madigan 9 p.m.

FOX Parkside Taraval at 19th
MO 1-940
LAST 7 DAYS
"THE ONE & ONLY GENUINE
ORIGINAL FAMILY BAND"
"THE GNOME-MOBILE"
Plus "THE THREE LITTLE PIGS"
Continuous from 1:00 p.m.

GRANADA Mission at Ocean
JU 4-6850
"SPEEDWAY"
"GUNS FOR SAN SEBASTIAN"

GRAND Mission-22nd
AT 2-1515
OPEN FRI., SAT., SUN. ONLY
3 HITS plus BINGO Sat. Nite

New ALHAMBRA Polk-Grn.
PR 5-5656
JACK LEMMON-WALTER MATTHAU
"THE ODD COUPLE"
Mats. Wed., Sat., Sun., Open 12:45
Feat. 1:30-3:25-5:40-7:55-10:10
Other days 7:30 & 10:00 p.m.

NEW MISSION Mission-22nd
MI 7-1261
CLINT EASTWOOD-INGER STEVENS
"HANG 'EM HIGH"
Science Fiction thriller
"LOST CONTINENT"

NEW ROYAL Polk-California
474-2131
Steve McQueen
Faye Dunaway
"Thomas Crown Affair"
Walter Matthau-Robert Morse
"GUIDE FOR THE MARRIED MAN"
Crown at 3:00, 6:30, 10:05
Man. 1:30, 5:05, 8:35

NORTHPOINT Bay & Powell
989-6060
JULIE CHRISTIE-GEORGE C. SCOTT
"PETULIA"
Filmed in San Francisco
Free Parking after 6 p.m.
Doors Open 5:30 p.m.

PALACE Columbus Ave. & Powell
392-8526
"PLANET OF THE APES" C. Heston
"2 MILLION YEARS TO EARTH"

SERRA Junipero Serra. PL 5-1455
Free Parking
"MAN AND A WOMAN"
"A THOUSAND CLOWNS"
& Mike Nichols-Elaine May
"BACH TO BACH"

INTERNATIONAL PICTURES

BELLA UNION K'rny-Wash.
421-4824
"YOUNG SWORDSMAN"
"SPELL OF HIDDEN GOLD"

BRIDGE Geary-Blake
SK 1-3212
Jeanne Moreau in
"THE BRIDE WORE BLACK"
Shown at 6, 8, 10

CENTO CEDAR Cedar-Larkin
PR 6-8300
8TH SMASH WEEK!
EXCLUSIVE BAY ENGAGEMENT
Uncut—Uncensored—Limited Time
"ULYSSES" 6:30, 9:10
"So lyrically & delicately handled
as to raise it above the level
of crudeness & obscenity" Eichel-
baum, SF. Exam. "SUPERB" Life
JAMES JOYCE
"ULYSSES" 6:30, 9:10
"THIS IS NOT A PICTURE TO BE
ENJOYED ONLY BY THOSE WHO
READ THE BOOK. Incredibly rich.
Superbly acted" SF Chron.
"ULYSSES" 6:30, 9:10
NO ONE UNDER 18 ADMITTED
Extra! Academy Award Short:
"REDWOODS"
Regular Prices—All Seats
Student Prices Mon. thru Thurs.

CLAY Fillmore near Clay St.
Phone FI 6-1123
"HAGBARD & SIGNE"
Shown at 6, 8, 10

GATEWAY 215 Jackson St.
& Battery. 421-3353
2 DAYS ONLY! PINTER'S
"THE CARETAKER" 7-9
Alan Bates-Robert Shaw

LARKIN Larkin at O'Farrell
Phone PR 5-3011
Ingmar Bergman's
"HOUR OF THE WOLF"
Shown at 6:15, 8:10, 10:00

METRO Union-Webster BA 1-8181
Anne Bancroft-Dustin Hoffman
"THE GRADUATE"
Shown at 6:15, 8:15, 10:10

METRO II Union nr. Fillmore
Phone 221-8181
"A SLICK BIT OF
BEDROOM DECEPTION ..."
Bosley Crowther, NY TIMES
"HUGS & KISSES"
Shown at 6:20, 8:10, 10:00

MUSIC HALL Larkin off Geary
Ph. OR 3-4800
Year's Surprise Hit
"ELVIRA MADIGAN"
Shown at 7:00, 8:35, 10:05

North Beach MOVIE Kearny Nr. Broadway
391-1073
GIGANTIC 6-UNIT
COLOR FILM FEST!
Male & Female Underground!
Shown 10 A.M. 'til 2 A.M.

PRESIDIO Chestnut nr. Scott
Phone WA 1-2931
"THERESE & ISABELLE"
OPEN 11:45 AM DAILY
Shows 12, 2, 4, 6, 8 & 10 p.m.
ADULTS ONLY

RICHELIEU Geary nr. Van Ness
221-8181
"Man & A Woman" 8:30
Jason Robards-Barbara Harris
"A THOUSAND CLOWNS" 6:30, 10:15

SURF Irving at 46th Ave.
MO 4-6300
TONIGHT ONLY!
Satyajit Ray's
"APU TRILOGY"
One complete perf. from 7 p.m.

VOGUE Sacto.-Presidio
BA 1-8181
MARCELLO MASTROIANNI
"Man With the Balloons"
Shown at 6:30, 8:10, 10:00

YORK 2789 24th Street
MI 8-1612—MI 8-7397
David Reynoso-Maria Teresa Rivas
"EL HIJO DESOBEDIENTE" color
Sonia Furio "EL POZO"

DRIVE-IN MOVIES

EL RANCHO El Cm. & Hickey
So. S.F. PL 6-5000
Elvis Presley-Nancy Sinatra
"SPEEDWAY"
Steve McQueen-Ann Margret
"CINCINNATI KID"

GENEVA Next to Cow Palace
JU 7-2884
"WITH & YOU GET EGGROLL"
"SHAKIEST GUN IN THE WEST"

MISSION Atop Guttenberg Off
5500 Mission JU 6-1234
"FIVE CARD STUD"
"WILL PENNY"

SPRUCE Spruce & R.R. Ave
South S.F. EC9-7965
"HANG 'EM HIGH"
"SCALPHUNTERS"

Andy's Thing

In addition, tremendous time and energy is wasted by critics attempting to "justify" Warhol for an uncomprehending preconditioned audience while the avant-garde arts move further ahead—just as radio has moved from vacuum tube to transistor to integrated circuitry before most people know what "solid state" means. There is, after all, a post-Warhol esthetic. The confusion is compounded by critics who insist that he has "rediscovered the essence of cinema" simply because he doesn't edit, or that he "reveals the decadent soul of America" through his bizarre characters. These could not be further from the truth. One would have to be entirely ignorant of Pop Art not to understand that the Pop artist must remain completely indifferent to his subject. Emotionless distancing is a central issue in Pop Art, with the purpose of focusing on the subject itself, in or out of context, and not an artist's interpretation of that subject. Warhol doesn't edit, therefore, because editing creates a new reality which has nothing at all to do with the reality being photographed. He is not "rediscovering the essence of the medium;" he is merely a good, faithful Pop Artist. And one need only look to the works of James Rosenquist, Tom Wesselman and Robert Rauschenberg to discover the source of Warhol's seemingly irrelevant close-ups; zooming in on Viva's hands, clasped behind a boy's neck while they kiss, instead of focusing on the kiss. Notation of incidental detail is a fundamental premise of Pop Art. The controversy over Warhol's cinema merely illustrates the gaping chasm which exists in public understanding of contemporary art.

Gene Youngblood.

Korty's *Riverrun*

Korty
Independent maker of feature films.

An interview with John Korty

How did you get interested in films?
I'm thirty-two years old, and I've been making films for sixteen years. So I started at an age which was younger than your college students would be. I was interested in graphic arts when I was in high school.
I read that you did some animation.
Yes, I got into film by doing art work first. It was an extension of graphic arts. From about sixteen to twenty-one all my films were animated, and then I gradually started photographing live people. And then I started making documentaries. I worked back and forth, did some children's films and finally a feature.
You've been independent all that time?
Yes. In fact I worked my way through college with my film business.
Where did you go to school?
Antioch, in Ohio. The college has a work-study program. It was a good chance for me to work on films and go to school.
Do they have film courses there?
I never took a film course anywhere. I don't mean to put down film courses. I think they have their place. But the surprising thing is that a school like Antioch which has never had film courses for a long time has had films being made there, and a lot that I've seen are better than others from schools which have loads of courses and equipment.

One important thing is the spirit of the school. Since students have to scratch for their materials and facilities they work harder and better than if they were handed everything.
There are certainly a lot out scratching!
This surge of interest in film making is going to result in a lot of disappointed students. There simply aren't going to be that many openings.
Unless an entirely new mode emerges. There's the idea of distributing feature-length 8mm films like books-of-the-month for home use. That could lead to a vast market. Do you think film has engendered this surge of interest because it is the art of today.
Yes, I think so. Even more so than television. I've worked in television myself. It's such a rat race and so inhibited by the general quality of the audience. But you can make underground films; you can make poetic films; you can make personal films.
It's very hard to do anything personal in television. The paradox is that even though television will probably get bigger and bigger quantitatively, you meet very few kids who want to be television directors.
I read that you set up a corporation for your first film. Is that the way you did the others?
Yes. Each film had its own investors. Generally we set up a company for film. But Korty Films itself is a kind of continuing structure.

How many people are involved in the continuing organization?
Sometimes only me. Sometimes when we're in production we might have up to ten involved. But it varies. When we get into editing it goes down to four or five. When we get into mixing and sound tracks we hire two or three more. So it's constantly fluctuating.
Do you edit your own films?
For the last two pictures we've had an editor. I did only a small amount of the actual editing, but I supervised the work. At this point I do direction and camera work, that's enough.
You do all your own camera work?
Yes.
What kind of camera do you use?
It's a 35mm Arriflex. We've used 35mm from the beginning. It's possible to shoot in 16mm and blow it up for theaters. But you get into some problems. If it's a fast-moving documentary or some kind of underground film, it's o.k. to shoot in 16mm. My films emphasize a visual quality, and it really makes a difference to use 35mm if you need a sharp, fine image. It's odd. In this country there's the approach that film schools should start with the cheapest material, 8 or 16mm, UCLA starts kids with 8mm, and they build up. But in Europe they feel that the student who is seriously interested in professional film-making should start at the very beginning with the best 35mm equipment. I think that's good for certain people. Not

Korty's *Funnyman*

everybody should do it. It's terribly expensive. But in England, in Poland, the serious student is started right at that level. It's important for a student to make decisions about what kind of films he wants to make. I'm very much a pluralist about films. I think it's a good thing that there are underground films, art films, TV commercials. All of these contribute to the total development. In the beginning a student should be exposed to possibilities, but he doesn't have to make up his mind prematurely. He shouldn't feel limited by problems of equipment. It's so easy to get hung up. Some people who get interested in film are simply equipment nuts. They don't want to say anything. They just like to hang around and look at cameras.

What about the director as someone who expresses a point of view?
Well, *Funnyman* was just an idea for a story. I had never worked with actors much, and after making one feature with actors I found it interesting to think about what it was like to be an actor. They must have a problem knowing when they are acting. So that was the germ of the idea for the story.

Where did the story come from?
It grew out of that initial question. It was not written down. In fact I had the idea four or five years before the film.

Is there a script?
For *Funnyman* there was never a script. There were about fifty three-by-five cards. The dialogue was improvised. Part of what I'm doing in these three films is simply exploring different possibilities. The third film is almost the opposite of *Funnyman*. It was highly scripted. I knew exactly what every scene was going to be beforehand.

Did you also know what kind of shot you would use?
Not quite. It was a script written in prose. It said nothing about medium shots, long shots, and the like. It might say, "Dan turns and looks closely at such and such." But it was up to me to interpret what that meant.

Did you originate that script?
It was totally my own.

We would like to use a few pages from your script and a shot analysis of the film to see how the original changed into the final film.
Yes. In the final editing you say, "Well, we really don't need this scene here. If we take it out, we could have a better transition. But we could use it effectively way down here." And vice versa. You find yourself juggling scenes in a drastic way. In all of our films that's happened. So for me this means that there must be a balance between planning and spontaneity. You have to know what you want to do to the point that you don't have chaos. But once you get seventy percent of it down, then you should have another twenty or thirty percent of it that's loose.

Did you feel this tighter script was restricting your freedom?
No. I felt good about it. I knew where I was going. I recall speaking at the University of California. Some students asked how much of a script I had. At that point I didn't work with scripts at all, and I made a point of saying this. I could see the teacher's face. He had probably taught them the opposite.

That's a Hollywood procedure.
My feeling is that until you've shot a film you can't write a script. The experience with planning shots and camera angles and especially with editing and footage is a prerequisite to script writing. If you tell kids that the first thing they have to do is write a script, it will be very tight and will have nothing to do with cinematic language. They haven't had that experience first. Now, in my next script, I might specify camera angles. But it took me three feature films and something like half a million feet of film.

How much of that did you retain in your finished films?
Our films have a seven- or eight-to-one ratio. We budget usually for ten-to-one. That's typical. Hollywood films go anywhere from six-to-one to forty-to-one, or even sixty-to-one. They just shoot like mad.

On a lower budget, do you feel hampered? Do you feel your movies would be better if you had more money?
The budgets on each of our features have gone up. But from here on out I think the costs should level off. The main thing is that low budgets don't have to

Korty's *Crazy Quilt*

be a limitation to anybody.
There's always a way to make a
film. You can't make film after
film on a tight budget; gradually
the more you want to do the
more it costs, but it doesn't have
to be a monstrous budget.

**You now have your own studio
and permanent equipment.
Do you have dollies and that
sort of thing?**

No, I use very little of the booms,
dollies, tracks. Our money has
gone into editing and sound
equipment. We have something
like $35,000 worth of equipment.
For us that's a lot; for a big company it's nothing. But it means
that in our studio, we can transfer our original tapes, we can
do all our own editing, and we've
even done our final sound mixing. Usually we end up with an
edited music track, an edited dia-
log track, a sound effects track.
Then we take this to a Hollywood
sound studio; they do the mixing. It costs about a thousand
dollars a day. If it's done well, it
takes several days. Well, we've
invested that money in equipment. As a result we took three
weeks to mix *Riverrun*. We had
plenty of our own time; we could
keep going until we got it right.

**How many tracks did you
have to mix for *Riverrun*?**

In this film it was between eight
and ten. There are eleven reels of
film. *Funnyman* was usually between six and eight. *Crazy Quilt*
was even simpler, between four
and five.

Is it all dubbed in afterward?

Crazy Quilt was mostly dialogue
and was dubbed later. *Funnyman*
was all location sound. With improvised dialogue, the only way
you can keep that spontaneous
quality is to do it on location.
But on *Riverrun* I wanted a classic clarity. There wasn't that
much dialogue, so we went back
to dubbing. I really like it better.
It's cleaner and more easily
controlled. If you work hard
enough, you can improve the
quality. The actors have a second
chance. On location, all they
have to worry about is the visual
side of the performance. And all
you have to worry about is
shooting. With location sound
you always have to worry about
keeping it on mike. So an actor
has to know where he's going in
advance. It puts him in a straight-
jacket. With dubbing, the actor
is free to move. He can speak
loudly or softly. I tend to advo-
cate dubbing.

Most kids starting out don't
know that it's even possible.
They get all tangled up with trying synchronous sound. But
many 16mm films could be
easily dubbed by the actors involved. And they would get
better sound.

Hype:
Did you know he's the number one
film star in Cambodia? In Iran they
released three of his films in one
week—regular Warren Beatty film
festival.
Guy McElwaine, press agent, to
Rex Reed, *Esquire.*

Sending the viewer out into the night
with the cinematic equivalent of a
Chinese dinner no longer suffices.
Arthur Knight.

Once he was telling me about an
unknown actor he hired for *Bonnie
and Clyde.* I asked if that was
dangerous for box-office. "The
only thing that is dangerous,"
he said, looking me straight in the
eye, "is boredom. I want to get out
and do things that are different—not
sit around and dwell on my own
excrement."
Rex Reed,
Esquire.

The Critic's Table
by Stanton Delaplane.

OFF TO THE movies the other spring evening to see *Bonnie and Clyde*. (We seldom go to movies until they reach the neighborhoods. It gives an advantage in evaluation plus easier parking.)
The film has caused a great deal of backyard, over-the-fence criticism in our suburbs.
Film critics are experienced people. But I think the criticism of the birds who read *Photoplay* under the drier should be considered, too.
So to press.
WE CAME out into a sparkling clear night. I asked: "Well, how did you like it?"

She said: "I think it glamorizes crime."

I said: "It didn't look very glamorous to me. Living in crummy motels. And in the end getting shot like a pigeon."

She said: "I guess that Faye Dunaway is a good actress, but she's all hung up. I read in the movie magazine that she goes to a psychiatrist."

"That's part of the status," I said. "As soon as you pass a certain figure on the paycheck, everybody gets a psychiatrist."

She said: "Do you think her legs are better than mine?"
AT BREAKFAST next morning, she said: "The people next door didn't like it either."

"Like what?" I asked. "Is there any more coffee?"

"The movie," she said. "They thought *Bonnie and Clyde* should have been prohibited."

"Let them write to Jack Valenti," I said.

"Do you think she's sexy?" she asked.

"Who?" I said.

"You know, Faye Dunaway," she said. "I guess she is. If you like that type."

"What type is that?" I asked.

"You aren't answering what I asked," she said.

"I think you DO think she's sexy."
I said: "For heaven's sake, it's only a movie."
AT DINNER time, she said: "I don't understand why they're making all the fuss about that movie. The papers are full of fashions based on it. And all those pictures of her on the cover of *Life.*"

I said politely: "Are we still working on *Bonnie and Clyde*?"

She said: "You know perfectly well what I'm talking about. Did YOU think she had good legs?"

"I was kind of watching the shooting and the picture," I said. "I really didn't zero in on her legs. She looked fine to me."

"I suppose you'd like to see the movie again," she said.

I said: "Well, not tonight. I can get along on TV tonight. Why in the world would I like to see it again?"

She said: "Oh, I don't know. I just thought you might like to look at that sexy female again. Men are like that."

I said: "Are there any martinis left?"
SHE SAID: "Anyway, I heard she dieted for that picture. Ordinarily I bet she has thick ankles."

"I'll bet she has," I said. "Probably pretty broad in the rear, too. Could you put more gin and less ice in the next one?"

She said: "That isn't what you said about Virna Lisi."

"What did I say about Virna Lisi?" I asked. "I only saw that mouse once."

"When you interviewed her," she said. "You said she had trim legs."

I said: "Holy cow! There were about a hundred reporters there. I couldn't get near enough to see her legs."

"Well, that's what you said," she said firmly.
SHE SAID: "I really don't see what you see in her."
I said: "I don't see anything in anybody." She said: "Does that include me?" I said: "Pass the jug."

"I don't know why you're having another drink," she said. "Unless you feel guilty. I just didn't like the picture. What's wrong with that?"

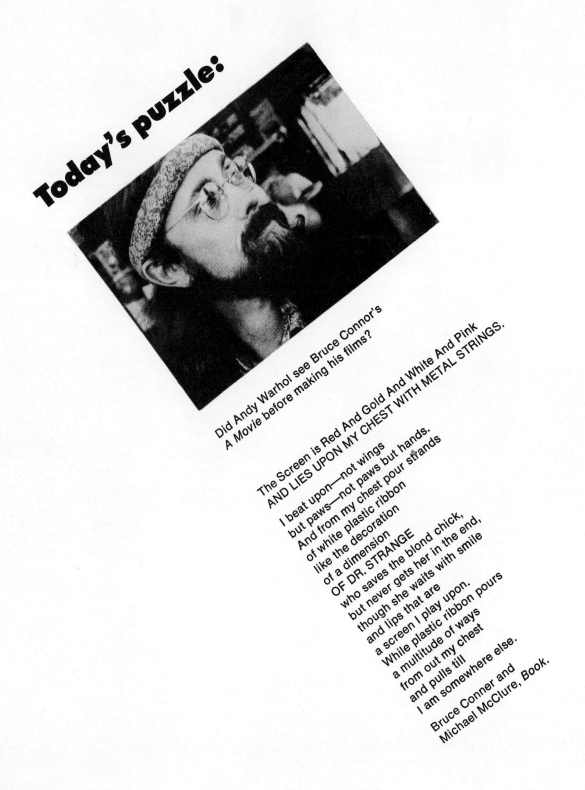

Today's puzzle:

Did Andy Warhol see Bruce Connor's
A Movie before making his films?

The Screen is Red And Gold And White And Pink
AND LIES UPON MY CHEST WITH METAL STRINGS.

I beat upon—not wings
but paws—not paws but hands.
And from my chest pour strands
of white plastic ribbon
like the decoration
of a dimension
OF DR. STRANGE
who saves the blond chick,
but never gets her in the end,
though she waits with smile
and lips that are
a screen I play upon.
While plastic ribbon pours
from out my chest
a multitude of ways
and pulls till
I am somewhere else.

Bruce Conner and
Michael McClure, *Book.*

Carl Linder

TRIPTYCH

This business of showing three films next to each other . . . three-screen technique. I can't concentrate on three separate images at once.

Try thinking of it as a symphony—or a ballet. Do you concentrate on each dancer separately or become confused when more than one instrument is playing in an orchestra?

I will never make that train.

NOT JUST FOR THE HELL OF IT.

Negative space

The real question, then, is whether contemporary structural innovations have not been essential for artistic reasons—whether, that is, the sacrifice of the kind of action "suspense" associated with the old narrative structures has not been obligatory for certain kinds of films.
Ernest Callenbach,
Film Quarterly.

The cutting works something like this: from a shot of Petulia lying in Archie's apartment we flash back to a brief crowd scene in Tijuana, followed by a scene of Archie and his sons on a Bay cruise. At another point the film wedges a segment of Petulia's past between two scenes of Archie's hospital routines. This intercutting of one character's present with another character's past—I can't think of any clear precedent in other films—gives us exactly the feeling that Lester must have wanted to convey, the sense of two lives being lived simultaneously, intersecting but essentially, perpetually disjointed. There is no way that Archie can *ever* reach Petulia's past, no way for him to know the experiences that have made her what she is. Time past and time present do not meet; they are like two parallel lines, fragments from different lives. A simple intercutting of the present experiences of both characters would not so poignantly render their separateness.
Stephen Farber,
Film Quarterly.

You are fragments from different lives. So are movies.

A 'B' movie tells more about the culture that produced it than a film classic does.

October, 1927:
***The Jazz Singer* opens.**

In *Mother*, Naruse had great fun with the mechanical nature of the motion picture. The film proceeds normally until all of a sudden, scenes start appearing on the screen upside down. The audience is confused but just before it has begun to think that the projectionist has made a mistake, Naruse cuts back to a normal view, a little boy looking at the world as he stands on his head.
Later when things are coming
to a climax, just as we hope that all of the diffi-
culties of the characters will be solved, the
title "The End" flashes prematurely on the
screen. We think the film has ended too soon;
then Naruse cuts to his central characters leaving
a theater. The title we saw belonged to a movie
they were seeing, and we feel all the closer to
his wonderful people because we thought when
we first saw "The End" that we would have to
leave them too soon.
Anderson and Richie, *The Japanese Film.*

Mother has no end.

Purpose: Antonioni explained that he did not think he would ever again make a picture in black-and-white. "But if color is used, it must have a purpose. In *Red Desert* it was to put the audience in the correct psychological mood. I discovered too that a fast pan can change the intensity of a color. It requires experimenting."

In one scene of *A Cat, Shozo, and Two Women*, Isuzu Yamada comes back home in order to kidnap the cat. There is a short shot where she reflectively runs her hand along the staircase balustrade. This strip of film tells us precisely what she is feeling: this is the house where she used to live; this is the bannister she used to touch every day when it was her house; now everything is different.
Anderson and Richie, *The Japanese Film.*

In my opinion, the responsibility for the spiritual stagnation of cinema lies with the amorphous mass, routine and conformist, that makes up the audience. If it were possible for me, I would make films which, apart from entertaining the audience, would convey to them the absolute certainty that they do not live in the best of all possible worlds.
Luis Buñuel, *Film, Book I.*

I Am Curious *seemed to be a cinematic* **Tristram Shandy,** *in the sense that it used the conventions of the film against itself; the attitudes toward sex, position of camera, putting the director in the film itself, etc. What were the ideas (social, sexual, cinematic) that you were working against?*

I had made four films, the last being *My Sister, My Love*, which, I felt, had led me into a dead end. With *My Sister, My Love* I was trying to do a well-made play, translated into cinematic terms.

You mean with a logical coherence?

Yes. Sort of beautiful lines and structure, in the period style that Bergman had invented for Swedish film. How do you deal with modern problems in costume?

Paris 1882: Emile Reynard uses his praxinoscope to project Eadweard Muybridge's succession of 24 stills of a horse running.

You must always keep both feet on the ground in the movies. True or false?

You have the *Seventh Seal* and others like it. So *My Sister, My Love* was really an exercise in his school. Although I think that the film had some feeling and emotions which were personal and not Bergman's, it was that school and that tradition I had to break out of. With its completion I felt freed, but I thought, "My God, what am I going to do now?" And I answered: "Try all kinds of things." You're not going to do a well-made movie; the most important thing is that it somehow stay alive. It could be awkward or a failure, but I had to try. These two versions of *I Am Curious* were experiment. I tried to get away from the old techniques.
Vilgot Sjöman, in
Evergreen Review.

Can plays of conversation be successfully filmed?
James M. Barrie: "The film play of the future will have no pictures
and will consist exclusively of subtitles."

The audience is the content of film.

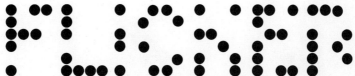

An optical exercise known as *Flicker* was
screened at Lincoln Center's Film Seminar
a few years ago. One half-hour of white
light flashing at varied frequency, ac-
companied by a deafening sound track
designed to infuriate, describes the
screen, but not what happened to the audience. As strangers turned to ask if it
was a put-on, if they had forgotten to
put film in the projector, they noticed
that the flickering light fragmented
their motions, stylizing them like the
actions of a silent movie. In minutes,
the entire audience was on its feet,
acting out spontaneous pantomimes for
one another, no one looking at the flashing screen. The happening precipitated
by *Flicker* could be called the film of
the future, but it was actually an anti-
environment that gives us an insight into
the past. By abstracting totally from
content, the director demonstrated that
the film is in the audience which acts
out personal and public dramas as the
screen turns it on. The delight of this
experience opened up the notion of film
as an environmental art.
Anthony Schillaci,
Saturday Review.

Right now you are in a movie.

Scissors:
The cutting room floor.

When the Marxes began in movies they missed the "feel" of a live audience that they had in musical comedies like *Cocoanuts*. One of their best pictures was *A Night at the Opera*. It started out as one of the worst. George Kaufman was one of the writers as well as supervisor of the film, along with Irving Thalberg, the reigning MGM genius; the director Sam Wood, later became famous when he served in the same capacity in the tearjerker *Goodbye, Mr. Chips*, but with the Marxes he was chosen because he was flexible and would let the brothers cavort as they wanted to on the screen.

When the picture was finished, Kaufman took it to a theater for a preview. It was a disaster. There was hardly a laugh in the audience. It was rushed indignantly to another theater. The audience reaction was almost exactly the same. So they took it back to the studio to ponder upon the phenomenon.

It was Kaufman who came up with the solution. What had been missing was the uncanny timing of the Marx Brothers on the stage. But this factor could be largely controlled by a pair of scissors. Kaufman and Thalberg spent days in going over the film again and again, snipping out perhaps nine minutes of a movie that lasted two hours. The result was a smash comedy success.

Oscar Levant, *The Unimportance of Being Oscar.*

View it, by day, from the back,
from the parking lot in the rear,
for from this angle only
the beautiful brick blankness can be grasped.
Monumentality
wears one face in all ages.

No windows intrude real light
into this temple of shades,
and the size of it,
the size of the great rear wall measures
the breadth of the dreams we have had here.
It dwarfs the village bank,
outlooms the town hall,
and even in its decline
makes the bright-ceilinged supermarket seem mean.

Stark closet of stealthy rapture,
vast introspective camera
wherein our most daring self-projections
were given familiar names:
stand, stand by your macadam lake
and tell the aeons of our extinction
that we too could house our gods,
could secrete a pyramid
to sight the stars by.

John Updike, *Verse.*

Missed It.

TITLE

1929:
It is the art of arts
because there is no
other medium that
appeals to so many
people.
Irving Thalberg.

. . . the photoplay
foreground is full of
dumb giants.
The bodies of
these giants are
in high sculptural relief.
Where the lights are
quite glaring
and the photography
is

bad,
many of the figures
in their impact on the
eye as lime-white plaster-casts,
no matter what
the clothing.
Vachel Lindsay,

Eternal Idol, 1922.

To show something as everyone sees it
is to have accomplished nothing.
V. I. Pudovkin.

Lime-white plaster casts

This painting has
a movie in it.
Find the movie.
Make the movie.

"It stinks, and nobody's shocked."

It's only a movie. What
beautiful words. At the movies,
you're left gloriously alone.
You can say it stinks, and nobody's shocked. That's something
you can't do with a Dickens novel
or a Beethoven symphony or even
a poem by Browning, and because
you can't, because they're all
. pre–selected and pre–judged and
graded for greatness, you don't
talk about them with the other
kids the way you do about movies.
Pauline Kael.

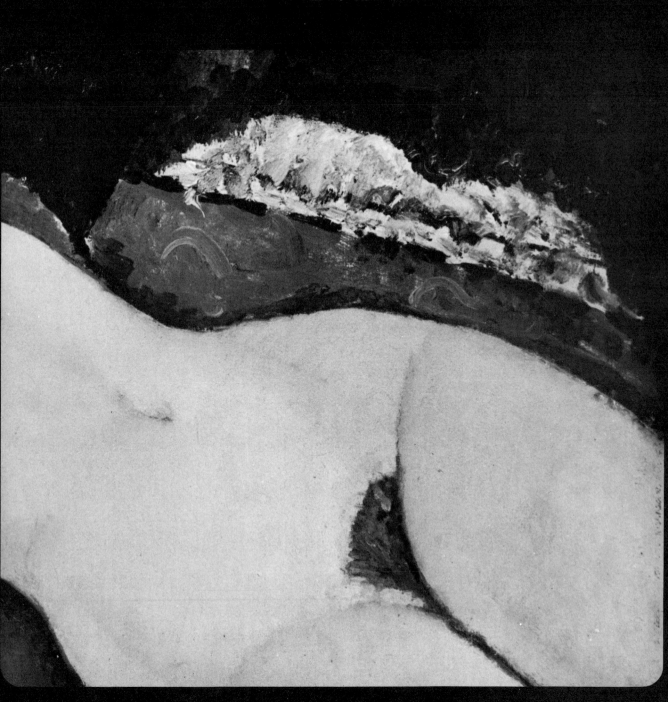

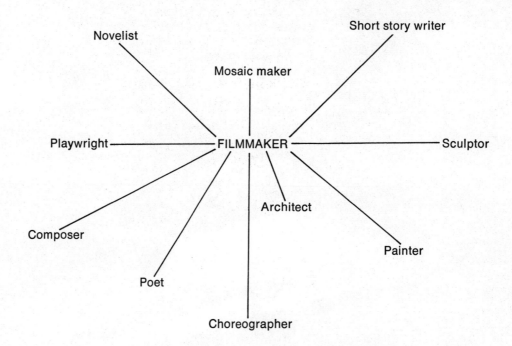

A good filmmaker is:

a) sometimes all of these.

b) always all of these.

c) sometimes some of these.

d) sometimes none of these.

e) all of the above always.

THE ARTIST/THE ARTS

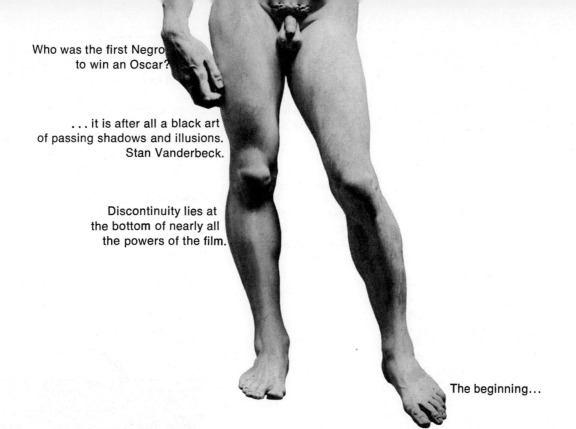

Who was the first Negro
to win an Oscar?

... it is after all a black art
of passing shadows and illusions.
Stan Vanderbeck.

Discontinuity lies at
the bottom of nearly all
the powers of the film.

The beginning...

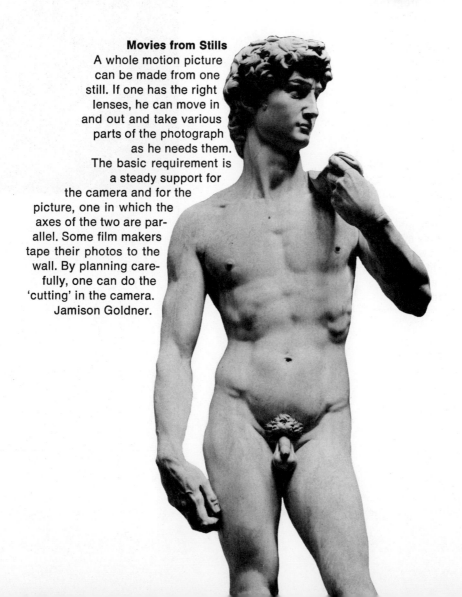

Movies from Stills
A whole motion picture
can be made from one
still. If one has the right
lenses, he can move in
and out and take various
parts of the photograph
as he needs them.
The basic requirement is
a steady support for
the camera and for the
picture, one in which the
axes of the two are par-
allel. Some film makers
tape their photos to the
wall. By planning care-
fully, one can do the
'cutting' in the camera.
Jamison Goldner.

47

Ask Titian to paint portraits in black and white.

You may ask me why I don't write scenarios for the movies, or knock up plots to enable our fascinating leading ladies and matinée idols to come on the stage and enchant the spectators into imagining all the depths of thought and importance of character that don't exist in the plot and the twaddle by which it is carried on. I can only say that it is easier for me to do the classic work. The plot and twaddle business would be to me the most repulsive drudgery: I had much rather write essays on economics, politics and so forth. The movies are more tempting: there is a new art there, and I may be tempted to try my hand at it; but after all, if one has the gift of language, asking me to write a dumb show is rather like asking Titian to paint portraits in black and white. Still, there is one sort of dumb show which is something more than a play with the words left out,

and that is a dream. If I ever do a movie show it will have the quality of a dream.
George Bernard Shaw, 1924.

Hattie McDaniel in *Gone With the Wind*

La Chienne was edited the way I wanted, and was shown first in a provincial town, in Nancy. The result was that the next day the picture was removed from the screen. They had to interrupt the presentation because the audience couldn't accept such a realistic story in a talking picture. Strangely enough they did accept them in silent films but when people in such sad, gloomy situations were *talking* they couldn't accept it.
Jean Renoir.

Changes are inevitable the moment one abandons the linguistic for the visual medium.

Movies reek of morality, but dare not touch virtue.
George Bernard Shaw.

Fish
Lady: That doesn't look like a fish.
Picasso: It's not a fish, madame, it's a painting.

Substitute
"critic" for "lady"
"novel" for "fish"
"director" for "Picasso"
"film" for "painting"

I looked now and then at Eduard Munch's lithograph 'The Kiss' . . . It seemed very cinematic, and I tried to make my own version of it in *I Am Curious—Yellow*.
Vilgot Sjöman.

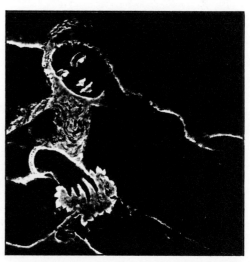

of all art . . .

Mary Stuart, a popular stage drama of the 1880's, reached its climax, naturally enough, as the headsman lowered his ax on Mary's neck. Out of consideration for the actress playing Mary, the curtain was customarily lowered somewhat faster. One of Edison's first Kinetoscope subjects was *The Execution of Mary, Queen of Scots* (1893). This little film, running just under a minute, begins as Mary approaches the chopping block. She kneels, the headsman swings his ax—and the audience is rewarded with the edifying spectacle of Mary's head rolling in the dust! At the crucial moment, of course, the film was stopped in the camera and a dummy substituted for Mary; but the gruesome bit of action continues on the screen without interruption. When the great Joseph Jefferson consented to do scenes from his stage success *Rip Van Winkle* for the Biograph camera in 1896, his theater performance was photographed in a real forest.

This difference between stage and screen is perhaps best pointed up in the popular May Irwin-John C. Rice *Kiss* (1896), a scene from the play *The Widow Jones.* Its few moments of magnified osculation resulted in the first scandalized attempt at film censorship. The "kiss" may have been harmless enough in the theater, but seen in full close-up, it suddenly became so much more "real."
Arthur Knight,
The Liveliest Art.

It's realer than life.
A lot realer.

Will Hindle

Larry Jordan

Carl Linder

Bruce Baillie

Painting and drawing directly on film:
Some labs let students have all the scrap film they want. Sometimes optical sound tracks are made on 35mm film and a sprocketed 16mm side is slit off and discarded. Experimenters find it a good, clear surface for painting or drawing. Some students like to leave the old images on used film stock, but dipping the film in Clorox will remove them.

Clear plastic leader gives a white background. Drawing and coloring with pentel pens results in frosted images.

Roughing up the film surface with various grades of sandpaper or emery boards gives a textured surface. Another effect can be created by covering that surface with shoe polish and then wiping off the excess. This re-

sults in an etched effect. Some artists draw on one side and flip the film over and color on the other. The colors are a trifle out of focus, and give an effect of depth to the image.

Print film can be bought for about a penny a foot, rolled out and made completely opaque. Or the film can be put in a pan of print developer and allowed to turn black. Rinsed off and dried, it can then be scratched white on black.

Useful tools include a magnifying glass, linoleum cutting tools, small screw drivers, dissecting tools. A lab can then make a print which will come out as a line drawing of black on white. Or a reversal print will maintain the original white on black.
Jamison Goldner.

We began shooting without having the slightest idea of what had to be done or what the film would be like. We had no idea at all. We didn't know a thing about technique: all we did was begin shooting. And once we'd begun we would never have been able to finish if all the people who participated in the film hadn't discovered one absolutely fundamental thing: that being an artist is nothing other than the desire, the insane wish to express yourself completely, absolutely.
John Cassavetes.

In the theater we sweep the scene, looking for a center of interest. In the cinema, the camera thrusts us into the depth of things. . . .
Marcel Martin.

When my motion picture camera broke down and the painting on the easel reached an impasse, I grabbed some old exposed and discarded film and threw it into the bath tub. For good measure I sprinkled different color dyes into the water and waited. When the stew seemed gooey enough, I marinated it with a dash of alcohol. (Cognac was all I had. But I left a sufficient amount in the bottle for other purposes.) After scraping all the muck from the film, I mangled it a little more by stomping and sandpapering the emulsion side. Then I hung it up to dry. Finally I cut it up into two-foot lengths and began to draw directly on the film with ink. When I glanced at what I had done under a viewer, I was shocked! I had made a film!! So

. . . I titled it *A Trip* and ran out to find some kind of music to fit, only to find I had the music I needed right here in the studio, a beat up old dusty record . . . somewhat scratched. After distorting the music by speeding up the turntable, I had it put on a soundtrack, cut the film to fit and had them married in one print. The whole production with three finished prints cost me the enormous sum of twenty-five dollars! Hollywood could do it all for a slightly larger budget.
Carmen D'Avino.

montage is conflict.

when planting a rice field . . .

Japan:
A character by the name of Shirano Benjiro once became so popular that most of those in the audience would have expressed disbelief upon learning that he was really the creation of a Frenchman named Rostand and that the French insisted upon pronouncing his name Cyrano de Bergerac.
Anderson and Richie, *The Japanese Film.*

He now says he doesn't want to return to the stage because, "I don't want to go through the mess of doing a play just to win the approval of four critics who decide whether you're going to be allowed to keep doing the play. That's a bore."
Warren Beatty.

The little faraway people on the old-fashioned speaking stage do not appeal to the plastic sense. . . They are by comparison with motion picture characters mere bits of pasteboard with sweet voices, while on the other hand the photoplay foreground is full of dumb giants.
Vachel Lindsay.

I had always believed that for the movies acting must be exaggerated, but I saw in this one flash that restraint was the chief thing that the actor had to learn in transferring his art from the stage to the screen. . . .
George Arliss.

The beginning of all art: a song when planting a rice field in the country's inmost part.
Basho.

. . . there can be an extremely intimate relationship between the screen actor and the audience, but it is not personal. In the theater it can be personal but not intimate.
John Howard Lawson.

In the theater, dialogue is continuous and may serve the functions of creating atmosphere, describing events offstage, revealing a character, and so on. All these things the cinema can do visually, and if they are also conveyed verbally there will be audio-visual pleonasm.
Ralph Stephenson and J. R. Debrix, *The Cinema as Art.*

Poetic speech is a means of extending the action beyond the physical limits of the stage.
John Howard Lawson.

In film you can really whisper. In theater you have to "stage whisper."
When Chaplin takes the clock apart in *The Pawnshop,* he performs an action which would be difficult and uninteresting in a theatre or circus arena.
John Howard Lawson.

I'm just now realizing that I can be completely seduced by a movie, but I've never been by a play. In the theater I am conscious that I have a wrist watch on my arm, that we're in the middle of the second act, or the third. Or I'm conscious that my arse hurts.
A moviegoer.

If the theater stands . . . for mankind, the cinema stands for the individual.
Allardyce Nicoll.

Language is a set of conventions. Film is a set of conventions.

In theatre dialogue is the play. In film .... is ....

What uses of dialogue in the theater are taken over by the camera in movies?

The theater stimulates the spectator's mind and only through it his sensitivity proper. Whereas the cinema urges him to proceed in the reverse direction.
The moviegoer works his way . . . from "below" to "above." Contrary to the theatergoer he does not consciously ask questions and grope for answers unless he is saturated physiologically.

51

Every object must, by editing, be brought upon the screen so that it shall have not photographic but cinematographic essence.
V. I. Pudovkin.

Substituting Frames.

. . . In about 1947–8, certain documentary film-makers (Luciano Emmer, Enrico Gras, Henri Storck, Alain Resnais, and Gabriel Pommerand) developed a new technique in such films as *Il Drammo di Cristo, The World of Paul Delvaus, Van Gogh* and *Légende cruelle.* The camera from the start is set right inside the world of the painting, as if it were a real world. It never goes outside the canvas and we never see the frame of the painting. The painting—or paintings—is cut into fragments, which, by rearrangement, contrast, linkage and visual synthesis are built into a new total effect. Further . . . the spatial relationships of the painting become, in film, relationships in time. The filmmaker dissects the painter's work, organized in spatial immobility, and transforms it into a moving temporal unity formed by cutting, montage and camera movement. The result of the camera never going outside the painting is that appears as unbounded in space. This is due to a curious psychological effect. Instead of the spectator's vision being limited by the frame of the painting which he knows is real, it is limited only by a boundary which he regards as conventional—the edge of the screen. By substituting its own frame for that of the painting, the cinema substitutes film space for pictorial space and by this trick it assimilates pictorial space into the unbounded space of nature which the camera usually shows us. This illustrates the quite arbitrary nature of our concept of space in the cinema.
Ralph Stephenson and J. R. Debrix,
The Cinema as Art.

The screen just started to talk when
——————— interrupted in 1930.
Dick Maney.

Koan:
Do I know life or
life's illusions?

most part.

___Claude Dukinfield	A.	Rita Hayworth
___Eunice Quedens	B.	Mitzi Gaynor
___William Pratt	C.	Jennifer Jones
___Francesca Gerber	D.	Mickey Rooney
___Ruby Stevens	E.	Eve Arden
___Doris von Kappelhoff	F.	Susan Hayward
___Margarita Cansino	G.	Charles Bogle
___Leonard Slye	H.	Doris Day
___Joe Yule Jr.	I.	Barbara Stanwyck
___S. Arlington Brough	J.	Boris Karloff
___Sarah Fulks	K.	Robert Taylor
___Phyllis Isley	L.	Jane Wyman
___Edythe Marrener	M.	Roy Rogers
___Bernie Schwartz	N.	Tony Curtis

Answer: GEJBIHAMDKLCFN

At two and one half million *Bonnie and Clyde* was considered a moderate budget film.

Start your own collection of great movie clichés.

Examples:
Audio: "Don't make me do something we'll both regret."

Visual: On the balcony she confesses to George that she really loves him but will marry instead Malcolm who has been so good to her all these years. Camera pans, picks up first a wisp of cigarett smoke and then behind a pillar stricken Malcolm.

Visual: 1.   Audio: 1.

2.   2.

3.   3.

4.   4.

. . . . A classic example is the leftist newsreel which scandalized Berlin in 1928. Issued by an association of red-tinged German intellectuals, it was composed exclusively of indifferent shots from UFA newsreels which had been exhibited before without annoying anyone. Only the arrangement of shots was altered. Kracauer.

Stay for the second feature on a double bill

Always: it will teach you how to love, how not to live,

And how to leave the theater for that unlit, aloof

And empty world again. "B"-pictures showed us: shooting

More real than singing or making love; the shifting

Ashtray upon the mantel, moved by some idiot

Between takes, helping us learn beyond a trace of doubt

How fragile are imagined scenes; the dimming-out

Of all the brightness of the clear and highly-lit

Interior of the hero's cockpit, when the stock shot

Of ancient dive-bombers peeling off cuts in, reshapes

Our sense of what is, finally, plausible; the grays

Of interiors, the blacks of cars whose window glass

At night allows the strips of fake Times Square to pass

Jerkily by on the last ride; even the patch

Of sudden white, and inverted letters dashing

Up during the projectionist's daydream, dying

Quickly—these are the colors of our inner life.
John Hollander,
Movie-going.

Tallulah

The film of tomorrow
seems to me even more
personal than a novel,
individual and auto-
biographical, like a
confession or a private
diary.
François Truffaut.

You kids are disgusting,
standing around all day
reeking of popcorn
and lollipops.
Chester Snavely.

We must shift from the
habit of data classifica-
tion to the mode of
pattern recognition.
Marshall McLuhan.

Pull yourself together.

Pierrot le Fou

1.
Suppose you stood facing
a wall
       of photographs
from your unlived life

as you stand looking at these
stills from the unseen film?

Yourself against a wall
curiously stuccoed

Yourself in the doorway
of a kind of watchman's hut

Yourself at the window
signalling to people
you haven't met yet

Yourself in unfamiliar clothes
with the same eyes

2.
On a screen as wide as this, I grope for the titles.
I speak the French language like a schoolgirl of the 'forties.
Those roads remind me of Beauce and the motorcycle
We rode from Paris to Chartres in the March wind.
He said we should go to Spain but the wind defeated me.
France of the superhighways, I never knew you.
How much the body took in those days, and could take!
A naked lightbulb still simmers in my eyeballs.
In every hotel, I lived on the top floor.

3.
Suppose we had time
and no money
living by our wits
                      telling stories
which stories would you tell?

Continued on Page 56

The Camera's View

To get the feel of the camera's frame-effect,
cut a small rectangle in a 3 x 5 card. Look
through it when you are planning location
shots, to save carrying a camera.
A Framing Device

The Frame

The Big Sleep
The Blue Dahlia
The Maltese Falcon

My films are circus shows.
. . . After the elephant comes the
conjuror, the bear. I even
arrange an interval around the
sixth reel because
people may be getting a bit tired.
At the seventh reel I take them
in hand again and
try to end up
with
the best thing in the show.
François Truffaut.

I would tell the story
of Pierrot le Fou
who trusted

        not a woman
           but love itself

till his head blew off
not quite intentionally

I would tell all the stories I knew
in which people went wrong
but the nervous system

was right all along

4.
The island blistered our feet.
At first we mispronounced each others' names.
All the leaves of the tree were scribbled with words.
There was a language there but no-one to speak it.
Sometimes each of us was along.
At noon on the beach our shadows left us.
The net we twisted from memory kept on breaking.
The damaged canoe lay on the beach like a dead animal.
You started keeping a journal on a coconut shell.

5.
When I close my eyes
other films
        have been there all along

a market shot:
bins of turnips, feet
of dead chickens

close-up: a black old woman
buying voodoo medicines

a figure of terrible faith
and I know her needs

Another film:
        an empty room stacked with old films
I am kneeling on the floor
it is getting dark
        they want to close the building
and I still haven't found you

Scanning reel after reel
tundras in negative,
the Bowery
all those scenes

but the light is failing
and you are missing
from the footage of the march
the railway disaster
the snowbound village

even the shots of the island
miss you
yet you were there

6.
To record
in order to see

To record
in order to forget

To record
in order to control

to record
for that is what one does

if you know how the story ends
why tell it

the surface is always lucid
my shadows are under the skin

the eye of the camera
doesn't weep tears of blood

climbing your stairs, over and over
I memorized the bare walls

This is my way of coming back

Adrienne Rich.

The thing is, I used to have
lots of ideas about film.
Now I don't, none at all. By
the time I made my second
movie, I no longer had
any idea what film was. The
more movies you make, the
more you realize that all
you have to work with—or
against, it comes down to
the same thing—is the
preconceived ideas . . .
Jean Luc Godard.

N A F K E H: Technique,
direction are only a sort of
prostitution that doesn't
interest me in the least.
Making a film, that is to say,
telling the story of a man,
of a woman, of two or more
people, in less than two
hours or in at least two
hours, is a terrifying business that deserves far more
than the mechanical
cleverness of a prostitute.
John Cassavetes.

Suffering
Sciatica

A statement by Carl Linder

More and more I find the best way to enter the water—to start a film and keep it started—is not through the idea . . . there is something all nourishing, defeating about the consciousness of the average guts, the intellect, the intellect . . . the idea produces chrome, the structure produces color, hence, I always enter the water most diffidently through the process, because I can educate my mind, fool it, in the Renaissance sense. . . .

I say this is a collage I'm using, or this is a stultifying reflection in a mirror, or this is a fine girl (a process-part)—with me it's mostly glitter, reflections, parts of things that downgrade my mind, that make my mind wonder what my body is up to . . . the most funny experience is to start with an idea that's precious, that is funny and totally simple-bodied . . . I try to start with what excites my eye, for that excites my spirit too . . . my mind is good for nothing, most of the the time . . . I start with the excitement, if I don't, I'm dead, and the film is dead. That is why when you see an idea movie, you've got the thing resolved in five minutes. . . . The idea is only good for one thing, comedy. Ben Jonson could never produce a tragedy because he was an idea-man.

I have found that film responds to my thinking like an anti-toxin . . . my mind won't take on film, like a foreign body, an arm of a hand grafted to another body, the body knows and must be drugged before it will accept . . . either the corpus of the film must be drugged before it accepts the mind, or the mind must be drugged. . . .

Process, then, is organic—and film responds to a spirited organicity . . . therefore films must be made from the structural inception, from the excitement of materials, from the medium . . . and if the film-maker has half a mind, and if it has a through passage to his hands . . . then his film will be informed, and the brain will be indecipherable from the body . . .

THE UNICORN FACTOR

Can movies
be profound?

I Didn't Know That, Olie.
When we finish a film like
Riverrun, after the end of all
the other dubbing, we have the
actors just give us a lot of wild
lines. 'Yes' and 'no' several different ways, I don't know—they
just talk to themselves. And this
gives us a reservoir of loose
lines which can then be inserted
anywhere in the film we need it.

For instance, in *Crazy Quilt*
there was a very awkward pause.
In a normal scene it would be
hard to do something with that
pause. But in the dub track we
had somebody outside the scene
implying that somebody was
walking up and down the stairs
putting garbage in the can. We
were able to sync that up cen-
trally so that we had a big,
clanking sound of the garbage
lid going down. We put that right
in the middle of the pause.
It worked.

There's another scene in *Crazy
Quilt* where the dialogue scene
seemed very choppy after we
finished cutting it. We had taken
out phrases and moved things

around. We decided what we
needed was a sound effect that
would bridge this whole scene.
Then I thought of something from
my childhood: I was always
amazed when planes would fly
over. So we just went outside
and waited for an airplane. We
got the sound of a small-engined
plane coming from a distance,
flying over, and away. We put
that under the dialogue and it
held the whole thing together. All
the choppiness of the dialogue
was overcome.
John Korty.

The Evil Eye.
Last night we sat with the
  stereopticon,
laughing at genre view of 1906,
till suddenly, gazing straight into
that fringed and tasselled
  parlour, where the vestal
spurns an unlikely suitor
with hairy-crested plants to
  right and left,
my heart sank. It was terrible.
I smelled the mildew in those

swags of plush,
dust on the eyepiece bloomed
  to freaks of mould.
I knew beyond all doubt how
  dead that couple was.
Today, a fresh clean morning.
Your camera stabs me unawares,
  right in my mortal part.
A womb of celluloid already
contains my dotage and my
  total absence.
Adrienne Rich.

Psycho cost no more than
eight hundred thousand to
make. It has grossed over 15
million dollars.

The old movies almost always
portrayed U. S. dreams—and
thus, indirectly, realities. Just
as the peasant tales retold by
the Grimm brothers spoke of
common maidens who could
spin gold from straw, Hollywood created its own folk
stories from the yearnings of
1930's audiences.
Time.

See page 77

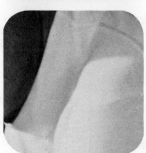

the micro–physiognomy of the screen image.

Persona

Once Andy Warhol invited Henry Geldzahler of The Metropolitan Museum of Art to be in a movie. Geldzahler sat on a couch in Warhol's studio in front of a running camera for an hour—without any directions or instructions whatever—while Warhol went off somewhere to listen to some records. When Geldzahler saw the film later, he thought it was the best portrait of himself he had ever seen.

Even without make-up the face is still a mask.

On the stage, the art of acting is essentially the art of controlled exaggeration.
In movies the camera does the exaggerating. It can magnify a smile, the tiniest scar.

Change the lighting and you see the very same face in a new light.

A terrain on which may be enacted dramas broad as battles.

On seeing himself on a tape of a TV panel show "cerebrating for the camera," Norman Mailer reports that the camera picked up one fatal taint about himself that he found insupportable: "the nice Jewish boy from Brooklyn."

Unlike many Japanese directors who break down everything into close-up, medium-shot, and long-shot set-ups, and then shoot only these parts, Toyoda first shoots the entire scene in one master-shot. Thus the actor plays the scene in its entirety and can build up emotion in a natural manner. Then, when the necessary short shots, repeating the master-shot actions, are inserted, there is much stronger continuity of mood and expression.
Anderson and Richie,
The Japanese Film.

Frames of Reference

Arriving at RKO to direct his first film, Orson Welles looked around the vast studio and its equipment and said happily, "This is the biggest electric train any boy ever had to play with."

Jean Cocteau believed that movies could never become a true art until the materials to make them were as inexpensive as pencil and paper. The era he predicted is rapidly arriving. Students can now make a short film for as little as $25, and a workable 16mm camera can be had for as little as $40.

1) *I Lost It at the Movies.*

2) *Kiss Kiss Bang Bang.*

The first, why you went there.
The second, what happens to them all the time and never to you.
But you can watch it happen to them.

In this country we encourage creativity among the mediocre, but real bursting creativity appalls us.
Pauline Kael.

Students can now experiment more easily with sound tracks because cassette recorders are available. With tape decks and stereos they can teach themselves to control sound.

Inadvertently, by closing the camera iris to the small diameter demanded by brilliant sunlight, Bitzer had brought the end of his lens hood into focus. When Griffith saw the projected film he was far from disappointed. 'He got very excited,' Bitzer told the writer, 'and asked me how I'd gotten the new effect.'
Iris Barry, in
D. W. Griffith.

THE ARCH

I don't really care where the material comes from . . . just like my friend Rauschenberg—when he paints, he may use any medium, any image, as long as they say what he wants. I use a lot of stock footage, because I like stock footage—I'm really addicted to it.
Emile de Antonio.

Documentary compilation.

The muse of the cinema is its apparatus.
Balazs.

Anyway Lena says that she is surprised at these two rehearsal evenings.

"I thought it would be frightfully difficult to pass the shyness barrier. But it wasn't."

P.S. Long afterward Lena told me about her fear of close-ups. Not until the summer, after she had been filming for some weeks, did the fear diminish. Yet she has been working in front of the camera since she was ten!

What is it that's so horrid when the camera creeps close up to the face? A quiver of vanity—one isn't pretty enough?

No, it's because the soul can be seen.

Moral: the body's shyness barrier is not the only one.
Vilgot Sjöman.

A student should have an 8mm camera, a splicer, a viewer. Some viewers and splicers can be bought for about $20.

Take, for example, a film of a child digging a hole in the ground. Show the child approaching the place to be dug, then make several medium shots of her digging with her toy shovel and at least one close-up to show the determination on her face. You can then make an effective dissolve by blowing smoke into the lens while the camera is running, then quickly stop the action. Move the camera to a neighbor digging a large hole, and start the action with the smoke again. As it clears away, photograph the large hole with someone (presumably the little girl) throwing dirt out of the hole. This basic type of format is simple and effective.

TE CT URE

AT THE FEELIES.

The scent organ was playing a delightfully refreshing Herbal Capriccio—rippling arpeggios of thyme and lavender, of rosemary, basil, myrtle, tarragon; a series of daring modulations through the spice keys into ambergris; and a slow return through sandalwood, camphor, cedar and new-mown hay (with occasional subtle touches of discord—a whiff of kidney pudding, the faintest suspicion of pig's dung) back to the simple aromatics with which the piece began. The final blast of thyme died away; there was a round of applause; the lights went up. In the synthetic music machine the sound-track roll began to unwind. It was a trio for hyper-violin, super-cello and oboe-surrogate that now filled the air with its agreeable languor. Thirty or forty bars—and then, against this instrumental background, a much more than human voice began to warble; now throaty, now from the head, now hollow as a flute, now charged with yearning harmonics, it effortlessly passed from Gaspard Forster's low record on the very frontiers of musical tone to a trilled bat-note high above the highest C to which (in 1770, at the Ducal opera of Parma, and to the astonishment of Mozart) Lucrezia Ajugari, alone of all the singers in history, once piercingly gave utterance.

Sunk in their pneumatic stalls, Lenina and the Savage sniffed and listened. It was now the turn also for eyes and skin.

The house lights went down; fiery letters stood out solid and as though self-supported in the darkness. *Three Weeks in a Helicopter. An All-Super-Singing, Synthetic-Talking, Coloured, Stereoscopic Feely. With Synchronized Scent-Organ Accompaniment.*

"Take hold of those metal knobs on the arms of your chair," whispered Lenina. "Otherwise you won't get any of the feely effects."

The Savage did as he was told.

Those fiery letters, meanwhile, had disappeared; there were ten seconds of complete darkness; then suddenly, dazzling and incomparably more solid-looking than they would have seemed in actual flesh and blood, far more real than reality, there stood the stereoscopic images, locked in one another's arms, of a gigantic negro and a golden-haired young brachycephalic Beta-Plus female.

The Savage started. That sensation on his lips! He lifted a hand to his mouth; the titillation ceased; let his hand fall back on the metal knob; it began again. The scent organ, meanwhile, breathed pure musk. Expiringly, a sound-track super-dove cooed "Oo-ooh"; and vibrating only thirty-two times a second, a deeper than African bass made answer: "Aa-aah." "Ooh-ah! Ooh-ah!" the stereoscopic lips came together again, and once more the facial erogenous zones of the six thousand spectators in the Alhambra tingled with almost intolerable galvanic pleasure. "Ooh . . ."

The plot of the film was extremely simple. A few minutes after the first Oohs and Aahs (a duet having been sung and a little love made on that famous bearskin, every hair of which—the Assistant Predestinator was perfectly right—could be separately and distinctly felt), the negro had a helicopter accident, fell on his head. Thump! what a twinge through the forehead! A chorus of *ow's* and *aie's* went up from the audience.

The concussion knocked all the negro's conditioning into a cocked hat. He developed for the Beta blonde an exclusive and maniacal passion. She protested. He persisted. There were struggles, pursuits, an assault on a rival, finally a sensational kidnapping. The Beta blonde was ravished away into the sky and kept there, hovering, for three weeks in a wildly anti-social *tête-à-tête* with the black madman. Finally, after a whole series of adventures and much aerial acrobacy three handsome young Alphas succeeded in rescuing her. The negro was packed off to an Adult Re-conditioning Centre and the film ended happily and decorously, with the Beta blonde becoming the mistress of all her three rescuers. They interrupted themselves for a moment to sing a synthetic quartet, with full super-orchestral accompaniment and gardenias on the scent organ. Then the bearskin made a final appearance and, amid a blare of sexophones, the last stereoscopic kiss faded into darkness, the last electric titillation died on the lips like a dying moth that quivers, quivers, ever more feebly, ever more faintly, and at last is quiet, quite still. Aldous Huxley, *Brave New World.*

What's the sound of a strawberry?

DISSOLVES LONG

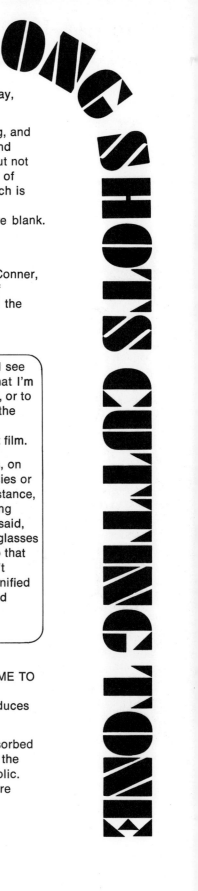

Despite appearances, cinematographic space-time is a mental rather than a physical entity and one which the artist can work with as freely as, say, the words of a language.

If the eyes are attentively watching a certain event, say a person speaking, and if another event, say a movement of the door handle, seems to the mind to be of superior importance, the eyes and head will indeed be turned, but not in the least way represented by the [panning] camera . . . At each end of the eye-travel, the field of vision is clear and definite about the area which is being attended to . . . But between the two positions is a space which is neither clear nor blurred. It is not apprehended at all; it is a mere blank.
Spottiswoode.

Cannibalized

When historians get around to adding up influences, the names of Bruce Conner, Ron Rice, and Jordan Belson are likely to loom larger than those of Richard Lester and Stanley Kubrick; for they are the men who invented the new forms that *Help!* and *The Trip* and *2001* later cannibalized.
Ernest Callenbach.

Truffaut: They show *The Lady Vanishes* very often in Paris; sometimes I see it twice in one week. Since I know it by heart, I tell myself each time that I'm going to ignore the plot, to examine the train and see if it's really moving, or to look at the transparencies, or to study the camera movements inside the compartments. But each time I become so absorbed by the characters and the story that I've yet to figure out the mechanics of that film.

Hitchcock: It was made in 1938, on one of the smaller Islington stages, on a set ninety feet long. We used one coach; all the rest were transparencies or miniatures. There are some very interesting technical things in it. For instance, in *The Lady Vanishes*, there was the traditional scene of a drink being doped up. As a rule, that sort of thing is covered by the dialogue . . . I said, "Let's not do it that way. We'll try something else." I had two king-sized glasses made, and we photographed part of that scene through the glasses, so that the audience might see the couple all the time, although they didn't touch their drinks until the very end of the scene. Nowadays, I see magnified props in many pictures. It's a good gimmick, isn't it? The giant hand in *Spellbound*, for instance.
François Truffaut, *Hitchcock.*

Rule of Thumb:

GIVE MORE TIME TO LONG SHOTS (there's more to see) AND LESS TIME TO CLOSE-UPS (your eye takes them in more quickly).
The dissolve, by slurring over the bridge from shot to shot, markedly reduces any cutting-tone which might otherwise be produced.

The scene is a little on the long side, but I feel that if the audience is absorbed in it, it is automatically shortened. I've always measured the length or the brevity of a scene by the degree of interest it holds for the public. If they're completely absorbed, it's a short scene; if they're bored, the scene is bound to be too long.
Alfred Hitchcock.

But people prefer that you condense; they find it quite natural for life to be condensed in films. And then you discover that people prefer that because they've already caught on to what you wanted to say and are ahead of you. So that there's a sort of competition between them and you, and you try to shake them up rather than please them: you show them that you know what they're going to say, so as to be more honest than they can imagine. John Cassavetes.

Joseph Gelmis: What is it about cutting that gives you so much pleasure?
Mike Nichols: You can take out things you hate. You can make things happen that never happened. You can have actors do things they never did. For instance, there is a scene in *Who's Afraid of Virginia Woolf?* that never happened. There was a long monologue of Elizabeth's that didn't work, through no fault of hers. And we took little tiny bits of it and put it on the sound track over that overhead shot of her yelling for George, going to the car, walking around the backyard, which had been a silent scene. We *made* a scene.

VERBAL VISUAL ASYMMETRICAL MONTAGE

The Rebel told a story of the opposition of the Bavarian peasants to Napoleon's invasion of their country in 1809. In the last sequence, the three rebel leaders, having been captured after a defeat, were sentenced to be shot. They were stood before a firing-squad while the sentence was read to them, the sound being realistic throughout this part. The squad fired, and the rebels were again seen, fallen sprawling in the dust. But now the sound of a patriotic song was faintly heard, ghostly figures of the three men rose from their prostrate bodies and, valiantly singing their song, marched at the head of the peasant forces, ascending along the rim of a distant cloud, until finally, as the song swelled to its conclusion, they disappeared into the skies. The noble devotion of the Bavarians, which had previously been well conveyed, conflicted strangely with the crude conception of spiritual values revealed by the final shots; but though montage of a sort in consequence took place, it did but demonstrate the contradiction of outlook which different parts of the film displayed. Spottiswoode.

Problem: Use the same sequence of images. Stop where the bodies fall to the dust. Handle the sound so that the conclusion is both powerful and consistent with the realism desired.

Compression

Toyoda leaves his imprint on everything he touches and precisely what this imprint consists of was perhaps best expressed by Akira Kurosawa, upon seeing Toyoda's section of the omnibus *Four Love Stories*, . . . for which Kurosawa had written the script. Kurosawa did not believe his script had been used. He almost did not recognize it. Then he went back to Toyoda still in the screening-room, and said: "Now I see what you've done. I understand now. I described the love of these young people merely psychologically; but you've described it physiologically." Anderson and Richie, *The Japanese Film*.

Spottiswoode's Solution:
Had the principles of simultaneous montage been firmly grasped, the following method would have shown a way out of the difficulty. The capture of the rebels would have coincided with the first faint strains of the marching song, which would have increased in strength while the men were led out to die and the firing-squad trained their rifles upon them. As they fell to the ground, the song would rise to its climax, seeming to come from a great concourse of Bavarian peasants, and the film would end.

The Feel.
I'll tell you something: It's hard to put violence on the screen. Real Violence. It takes special effects. It takes doing over and over again. The scene in the end when Bonnie and Clyde are shot—what makes that scene is the fact that you can see the shots as they go into the bodies. I mean, in most other gunshot scenes, it's like, "Uhhhh," and then they fall over and they're dead. It's so much easier to put a little blood on the stairs and fall down or something. But that's not the question. The answer is: Yes, we knew what we were intending. How do you make a picture about Bonnie and Clyde and not make it violent? There's been some talk, though— people concerned that they identify or sympathize with Bonnie and Clyde. People saying, "I really care about them and I don't think I should." I think that this kind of reaction—if you took Richard Speck or Caryl Chessman or Oswald, or if you took anybody, and really exposed these people to the movie camera, they would have moments of vulnerability. They would have moments—psychotic moments and non-psychotic moments. And if you exposed these people to the camera for the length of time it takes to see the usual motion picture, about two hours, you are going to be pretty upset when they are finally hung or fried in the electric chair. People avoid these feelings of personal involvement with, let's say, well-known criminal cases. They avoid the feelings; they don't really investigate the character; they don't really study the person, so that when the criminal is finally sent to the chair, they say, "Well, they finally got so-and-so and he deserved it because he did such-and-such." Well, it's not that easy, and if they were really exposed to the character, they would get all caught up about capital punishment and a hundred other things that they are not really caught up about. You see, some people—and maybe you're one, maybe I am— have very strong feelings about capital punishment, think killing people is wrong. And I would say that the person who doesn't have a very strong feeling or revulsion or isn't traumatized by someone's death is a person who is sick and maybe a little different.
You know, those gangster pictures that picked the criminal and made him a heavy and said: You've got to hate this guy, and you got to the end of the picture and you wanted to throw your popcorn at the screen— I think that's kind of not very realistic. You read magazine interviews now with Richard Speck, and you can't help but think: Gee, killing the guy—that isn't the answer. And that, by the way, is the other objection I heard to this movie by the critic—you mentioned Bosley Crowther—who has been such a wonderful father-figure for us: that the characters had charm and how could they have had charm because they were these evil varmints and foul-smelling young toughs. Warren Beatty.

In the middle
In the neighborhood movies
Watching the men of steel and the lovers
And the sacrificial wars
I settle back.
I look for a face.
This is how it is in the huge
Auditorium after the lights dim.
Laughter breaks over the faces like rain.
Somewhere hands are moving alone.
And my mother calls, "I told youuu . . ."
My father winks, "She knows . . ."
I sit up late, eating a sandwich
The children ride out of me.
Stephen Berg.

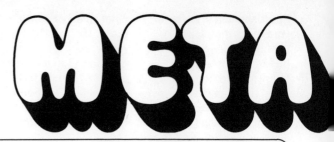

1926:
Abel Gance used three projectors and three side-by-side screens for his film *Napoleon*, augmenting a central close-up, for example, with flanking scenes of men riding into battle.

Strobe Effect

Split Screen

Splicing

Detail

Perspective

Multiple perspective

1) Take some film.

2) Heat it in the oven.

3) Run it through the projector.

4) See.

The Unicorn in the Garden.
Once upon a sunny morning a man who sat in a breakfast nook looked up from his scrambled eggs to see a white unicorn with a gold horn quietly cropping the roses in the garden. The man went up to the bedroom where his wife was still asleep and woke her. "There's a unicorn in the garden," he said. "Eating roses." She opened one unfriendly eye and looked at him. "The unicorn is a mythical beast," she said, and turned her back on him. The man walked slowly downstairs and out into the garden. The unicorn was still there; he was now browsing among the tulips. "Here, unicorn," said the man, and he pulled up a lily and gave it to him. The unicorn ate it gravely. With a high heart, because there was a unicorn in his garden, the man went upstairs and roused his wife again. "The unicorn," he said, "ate a lily." His wife sat up in bed and looked at him, coldly. "You are a booby," she said, "and I am going to have you put in the booby-hatch." The man, who had never liked the words "booby" and "booby-hatch," and who liked them even less on a shining morning when there was a unicorn in the garden, thought for a moment. "We'll see about that," he said. He walked over to the door. "He has a golden horn in the middle of his forehead," he told her. Then he went back to the garden to watch the unicorn; but the unicorn had gone away. The man sat down among the roses and went to sleep.

As soon as the husband had gone out of the house, the wife got up and dressed as fast as she could. She was very excited and there was a gloat in her eye. She telephoned the police and she telephoned a psychiatrist; she told them to hurry to her house and bring a strait-jacket. When the police and the psychiatrist arrived they sat down in chairs and looked at her, with great interest. "My husband," she said, "saw a unicorn this morning." The police looked at the psychiatrist and the psychiatrist looked at the police. "He told me it ate a lily," she said. The psychiatrist looked at the police and the police looked at the psychiatrist. "He told me it had a golden horn in the middle of its forehead," she said. At a solemn signal from the psychiatrist, the police leaped from their chairs and seized the wife. They had a hard time subduing her, for she put up a terrific struggle, but they finally subdued her. Just as they got her into the strait-jacket, the husband came back into the house.
"Did you tell your wife you saw a unicorn?" asked the police. "Of course not," said the husband. "The unicorn is a mythical beast." "That's all I wanted to know," said the psychiatrist. "Take her away. I'm sorry, sir, but your wife is as crazy as a jay bird." So they took her away, cursing and screaming, and shut her up in an institution. The husband lived happily ever after.
Moral: Don't count your boobies until they are hatched.
James Thurber, *Fables for Our Times.*

MORPHOSIS.

Stills into Movies:
One film maker got the film rights for a series of children's books. He bought two copies of each book. He plotted out on the first copy exactly where he would shoot, how much of the drawing he would use, and the duration of the shots: Shot one, a long shot of the whole picture; shot two, the medium shot; a series of close-ups; and so on. He used his second book for the actual filming. He was able to make little eight-minute films that were quite effective.
Jamison Goldner.

See the eight-minute animated version of *The Unicorn in the Garden.*

Film as Environment:
Film may be used to paint the walls with moving colors and shapes by throwing the projector slightly out of focus. Educational science films on cell structure, crystals, molds, etc., are good for this purpose Experiment with appropriate sound accompaniment. By fixing a piece of glass just right in front of the lens, (he piled up some books to the right height and stuck the piece of glass in an orange peel), one student managed to deflect the light beam so that two images appeared on the wall.

Multiple perspective, not single perspective, reflects our present concept of self. The thief doesn't run directly, steadily toward the movie camera. We see his feet racing, a window opens, he glances back, a garbage can crashes, a shot, an infant blocks his path. The montage, the juxtaposing of images, was offensive to Milton so his single perspective is alien to a generation whose poets are Pound and Eliot. And if these masters are too heady for today's average student, like the man who scoffs at modern art while enjoying the newspaper, blowing cigar smoke into abstract forms, and listening to jazz, he can find the principles of multiple perspective in all the popular media.
Charles Carpenter

Bolex has a splicer which eliminates the jiggle of the image at the splice. Instead of overlapping, it cuts both shots and scrapes them on a bevel so that instead of overlapping they butt together at about a forty-five degree angle. But mostly, splicing is a matter of taking care and of using fresh glue.

Lester uses detail effectively to reinforce the feelings of isolation, incongruity, melancholy that define the relationship of Petulia and Archie. His camera often settles for a moment on what seems a gratuitous face or group—laundresses working silently in the basement of the Fairmont Hotel, a clown selling balloons outside a supermarket, a Negro sitting alone in the furnace room of a hospital, gardeners spraying plants in front of Petulia's mansion, actors filming a commercial in Muir Woods, a group of nuns in the Japanese gardens or priests on the tour boat to Alcatraz. But this pageant has relevance: Lester is persistently calling our attention to the faces of strangers, faces from lives we will never know or understand, but that we glimpse and puzzle over for a moment as they pass us.
Stephen Farber,
Film Quarterly.

One technique is to scratch some images on a loop, with a repetitive sound track. The projector then becomes the light source, flashing like a strobe-light on dancing couples.
Jamison Goldner.

Trivia:
List all the films which begin
with an airplane view, moving in
until the place of action is fixed.
1. *Triumph of the Will*
2. *Rosemary's Baby*
3. *West Side Story*

ESTABLISHING SHOT.
Lack of orientation: You
can avoid having to
explain to your audience
what is happening on
the screen if you start
off each activity with an
"establishing shot." If
you're going to film the
children ice skating, for
example, start off with a
long shot of the rink
and people skating, then
make a shot of your
children putting on their
skates. If you're filming
a visit to a national park
or a zoo, start off with a
shot of the sign at the
entrance.

TRACKING.
If it is necessary to track up several miles to an
object (say, a house among the hills) which was just
discernible in the first shot, a series of dissolving
shots taken from fixed points along the line joining
the first to the last shot of the series will admirably
produce the required effect.
Spottiswoode.

PANNING.
If you feel it's necessary
to scan a landscape,
establish it as a "point-
of-view" shot by first
showing someone look-
ing at the scene. And
make sure you pan
slowly.

FLICKER
AND THE EARTH WAS WITHOUT FORM,
AND DARKNESS WAS UPON THE FACE OF THE DEEP,
AND THE SPIRIT OF GOD MOVED UPON
THE FACE OF THE WATERS.

GOD SAW, AND WHAT HE SAW WAS GOOD,
LET THERE BE LIGHT,
Focus, Shoot, Pan,
AND THERE WAS LIGHT AND ACTION,
AND GOD SAW THE LIGHT AND ACTION,
AND GOD SAW THAT THEY WERE GOOD!

Cut, print it!

AND GOD SAW WHAT HE HAD DONE,
AND GOD WAS HAPPY,
Focus, Shoot, Pan,

Develop!

AND THEN A DARK CLOUD CAME OVER GOD,
AND GOD WAS SAD.

Edit, Piece, Edit,
STRIPS AND STRIPS OF NEVER ENDING CELLULOID,
Edit, Piece, Edit,
GOD TOOK THE CELLULOID IN HIS HANDS,
AND SAW THE CELLULOID NEEDED SHAPE,
Edit, Piece, Edit,
GOD SHAPED,
GOD FORMED,
Edit, Edit, Print!
GOD SAW THE FORM, GOD SAW THE SHAPE.
GOD SAW THE FORM AND SHAPE WERE GOOD,
AND GOD WAS HAPPY ONCE MORE.

ON THE SIXTH DAY GOD RESTED,
AND WHEN GOD WAS DONE RESTING,
HE LOOKED,
AND WHAT GOD SAW WAS BEAUTIFUL,
AND GOD BREATHED LIFE INTO WHAT HE HAD DONE,
AND CALLED WHAT HE HAD DONE A MOVIE!!!

Fred Moeller.

Eisenstein's 'Ten Days That Shook the World' Returns

By Norman K. Dorn

'TEN DAYS THAT SHOOK THE WORLD'
The film took seven years to reconstruct

It has taken seven years to put together this version of the film. There was no longer an existing negative. Eisenstein's co-director, Grigori Alexandrov, has gathered pieces from different parts of the world, putting them together according to the original Eisenstein plan. To accommodate sound with the Shostakovich score, each frame of the film had to be optically reprinted so as not to distort the visual flow when the sound track was added.

1887:
Hannibal Williston Goodwin
applies for a patent on a
celluloid film.

Science! true daughter of Old Time thou art!
Who alterest all things with thy peering eyes.
Why preyest thou thus upon the poet's heart,
Vulture, whose wings are dull realities?
How should he love thee? or how deem thee wise,
Who would not leave him in his wandering
To seek for treasure in the jewelled skies,
Albeit he soared with an undaunted wing?
Hast thou not dragged Diana from her car,
And driven the Hamadryad from the wood
To seek a shelter in some happier star?
Hast thou not torn the Naiad from her flood,
The Elfin from the green grass, and from me
The summer dream beneath the tamarind tree?

Edgar Allan Poe.

SOLVING FILM PROBLEMS

TECHNIQUE

LIKE IT IS

IF YOU'RE JAPANESE
YOU SEE THE WORLD
DIFFERENTLY

CAMERA ANGLE

Antonioni: I have learned now
that I can no longer use anything
I learned at school. My favorite
picture right now is the one I
am making.

Ozu almost habitually shoots all his scenes from the same viewpoint,
the eye level of a person sitting on tatami. The camera angle is
correspondingly low, with ceilings, since the ceilings show in low-angle
shots. As early as 1930 he had begun to give up optical devices
which other directors rely on. He says that his silent *Life of an Office
Worker* "was a rare film for me—I used several dissolves. But this was
the only time I ever did. I wanted to get the feeling of a morning
beginning. The dissolve is a handy thing, but it's uninteresting. Of
course it all depends on how you use it. Most of the time it's a form
of cheating."
Anderson and Richie,
The Japanese Film.

Charlie Chaplin:
Comedy is life in longshot.
Tragedy is life in closeup.

Geraldine Chaplin agreed that symbolism often was in the eyes of the movie critic rather than the director.

"Right. When I was working on that film with Belmondo, he told me a funny thing about the final scene in *Breathless*. You remember, he's running, running and finally falls on that zebra-striped crosswalk? He said the critics had a field day interpreting the significance of falling on that crosswalk—like the stripes were symbolic prison bars—all that junk."

"Well, Belmondo told me what really happened. He said Godard (the director) told him to run until he was absolutely exhausted, until he fell down. He happened to fall in the crosswalk."
On View.

You said it was great and we hated it.

A style sets up an horizon of experience.
E. H. Gombrich.

Movies cause public nudity.
True or False?

Rapidity of rhythm has been elevated to the level of an aesthetic law. . . . The spectator has no time to realize at what point the film that one offers him is crude, false, untruthful.
Louis Daquin.

The films had a look about them that was unmistakably M-G-M. Mayer and Thalberg had assembled a staff of stylists who gave each production a distinctive mounting. The female stars were gorgeously outfitted by Adrian, whose simple, flowing creations set the standard for sophistication; his square-shoulder suits for Joan Crawford and satin gowns for Greta Garbo were coveted by women everywhere. The sets and furnishings designed by Cedric Gibbons were in advance of their time and had a profound influence on styles of the 1930s. The sound, supervised by Douglas Shearer, was the best in Hollywood, and the photography had unusual clarity; Thalberg had eliminated the soft focus that earlier film makers had considered to be artistic.
Bob Thomas.

Shoot the Piano Player is a respectful pastiche of the Hollywood B-film, from which I have learned a lot.
François Truffaut.

Any form is allowable.

I'm only interested in the superficial.
Andy Warhol.

The stars of Zeiffirelli's *Romeo and Juliet*, Leonard Whiting and Olivia Hussey, came to Boston to meet a cinema full of especially selected high-schoolers and later the press. A great divulgement took place. Whiting (17) and Hussey (16) did not know when they signed their contracts that they were to do a nude scene. (They didn't say why they missed it in reading the script). They were embarrassed (tender British secondary-schoolers) but by the end of the production, after they got better acquainted, they didn't mind doing it. Unfortunately, the scene is conceived after the back styles of Charlton Heston, Burt Lancaster, and about every other hunk of Hollywood meat of the last two years so that it jumps right out of the nice period feel of the film.
Robert Steele.

". . . loved the bits he's lifted from Bergman, Bunuel, Fellini, Resnais and Truffaut—hated the bits he's lifted from Preminger, Hitchcock, Donen, Huston and de Sica."

Short Story.

I intend for my films to not only bear repeated viewings but to almost require it and in this way I suppose they are more related to the plastic arts than to literature. There is usually no denouement in my films in the usual dramatic sense but more of a formal structure appealing (I hope) directly to the senses. My ideal public, therefore, is the art-collector type who would own a print of the film and run it from time to time for the same kinds of kicks he might get from a painting.
Robert Breer.

I myself have never had any ambition to be an author. I do not want to write novels, short stories, essays, biographies, or even plays for the theatre. I only want to make films—films about conditions, tensions, pictures, rhythms and characters which are in one way or another important to me.
Ingmar Bergman.

Moby Dick.

Hitchcock: A film cannot be compared to a play or a novel. It's closer to a short story, which as a rule, sustains one idea that culminates when the action has reached the highest point of the dramatic curve.

Art is amoral.

If I was going to make films, I wanted to believe in them. I didn't want to turn out products for mass consumption. I didn't— and still don't—want to titillate audiences in my films, but rather give them something that was seriously lacking in the vehicles I once played in: an honest, realistic picture of life.
Cornel Wilde.

Naked Prey.

When a student is instructed to read *Moby Dick* without any warning that it's written in another language, addressed to another society, expressing values alien to him, he ends up understanding the words, but not hearing the music. The film of *Moby Dick* was in many ways an improvement on the book, primarily because of its explicitness. For *Moby Dick* is one of the admittedly great classics, like *Robinson Crusoe* or Kafka's *Trial*, whose plot and situation, as distilled apart from the book by time and familiarity, are actually much more imposing than the written book itself. It's the drama of Ahab's defiance rather than Melville's uncharted, leviathan-than meanderings that is the greatness of *Moby Dick*. On film, instead of laborious tracks through leagues of discursive interruptions, the most vivid descriptions of whales and whaling become part of the action. On film, the viewer was constantly aboard ship: each scene an instantaneous shot of whaling life, an effect achieved in the book only by illusion, by constant, detailed reference.
Charles Carpenter.

Repeated viewings.

Movies still make moral points, but the points are rarely driven home in the heavy-hammered old way. And like some of the most provocative literature, the film now is apt to be amoral, casting a coolly neutral eye on life and death and on humanity's most perverse moods and modes.

The Graduate.

Which of the following are valid criticisms of film versions of novels?
a. It cuts out key passages, but it's still a good film.
b. It's incredible how they butchered the novel.
c. The film is true to the spirit of the book.
d. They ruined the ending.
e. Now I don't have to read the book.
f. The director never even read the book.

Going by most lists I know of,
not one of the ten or twenty
best films since the invention of
the art has cost more than one
million dollars to produce. Yet a
picture with that small a budget
is almost impossible to finance in
the American film industry today.
Americans think big. It is only
the results whose size is
questionable.
Ernest Callenbach.

When young Charles Webb
finished writing his first novel,
The Graduate, in 1962, he grate-
fully collected a $2000 advance
from his publisher. The book
caused no literary thunder-
storms, and Webb was pleased
when he was able to sell the
complete film rights for $20,000.
In its first six months the film
grossed more than $35 million,
and it may eventually out-earn
even *The Sound of Music* (the
all-time box-office champion with
$66 million at the end of the year).
Between *The Graduate* and *Love
Roger* Webb wrote another
novel called *The Journey of
Mary Godfrey*, which is now
with his publisher. He is,
obviously, a hot literary property,
since the momentum of the
movie has sold almost one million
paperback copies of *The Graduate*.
Nolan Davis.

A list of words making a poem
and a set of apparently equivalent pictures forming a photoplay
may have entirely different
outcomes. It may be like trying
to see a perfume or listen to
a taste.
Vachel Lindsay.

Some of the miniatures in *North
by Northwest* and many of the
special effects in *The Birds* have
all the poetic flavor of experi-
mental cinema that Jiri Trnka
achieves with his puppets and
Norman McLaren with his four-
minute shorts designed directly
on film.

"How many times have I got to tell you,
Gilbert, no *cinéma vérité.*"

CARTOON

The animated rabbits munching lettuce stare
Without suspicion at the hunter. There is nothing to fear
In Technicolor. One image with a wilted ear
Seems to wait the inevitable foe; yet unaware

His feast will end in fire, he relishes the leaves.
Bullets riot and shake the purple wood with drama.
Panic and white smoke circle the trees. A panorama
Similar to Bull Run in confusion somehow achieves

What we have never made amusing in a war:
Rabbits chasing their heads down a hill without surprise;
Stuffing the holes in their fur with motion, as if exercise
Had become, miraculously, the hilarious bailor

Of protoplasm. The hunter in his piglike stance,
Gun cocked and snout poised like a statue, sniffs the air.
He is about to embark skyward, riding the hot glare
Of dynamited vengeance while the rabbits dance.

I, who snicker in the theater, wait disaster.
Oh it may come tomorrow with its crimson flashes,
With its piggy dangers and rabbit-hopeful dashes;
It may come like the laugh from the dark without a master.

John Stevens Wade,
Film Quarterly.

Haiku-Vision:
The visual metaphor

Taihei Imamura, the motion-picture critic, has pointed out that the Japanese film is full of haiku-like images. "Japanese films in general portray nature and its necessity is not as a part of society. A situa-tion which elucidates a man's behaviour and its necessity is never shown in Japanese movies." Japanese films filled with these small scenes often have no direct relation to the story as such. Foreigners who were puzzled at Hiroshi Inagaki's intercutting his love scenes with shots of running wa-ter in Musashi (better known abroad as Samurai) failed to make the connection Inagaki expected of his audience: earthly passion was being contrasted with the im-ard poetic image of life on this earth.

—Anderson and Richie, *The Japanese Film*

DESCENDING SEAWARD
FAR-OFF WATERFALL . . .
WINTER NIGHTS ARE STILL.
Kyokusui.

Critic Imamura gives a particu-larly beautiful haiku-like image which occurred in the opening scene of Sadao Yamanaka's pre-war *The Village Tattooed Man*. A rough outlaw, "Just at this scene of the Village is walking outlaw through he meets each other, their They pass each other, brushing sleeves, the surroundings. instant, the grand temple bell strikes the hour, breaking the stillness of the surroundings. Stabbed mortally, the man falls; the other one of the camera is turned hastily disappears reverberation gate. As the prostrate figure dies out. upon the resonant reverberation of the bell returning to the long quility returning to the temple precincts." The Japanese, says Imamura, associate the temple bell reverberation. The dagger flashed with death. reverberation. The dagger flashed just as the bell was struck, the man has died just as the last rever-beration has been symbolized.

—Anderson and Richie, *The Japanese Film*.

Laugh In.

Certain film students are not the least bit interested in the esthetics of art. They're mad for the filters and gadgets. That's valuable, but that's where the collaboration comes in. A director can learn things from a good cameraman that can be very important.

—San Francisco Filmmaker.

. . . this kind of thing is very rare in the West and yet so common in Japan that even the dullest of the period thrillers make constant use of it.

Juggling a time sequence to no purpose seems to me exactly as tiresome as keeping a time sequence to no less.

—Ernest Callenbach.

THE SCENT OF FLOWERS
SILENT THE OLD TOWN . . .
FLOATING
AND EVENING BELL
Basho.

He will flash epigram after epigram at the spectators.

Virtue is the lifeblood of high drama.

—G. B. Shaw.

Ozo treats environment in yet another way. Very often he cuts back to the setting previously occurred. This time the setting is absolutely empty. In the few seconds it appears on the screen, it serves as an abstraction to recall the scene that was played there. There is no need to make any reference to the dialogue of the previous scene, no need to flashback to a recapitulation of the previous short shot of the "dead," set recalls everything. Just a simple

—Anderson and Richie,
The Japanese Film.

The visual metaphor.

Often nature—literally—the physical environment—dominates Japanese films; it sets the atmosphere, and, to the Japanese director, atmosphere is often more important than plot. Kinoshita uses locations, making the scenery itself comment, often constantly as location. A *Japanese Tragedy* is set in Atami, the Miami Beach of Japan. Ironically, upon the action is played against the scenery representing the most obvious kind of pleasure that money can buy. In *Carmen's Pure Love*, the heroine's penniless friend wants to abandon her baby, for after all, does it not represent, in front of the Diet Building, the welfare state? In the 1955 *Distant Clouds* (*Toi Kumo*), a widow meets the man she once loved. They meet in a place they both know but now the trees are dead and the grass is dry. Since the audience too knew the location when it was in full flower, the utter bleakness and sterility of the lover's fate is emphasized in a truly moving sequence.

The piercing chill I feel:
my dead wife's comb, in our
bedroom, under my heel...
Buson.

In Kyō I am
and still I long for Kyō—
Oh, bird of time.
Basho.

___ 1. "a pouting marshmallow."

___ 2. "The only way to stop her is to drive a stake through her heart."

___ 3. "A parrot around him/her must feel as frustrated as a kleptomaniac in a piano store."

___ 4. "a pizza waitress."

___ 5. "those sexy nostrils."

___ 6. "those gums."

___ 7. "Greer Garson with fur."

___ 8. "an eight by ten glossy."

___ 9. "the iron maiden."

___10. "the iron butterfly."

___11. "the singing capon."

A. Tallulah (Fred Allen's comment).

B. Robert Goulet.

C. Nelson Eddy (S. J. Perelman's comment).

D. Lassie.

E. Lana Turner.

F. Jane Morgan (Rex Reed's comment).

G. Sandy Dennis.

H. Anne Heywood (Marlon Brando's comment).

I. Jeanette MacDonald (S. J. Perelman's comment).

J. Joan Crawford.

K. Nancy Sinatra (Rex Reed's comment).

CASABLANCA

If you can play it for her, Sam, you can play it for me.

Holding its huge life open to the sky
snow fringes the scaly cones on this hilltop;
I can see it cupped and pierced by the rich needles.
This far from the city, it takes weeks to melt,
and nothing passes on the road that reaches me here
at the back of my house, planted above the river
of headlights. Do you remember that sad movie
where Bogart loses everything and begins
a new life after his plane takes off through the fog,
where he becomes an underground fighter, and poor?
It haunts me tonight because I am not myself
and, wedged between ceilings and floors,
I can feel the tight path of my hands over the keys
get wider. Because those bare, lasting pines
are understandable, because I am here
and not there, because of the silent breath
rising from different lungs,
because these hands are yours, I remember
something no one will ever tell us. Our life,
more like those trees than we are, is the snow;
the stars know it, the dirt road says it again
each time I stop for a minute and listen to the strange
human words of the hedges scraping together, and go in
where the moonlit weedy spaces continue.
Stephen Berg, "To My Friends."

Life imitates art.
Oscar Wilde.

Pure music (cinema?) can stir
us to the depths without arousing
specific thoughts or emotions.
True or False?

Flatt and Scruggs at hungry i

Flatt and Scruggs, popular exponents of traditional American music, will open July 1 for two weeks at the hungry i.

Lester Flatt and Earl Scruggs' latest release is the Columbia album, "The Story of Bonnie and Clyde." Scruggs wrote the background "chase" theme used in the motion picture.

Pygmalion:
By 1969 the film *My Fair Lady* had earned over 55 million dollars.

Movies do more to educate people musically than concerts, radio, or recordings.
True or Falsetto?

Filmmusic:
In 1953 Miklos Rozsa composed the music for the film version of Shakespeare's *Julius Caesar*.

PROBLEM

Should he have tried:

1) An approximation of Roman music to accompany the period to which the play refers.

2) Elizabethan music (which probably was used with the play in Shakespeare's day) to match the language and themes which the 1599 play incorporates.

3) Modern musical language for a modern audience.

(Rozsa's solution is on page 81).

The Gold Rush
The design of the story is not solely determined by the inter-woven stories . . . The progression starts with gay fantasy. . . . Each section has a distinctive mood and tempo that suggest a musical pattern: Part 2 (beginning the progression)—*scherzo*; Part 3—*allegro*; Part 4—*adagio*; Part 5 begins slowly and develops to a furious *presto*. This design has a dynamic development which does not depend on suspense, and which has more scope and imagination than the plot.
John Howard Lawson.

Humoresque

Spellbound

Max Steiner

Franz Waxman

Film as Music

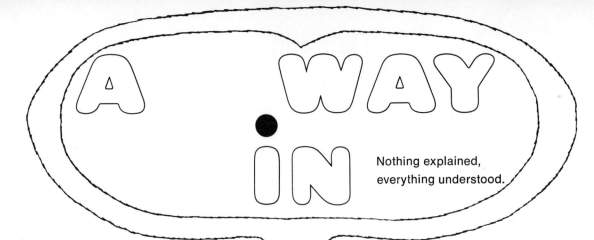

A WAY IN

Nothing explained, everything understood.

The Visual Prelude.

The introduction to *Mickey One* is a rapid montage of shots. The first flash is a steam bath. Mickey in among flabby, towel-draped men who laugh and laugh.

Then a rapid succession of images from which the viewer gets the feel of Mickey's life. He is a successful night club comic with money, girls, cars, drinks and clothes. He devours life as though he were starved.

The screen whirls with shots of night club interiors, Mickey on stage with a cigar, applause, laughter, makeouts, pool parties, more and more frantic and raw.

Punctuated throughout are quick shots of a man's attentive face, another man making a phone call and a bearded man watching.

The obscene laughter from the steam bath, the rising frenzy of image-shifts, the sinister watchers and the hollow night club audiences build the impression that the party has gone too far and has lasted too long. Some imminent danger hovers.

The final montage is a deserted club; Mickey's girl whirls in a slow dance; Mickey stands by with his collar open, a drink in his hand, only the drummer in the bandstand. It is very, very late.

The ride was over.

Three and a half minutes have elapsed.

The Musical Key.

Eddie Sauter's score begins with a soft jazzy background beat dominated by a single flute carrying a mysterious and melancholy theme punctuated with dart-like flutters of trombones and piccolos.

Stan Getz's tenor sax takes up the dominant theme, strong, mellow, lonely and blue. The background strings, in dinner-music counterpoint, gradually rise in volume and prominence. Discordant instruments punctuate the background. Sections of the orchestra pick up the dominant theme and improvise around it. The sax tones become more strident and urgent.

Now a third mood comprised of the first two themes amplified and agitated with sharp trumpet interjections emerges and rises to a peak with the full orchestra merging in a climax.

The elements gently untangle with the French horns dominant and the solo sax guiding us to a clear termination.

The ride was over.

Three and a half minutes have elapsed.

Those who tried to understand *Mickey One* as literature were confused.
Those who treated it as a sonata were exhilarated.

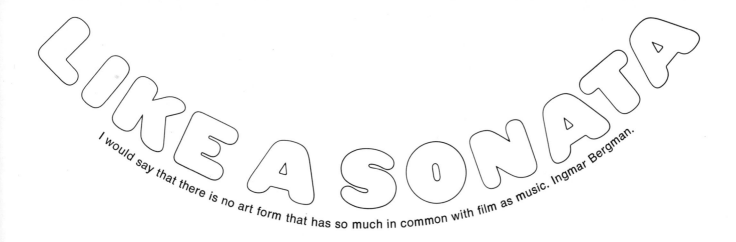

LIKE A SONATA

I would say that there is no art form that has so much in common with film as music. Ingmar Bergman.

The musically ignorant man watching a movie in a theater or before his television set receives a musical education subconsciously. The film-music composer bears a large responsibility for the musical taste of the present generation and its successor.
Miklos Rozsa.

1. *Elvira Madigan*

2. *2001*

3. *A Song to Remember*

4. *Woodstock*

5. *The Graduate*

6. *Performance*

7. *Yellow Submarine*

8. _____

9. _____

10. _____

Rozsa's Solution:
A Roman style would have been wrong for Shakespeare . . . An Elizabethan style would have been anachronistic for us. I decided, therefore, to regard the film as a drama about the eternal problem of dictators. I wrote the music I would have written for a modern stage presentation: interpretative incidental music, expressing, with my own musical language for a modern audience, what Shakespeare expressed with his own language for his own audience 350 years ago.

Beautifully symmetrical shots are not the essence of cinematography. Some of the best shots are not resolved. It's like a Bach fugue when it finally gets to a major chord; that's exciting. You have to compose so that there is something for the viewer to do, and he can really sit on the edge of his chair. Many photographers don't understand this. You can make a shot teasing and nasty. You can take the same material and make it sneering or you can make it joyous.

My main satisfaction is that the film had an effect on the
audience, and I consider that very important. I don't care about
the subject matter; I don't care about the acting; but I do
care about the pieces of film and the photography and the sound
track and all of the technical ingredients that made the
audience scream. I feel it's tremendously satisfying for us to be
able to use the cinematic art to achieve something of a
mass emotion. And with *Psycho* we most definitely achieved
this. It wasn't a message that stirred the audiences, nor was it a
great performance or their enjoyment of the novel. They
were aroused by pure film.
Alfred Hitchcock.

DIRECTLY ON YOUR FEELINGS

Art consists in the removal of surplus . . . the finished work
lies somewhere hidden in the block of stone.
Michelangelo.

The sequence of pictures plays directly on our feelings. Music
works in the same fashion; I would say that there is no
art form that has so much in common with film as music. Both
affect our emotions directly, not via the intellect.
Ingmar Bergman.

Both the novel and the
film are time arts, but
whereas the formative
principle in the novel is
time, the formative prin-
ciple in the film is space.
Bluestone.

The very length of the strips of film cemented together causes a rhythm or a lack of it. Long strips cemented together, slow tempo; short strips, fast tempo. This visual tempo needs to change to stay in harmony with the story being told at any given instant.

STRIPS OF FILM

Jean Renoir:
That's our big task. That's what makes our profession wonderful. It is just to discover the obvious reality. But the obvious reality is in front of our eyes and we don't see it unless we dedicate our lives to discover it.

1889: William Freise-Greene in England and Marey in France invented motion picture cameras.

Multiple Images:
The Boston Strangler was shot with multiple images. One scene shows at the left an elderly woman watching TV; at bottom center, a detective interviews a witness; on the right, the strangler drives his car slowly through the streets to the elderly woman's house.

Joseph Conrad:
My task which I am trying to achieve is, by the power of the written word, to make you hear, to make you feel—it is, before all, to make you *see.*

D. W. Griffith:
The task I'm trying to achieve is above all to make you see.

A good many years ago a Russian director took a strip of silent film showing an actor, in close-up, expressionlessly staring downward at a point below camera angle. Then the director spliced this shot—a repeat of the same one every time—in between other silent shots; one of a steaming bowl of soup, one of a dead woman in a coffin, another of children at play, and so on. When he screened the completed reel for a small audience, pretending it was a screen test, the viewers praised the unknown actor . . . They were impressed by the subtle way in which he expressed "desperate hunger" at the sight of the soup, "heartbroken grief" as he gazed down at the dead woman, "gentle amusement" as he watched the children playing. Gary Jennings.

THE CELLULOID WOMB

Reelity.

GWTW
Katie Hamilton Kennedy Butler
was better known as _____.

Close to 80,000 students are
enrolled in 3,000 film courses in
some 200 colleges and universities. Third-graders are cranking
out cartoons; middle-class kids
are exploring alienation; ghetto
boys are focusing on roaches
and rats. The subject matter of

the young film makers is no less
than an encyclopedia of their
society. No wonder that where a
youth might once have dreamed
of writing the Great American
Novel, today he wants to make
the Great American Film.
Life.

I . . . learned, to my surprise,
that a picture is not at all like a
play; that on the contrary, it is
like a novel, but a novel to be
seen, instead of told.
Robert Nathan.

The filmist becomes not a trans-
lator for an established author,
but a new author in his own right.
Bluestone.

Name that Movie:
It created great excitement,
winning both raves and criticism.
President Woodrow Wilson
praised it, saying it was "like
writing history with lightning."

Oh, Van!

Back in the corner, he held
Charlene's hand and they
smooched a little, but not much.
Sonny really wanted to see the
movie, and it was easy for him
to hold his passion down. Charlene had not got all the sweetness
out of the stick of Doublemint
and didn't want to take it out of
her mouth just to kiss Sonny,
but after a few minutes she
changed her mind, took it out,
and stuck it under the arm of her
seat. It seemed to her that Sonny
looked a little bit like Steve
Cochran, and she began to kiss
him energetically, squirming and
pressing herself against his
knee. Sonny returned the kiss,
but with somewhat muted interest. He wanted to keep at least
one eye on the screen, so if
Ginger Rogers decided to take
her clothes off he wouldn't miss
it. The posters outside indicated
she at least got down to her slip
at one point. Besides, Charlene
was always getting worked up
in picture shows; at first Sonny
had thought her fits of cinematic
passion very encouraging, until
he discovered it was practically
impossible to get her worked up
except in picture shows.
The movies were Charlene's life,
as she was fond of saying. She
spent most of her afternoons
hanging around the little beauty
shop where her mother worked,
reading movie magazines, and
she always referred to movie
stars by their first names. Once
when an aunt gave her a dollar
for her birthday she went down to
the variety store and bought two
fifty-cent portraits to sit on her
dresser: one was of June Allyson
and the other Van Johnson.
Marlene copied Charlene's pas-
sions as exactly as possible, but
when the same aunt gave *her* a
dollar the variety store clerk's stock
of portraits was low and she had
to make do with Esther Williams
and Mickey Rooney. Charlene
kidded her mercilessly about the
latter, and took to sleeping with Van
Johnson under her pillow because
she was afraid Marlene might
mutilate him out of envy.
Larry McMurty, *The Last
Picture Show.*

The Eye of God.

Traditional documentaries never lost the luster of artfulness; Flaherty's skies were filtered and Grierson's workers were posed. *But we know, from the direct cinema films, what life looks like when it is captured with very little interference. We know instinctively, by the feel and movement of the image, that the theatrical film is built upon interference, control, preparation.* We accept the presence of the camera there too, but we demand that the artist acknowledge its presence. In return we accord the artist certain new freedoms. His performers may now look at the lens—formerly a sacred taboo. His film may bear visible marks of having been worked upon: obtrusive editing, special titles. Most precious of all, he is no longer obliged to pretend that his film came into existence automatically or magically. The modern film is visibly constructed by the hand of man, and not by the eye of God. It has become, for sensitive viewers, slightly embarrassing to watch a film built on other assumptions—like watching a man who doesn't realize that he has a hole in his pants. The modern artist whom we find comfortable has sewed on a bright-colored patch or is busy exploring the hole with his finger. With him, we know where we are.
Ernest Callenbach.

How many novels about Hollywood are not critical or sardonic? How many are?

Presently . . . the Ethiopian called out, "I've caught a thing that I can't see. It smells like Giraffe, and it kicks like Giraffe, but it hasn't any form." "Don't you trust it," said the Leopard. "Sit on its head till the morning—same as me. They haven't any form—any of 'em." Rudyard Kipling to Sam Goldwin.

When Stephen Leacock wrote that every story must have a beginning, a middle and an end, he was addressing a literate audience. An Eskimo narrator will give his autobiography with complete disregard to chronology. He is uninterested in narrating a story from the ground upward, for he begins with the crisis, so to speak, and works backward and forward, with many omissions and repetitions, on the tacit assumption that your mind moves in the same groove as his and that explanations are needless. It produces the most extraordinary effect, one reminiscent of that achieved by Joyce and other sophisticated writers who deliberately reject sequential time. The Western listener, in order to understand and appreciate, is forced to rearrange images so that they represent an historical sequence.
Charles Carpenter.

Most screen writers prefer to work on an ill-written second-rate book, towards which they have no conscience.
Margaret Kennedy.

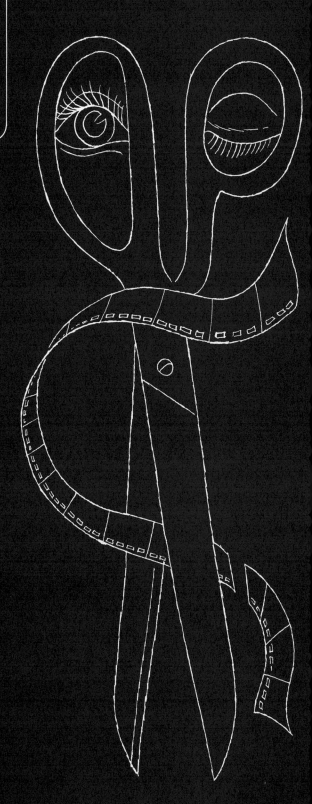

WHO are just touched with dreams
And never are forgetting;
Who are entombed through all their glamorous days
Amid dead things,
And seek the dusk for freedom
At the end?
These are the pathetics—
Who have no dreams worth telling
And yet would dream.
Florence Keady, "The Pathetics."

2001, A Space Odyssey is the first book to be published at the
same time as the film release.

One Hollywood director buys up enough copies of the book from
which he makes a movie so that it will remain on the best-seller list and
keep his film before the public.

*When a new media goes around an old media, the old media becomes an
art form. When the novel was new it was looked down upon. When the novel gave
way to the movies the novel became an art form. When movies gave way
to TV the movie became an art form. The novel is now dead.*
David Kerr.

It is estimated that for every book the average college student reads, he sees 20 movies.

Influence:
"I love making pictures," Mailer said after the screening of *Beyond the Law*.
Discussing the immediacy and power of the cinema, Mailer said it
had also changed his literary approach.

"It changed *Armies of the Night*. I was cutting *Wild 90* (Mailer's first film,
in which he appears) and got so used to looking at myself as an object that it
was natural to write about myself in the third person."

"Working with yourself as a piece of film cuts through any vanity you might
have. Making films also makes me write with more attention to how things look."
Jim Haagland.

According to Hollywood movies, which of the following are true?

_____Atheists are evil.

_____Injustice can be trying but it does not triumph.

_____Problems of labor, politics, domestic life and sexual abnormality can be solved by a simple Christian phrase or a fine American motto.

_____Fornication can be pleasurable and need not have damaging effects on one's life.

_____Only institutionalized sex is fun.

_____Law breakers must die, go to jail, return the money or become monks.

_____A philanderer will lose the one girl he eventually falls in love with.

_____The most potent and brilliant of villains are powerless before little children, parish priests or young virgins.

Terry tells Edie what he knows of her brother's murder, we see a close-up of Edie's face, and then a close-up of a steam whistle blowing, and we feel the pressures bursting in Edie's spirit.
Edward Fischer.

Somehow we don't resent these clichés. In fact, we find them satisfying. It is the satisfaction that lies in any art form that has unities of time, place and action. Greek tragedies and Molière comedies, Shakespearean plays and grand operas, classical ballets and Oriental dances, bullfights and baseball games—we like them *because* they follow fixed patterns and use stylized gestures.
William Zinsser.

List three of your favorite Hollywood conventions:
1._____
2._____
3._____

Economy of Means:
In the breakfast table sequence in *Citizen Kane*, the publisher √ and his wife are shown to grow apart in a film duration of slightly more than two minutes' time.

Film origins: side shows, slapstick, pornography, melodrama, _____, _____, _____, _____.

After the release of the film *Wuthering Heights*, the pocket book edition sold over 700,000 copies, more than all the copies sold in its previous 92-year existence.
Jerry Wald.

For me there is only one way [to get a perfect script]—write and correct, write and correct, day and night. In this way only can you make progress.
Ozu.

In *Brief Encounter* . . . a very poignant love story is heightened immeasurably by being told against the most meager backgrounds, and a Rachmaninoff concerto forms the accompaniment throughout. The whole was very satisfying.
Oscar Levant.

. . . most of the television I've seen, including productions that are much more expensive than mine, have an essentially lazy feeling about them. They always lean on narration—often of a very didactic nature. They get to a filmic problem and they solve it by putting a face in that bridges you from here to there. My work, from the beginning, has been characterized by the elimination of narration. *Point of Order* was the first film of feature-documentary length in which everything fitted together and there wasn't one word of explanation.
Emile de Antonio.

'B' movies are American documentaries.

Was I in here last night and did I spend a twenty dollar bill?

Yeah.

What a load that is off my mind. I thought I'd lost it.

Mahatma Kane Jeeves.

88

I think one of the things they should realize as an audience is the difference between a story film and one which may be a philosophic viewpoint. John Korty.

Joyce wrote *Ulysses* in the form of a movie and that's probably why so many people, including Joyce himself, thought it should be made into one.

Hitchcock: Well, I shall never do the screen version, precisely because *Crime and Punishment* is somebody else's achievement. There's been a lot of talk about the way in which Hollywood directors destroy literary masterpieces. I'll have no part of that! What I do is to read a story only once, and if I like the basic idea, I just forget all about the book and start to create cinema. Today I would be unable to tell you the story of Daphne du Maurier's *The Birds*. I read it only once, and very quickly at that. An author takes three or four years to write a fine novel; it's his whole life. Then other people take it over

The Definitive Form

completely. Craftsmen and technicians fiddle around with it and eventually someone winds up as a candidate for an Oscar, while the author is entirely forgotten. I simply can't see that.

Truffaut: I take it then that you'll never do a screen version of *Crime and Punishment*.

Hitchcock: Even if I did, it probably wouldn't be any good.

Truffaut: Why not?

Hitchcock: Well, in Dostoyevsky's novel there are many words and all of them have a function.

Truffaut: That's right. Theoretically, a masterpiece is something that has already found its perfection of form, its definitive form.

New York, April 23, 1896: Thomas Edison shows his first movie.

Language has become a a character in novels.

Technique has become a character in film.

Heard any good movies lately?

The cinema is the representative art of today as
painting was of yesterday. Painting is buried.
Eisenstein.

Jean Varda wanted to invent a machine which
would force the spectator to face the painting
and nothing but the painting and would prop the
eyelids open so that he was forced to perceive.
Such an instrument is the motion picture projector.

Great films like great novels
have to achieve a kind of
melding. It's like making two
metals hot enough that they just
melt into each other. And in a
really great film you shouldn't
be able to separate the two. The
story should be told not just
appropriately; the message must
be part of the story. They really
are one piece. But perhaps one
film out of 500 ever does that.
Films that fail over-emphasize
one or the other. They can have
too much of the philosophy explicit.
John Korty.

You will find, in every novel, the
counterparts of long shots and
close-ups, tracking shots and
dissolves; but you will find them
in words addressed to the ear,
instead of in pictures meant for the eye.
Robert Nathan.

GWTW: Who played Scarlett's father?   Sara Bernhardt   Merle Oberon   Calpurnia   Becky Sharpe

Linda Darnell   Miriam Hopkins   Greer Garson   Cathy   Phaedra   Emma Bovary

Jennifer Jones   Norma Shearer   Margaret Rutherford   Miss Prism   Marie Antoinette   Amber

The Big A

I was furious. I told him that if a common "greaser" like Magdalena Montezuma could have her pick of such famous writers as Ernest Hemingway, William Faulkner, Willa Catha and Elinor Glyn why should I, his own wife, have to put up with a nobody like Sheldon? I said that I intended to have a "name" author, too. With that Morris tossed a copy of *The Scarlet Letter* at me and said that I could probably play it to perfection. I asked Momma, Helen Highwater, Vivienne Vixen and some of the other girls in my set if they had ever heard of this Hawthorne and they said they thought they had. Lynn Caine was almost sure of it. Dudley du Pont had read the book and explained the story to me and I thought it was cute and certainly had some good scenes in it for the leading lady. The only thing I objected to was that it was so old-fashioned. I had been in so many costume pictures recently that I felt a change of pace would be good for me. So I told Morris that I liked the story and to go ahead and buy it for me, but that I did want some changes made and to get hold of the author for some story conferences. Morris just laughed and said something to the effect that Hawthorne didn't live in Hollywood but was eccentric, and hung around a Public Domain where they couldn't call him, and that I could do anything I liked with the script.

What a challenge! I admired the character and the nobility of

Hester   Prynne and I thought the title was very catchy. Otherwise I wanted a free hand to bring the story up-to-date and to make a lot of changes. So many men in the story department at Metronome said that *The Scarlet Letter* was a great classic and that it was a sacrilege to touch it that I decided to handle the script myself. (They'd certainly taken liberties with The Bible, but just try to change one comma in some old book about a girl having a baby in Massachusetts and they're all up in arms! That's the sort of help one used to be forced to endure on the Metronome "lot!").

What I did to *The Scarlet Letter* is now history. I have been both lauded and criticized for "taking liberties" with the work of "Nat" Hawthorne, who was the only person involved not to make any comments, either "pro" or "con," about my film. Suffice it to say that I transformed it from a dusty classic, about dead people in a dead age, to a vital, living story about a girl everyone could understand. In modernizing the story, I kept the essentials—Hester Prynne is a good, lively spirited girl who makes a mistake, pays the price and ends up happily married—and mercilessly cut out the "deadwood." As this was my first real starring vehicle, I wrote in parts for the people on the Metronome "lot" whom I knew I could trust (too many others had made the mistake of "showing their hands" to me in the past). Helen Hightwater was scheduled to appear but suffered

an unfortunate relapse and was once again placed in a sanitarium. I gave Carstairs Bagley a "fat" character rôle and offered a specially written part to witty Dudley du Pont. However, he said that he had been put out on loan to Alexander Korda (later Sir Alexander Korda) and had to go to England for a long time on the very next boat. I was sick with disappointment, but that, alas, is life in show "biz." I went to Morris and demanded—and got—Letch Feeley as my leading man. With a "team" like that how could any picture help but be a huge success?

As you may remember, *my* version of *The Scarlet Letter* was a college musical set in a big co-educational university called Allstate. Hester, the daughter of a man who renounced a fortune of millions to become a minister, is working her way through college (this was the time of the depression and I felt that she would lose sympathy and "audience identification" if she was just a pampered coed in some radical school like Vassar or Foxcroft) selling subscriptions to *College Humor* and she is also captain of the cheer leaders' team. She meets Brick Barclay (the new name I gave the hero, as Letch didn't like the one "Nat" chose), who is captain of the football team. They fall in love at a beautiful formal ball held in his fraternity house and, having drunk too much "spiked" punch, Hester allows Brick to take liberties with her that she would never have otherwise per-

Sam Peckinpah.

Little Me (cont.)

mitted. The next day she is horrified when she finds out what she has done and realizes that she is pregnant, and that a hard society girl is wearing Brick's "frat" pin and that he is the son of a millionaire and would never consider finding happiness with a poor girl. Hester is sick with worry but she puts on a brave face, avoids Brick whenever he tries to "date" her or even "cut in" at a dance, and she goes out to cheer the Allstate team on to victory against Plymouth U. It is then that she faints and Brick, realizing how much he loves her and that her unborn child is his, picks her up in his arms, tells his millionaire father that if he can't marry Hester he won't finish the game for the old *alma mater.* The father recognizes Hester as the daughter of his old college roommate, the man who lent him enough money to get started in business and gives the young people his blessing. With Hester cheering him on, Brick goes in to make the winning touchdown in the last minute of the game. Then Hester, wearing proudly the big red "A" of Allstate, leads the team and student body in a big victory snake dance culminating in their wedding under the visitors' goal post. I felt that it brought home a real message for the youth of America.

It took us more than four months to film *The Scarlet Letter*, I insisted on a closed "set" with only Manny, head of the publicity department, permitted to visit. Morris ranted and raved about

the budget, but I wanted my *chef-d'oeuvre* to be the one flawless film of my career. And it was. Why should I, a serious *artiste*, care for Morris' hysterical outbursts over deficits when I have in my scrapbook reviews such as "Devastating . . ." "An unbelievable four hours in the theatre . . ." "Belle Poitrine brings to Hester Prynne all the innocence and virtue of a John Held flapper . . . ."

After a carefully planned campaign of advertising, publicity, personal appearances and interviews, *The Scarlet Letter* had its *première* at the Buchsbaum Baghdad in New York's fabulous Times Square on New Year's Eve. The *première* was a very exclusive invitational affair. All the top stars of the Metronome "stable" were invited (with one glowing exception) as were rival producers, stars, international celebrities, critics and leading "opinion-makers." I was terribly disappointed when Louella O. ("Lolly") Parsons telegraphed that she had suddenly been taken ill. Walter Winchell was also suddenly unable to attend and President and Mrs. Hoover regretted that they had a prior engagement. Otherwise it was a *succès fou.* The showing began promptly at eight (I am one star who won't put up with latecomers) and ended on the stroke of midnight. Although I had seen "rushes" and screenings of *The Scarlet Letter* many times before, I was dissolved in tears at the beauty of my performance and even my "hardboiled" husband,

Morris, sobbed brokenly in the seat beside mine, muttering softly in his quaint native tongue. The rest of the audience was so touched that they were unable even to applaud at the end of the film.

When I stepped out of the theatre onto Times Square, pandemonium broke loose. From the wildly cheering populace of New York I knew that I had arrived. Never before was any actress given such an ovation. As the shouts, whistles, horns, sirens, serpentine and confetti swirled around me, I knew that this was something more than the work of Manny and the "boys" in the P.R. department. This demonstration was far beyond something staged in the name of publicity. "Morris," I breathed. "The shouting! The cheers!"

"It's 1932, *nafkeh*," he said affectionately.

Patrick Dennis, *Little Me.*

GWTW:
Who played Prissy?

Now that I have finished *Deserter* I am sure that sound film is potentially the art of the future. It is not an orchestral creation centering round music, nor yet a theatrical dominated by the factor of the actor, nor even is it akin to opera, it is a synthesis of each and every element—the oral, the visual, the philosophical; it is our opportunity to translate the world in all its lines and shadows into a new art form that has succeeded and will supersede all the older arts, for it is the supreme medium in which we can express today and tomorrow.
V. I. Pudovkin.

The impulse to film realism denied silence while creating it. Ironically, in contemporary cinema the great directors and innovators Antonioni, Fellini, Bergman, have rediscovered this economy, capitalizing on the trance state of film.

Gosho's idea of a talkie is a film which contains a lot of silence. Anderson and Richie, *The Japanese Film.*

What is the difference between a talking film and a sound film?

Speech can be used like paint to form a shadow across a soundtrack.

I prefer silence to sound, and the image produced by words occurs in silence. That is, the thunder and the music of the prose take place in silence.
William Faulkner.

Insects one hears— and one hears the talk of men— with different ears. Wafū.

The retreat toward silence, the appreciation of it as an active philosophic and human force, is a modern phenomenon.
John Lahr, *Evergreen Review.*

Well, the movie went on its rounds and I began getting letters from all over the country plus at the same time reactions which made me take the letters a little more seriously from my brother who was in Michigan and a friend who was living upstate saying this is a dirty movie, are you mad? So then, thanks to my friend and my brother tipping me off, I realized they were seeing *Dear John* with a sound track dubbed. *Dear John* had come here with subtitles. It was being shown around the country with an English dubbed track that according to the best witnesses was turning this movie into just a dirty sex exploitation movie. It had destroyed whatever sensitivity there might have been in the film. . . . . Judith Crist.

Adding sound to a print increases the cost of printing about 3½ cents a foot provided you have already put the sound on 16mm sprocketed tape.

Silent film always had sound. Talkies always have silence. True or False?

After a picture is cut, I dictate what amounts to a real sound script to a secretary. We run every reel off and I indicate all the places where sounds should be heard. Until now we've worked with natural sounds, but now, thanks to electronic sounds, I'm not only going to indicate the sound we want but also the style and the nature of each sound.
Alfred Hitchcock.

The sound of sound.

SCREEN IMAGE AS METAPHOR

Kurosawa is not interested in Sugata's prowess, however. He is only interested in Sugata's education—which is a much more interesting subject.

This, the next sequence illustrates. Some time has passed. Sugata has apparently gotten very good indeed and we watch him break up a village festival. He is using all of the correct judo procedures, besting one man after the other. All of this is shown with fast cutting at its most seductive. It is an exhilarating passage. It is like something from the ordinary Japanese fight-picture, only much more skillfully done. We—not yet guessing what the picture is about—think: that Sugata is a real man, a real hero. The crowd thinks so. There are cries of how wonderful he is, how marvelous. Sugata, carried away, attacks one man after the other, always winning.

There is a cut to the judo teacher's room. Everything is still. He does not move, there is no movement on the screen, and after the furious motion of the sequence directly before it is like an admonition. He sits there, as though waiting, the seconds pass. Then Sugata, his kimono torn, comes in.

Teacher: Well, you must feel good after having thrown so many people around.

Sugata: I'm sorry.

Teacher: I rather wanted to see you in action. You're very strong, really very strong indeed. Maybe you are even stronger than I am now. But, you know, there is very little similarity between your kind of judo and my kind of judo. Do you know what I mean? You do not know how to use it, you do not know the way of life. And to teach judo to someone who does not know that is like giving a knife to a madman.

Sugata: I know it.

Teacher: That is a lie. To act as you do, without meaning or purpose, to hate and attack—is that the way of life? No—the way is loyalty and love. This is the natural truth of heaven and earth. It is the ultimate truth and only through it can a man face death.

Sugata: I can face death. I'm not afraid to die right now, if you order it.

Teacher: Shut up, you're nothing but a common street-fighter.

Sugata: I'm not afraid to die.

Teacher: Then go and die.

Then Sugata does an extraordinary thing. He opens the *shoji* and without a look backward or below he leaps.

This extraordinary leap, right out of the house, lands him—as it did the jujitsu men—in the water, only this water is the lotus pond and we see that the teacher has been living in a temple. The nuances and hidden meanings in this sequence are worth investigating. Death is introduced as the great adversary, and this is something Sugata will discover at the end of the film where he is almost killed. What saves him then is a remembered vision of this scene with the teacher and later, in the pond. It is there, if anywhere, that he comes to realize "the way of life." At the same time, now, his teacher has thrown him into the water just as surely as he did the jujitsu men. Water is always a purification, a baptism; and, as in Christian baptism, it is also an initiation. That the teacher has been living in a temple is no accident for a temple is the home of initiation, and of faith, and Sugata's extraordinary leap can be understood as that—a leap into faith. The

Bring Back the Auk.

Because you don't seem quite real
   when I'm not with you,
I miss you.
I think of you in one pose always,
With your arms folded,
Your glasses down on your nose.

How long can I keep my balance
Waiting for you on this precipice?
My nails ache.
And you sit there as I would have
   imagined
Had I been inventive enough to remember.
I remember the ducks, kid.
Yes, they're nice.

"Bring back the Auk!"
That's wonderful. Yes, that's wonderful.
But in the meantime, what role do I play?
I've got fourteen lovers.
And the trains go by.
We watch for the caboose.
I've got fourteen lovers.

Don't you care?
Kid, don't you care? Even though it's
   raining,
Even though you're singing "A Thousand
   Clowns"
I've got fourteen lovers.
And you want to bring back the Auk.

Mary Pohland.

The guarantee against limits
is a sense of alternatives.

1893:
Thomas Edison's *The Ex-
ecution of Mary, Queen
of Scots* lasting less than
a minute is shown on the
kinetoscope.

shoji opens—there is the lotus pond, he chooses to leap.
After the leap comes the trial. Sugata has gotten himself into the water, it is up
to his shoulders, it is cold. The teacher may have thrown him but he himself chose
to be thrown. He had thought to prove that he was not afraid to die but, once in
the pool, it becomes apparent that all he can prove is that he is not afraid to live.
This sequence, Sugata in the pool, is of a beauty that even now, a whole war
and over two decades away, can move almost to tears. He grasps a post, holding
himself to it, and—clinging there—stares. Lost, confused, afraid, unsure, he can
only cling to this post, the cold waters around him. Later one of the priests points
to the post and tells him that that was his staff of life—and so it was. Without it to
center himself upon he might have climbed out of the pond, it was easy enough
to have done. But he does not. He clings and waits. The priest tries to talk with
him. Sugata, unsure, shows defiance, refuses to answer, and the priest says:
"Judging from the fact that you refuse to answer, you still have not received
enlightenment. All right, you can spend the night looking at the moon."
The camera watches Sanshiro. He stays in the water, holding onto the post,
looking up at the moon. There is a particularly beautiful transition as the last light
of evening fades from the *shoji* of the teacher's room and the light appears—he
is there, just on the other side of the paper. Outside it is night. Sanshiro
looks at the moon.
There is a close-up of the moon, and over it the sound of frogs, followed by a
direct cut to Sanshiro in the pond, faintly lighted, mists around him, and the distant
call of a rooster. It is dawn. He turns, then looks. Before him a lotus is open.
There is a short scene of Sugata looking at it, uncomprehendingly, the look of an
animal. Then—and the beauty of the scene is such that no description can
suggest it—Sugata understands. He has seen truth and beauty and this he shows.
He races from the pond, he pounds on the teacher's door—it opens at once, the
teacher was not asleep. The priests and other students appear. Sugata has
understood, the trial is over.
If this film were about boxing or wrestling, or almost any other kind of sport, such
mystical overtones would seem irrelevant and ostentatious. But there is a
mystique about judo and judo is a discipline just as much as zen is. It is not
accidental that so many young enthusiasts are given to lives of meditation and
self-denial. The way of life is a known route.
And it is precisely this which appealed to Kurosawa in the original book and which
he underlines in his film. The entire lotus-pond passage did not appear in the
book. Kurosawa wrote it. As later in *Rashomon*, he adds to a literary conception
something of which only film is capable. Sugata's vigil is something to be seen,
to be lived through, and to be remembered. And it is, tellingly, this image which
—above all others—remains alive in the memory long after the film has been
experienced. That is, after all, what remains of all films—these separate images,
alive in the mind long after the film itself may be forgotten. When Kurosawa said
that he wanted to make a really movie-like movie this is what he meant. The
construction is superb, the cutting is marvelous—but it is the inexplicable, the
unexpected, the truly moving which remains behind.
Donald Richie.

Butterfly McQueen

For in the end, the rhythm of the
picture depends less upon words than
upon direction and cutting.

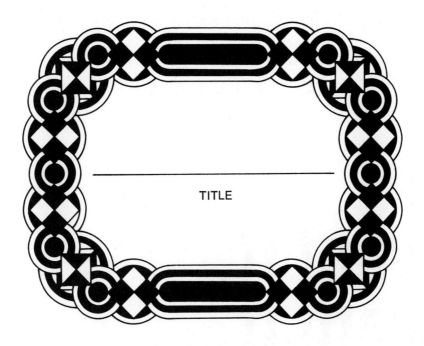

TITLE

Drive-ins are out, to start with. One must always be
Able to see the over-painted Moorish ceiling
Whose pinchbeck jazz gleams even in the darkness, calling
The straying eye to feast on it, and glut, then fall
Back to the sterling screen again. One needs to feel
That the two empty, huddled, dark stage-boxes keep
Empty for kings. And having frequently to cope
With the abominable goodies, overflow
Bulk and (finally) exploring hands of flushed
Close neighbors gazing beadily out across glum
Distances is, after all, to keep the gleam
Alive of something rather serious, to keep
Faith, perhaps, with the City. When as children our cup
Of joys ran over the special section, and we clutched
Our ticket stubs and followed the bouncing ball, no clash
Of cymbals at the start of the stage-show could abash
Our third untiring time around. When we came back,
Older, to cop an endless series of feels, we sat
Unashamed beneath the bare art-nouveau bodies, set
High on the golden, after-glowing proscenium when
The break had come. And still, now as always, once
The show is over and we creep into the dull
Blaze of mid-afternoon sunshine, the hollow dole
Of the real descends on everything and we can know
That we have been in some place wholly elsewhere, a night
At noonday, not without dreams, whose portals shine
Peculiarly, being made, in ever-changing shapes,
Of some translucent substance, not often used for gates.
John Hollander, *Movie-Going.*

May, 1896:
Auguste and Louis Lumiére
filmed the coronation of
Nicholas II in 420 feet of film.

I want it, I want it, I want everything I've ever seen in the movies!

Leo Bloom in *The Producers*.

Paul Bunyan

How hard it is, when
everything encourages
us to sleep, though we
may look about us with
conscious, clinging eye,
to wake and yet look
about us as in a dream,
with eyes that no longer
know their function and
whose gaze is turned
inward.
Antoine Artaud.

Yes, We Have No Ritchard.
Bruce J. Friedman

Since Mr. Dalton had seen many films and plays and read a good deal on the subject, he expected, after he died, to find himself before a Cyril Ritchard-type clerk, wearing white and seated at a desk. Wings were optional. Droll remarks would follow, in British accent, such as, "We've got your records right here; what took you so long?" There would be a file cabinet and much shuffling of papers and talk about "bringing your records up to date." The "front office" would be mentioned and sooner or later the "boss," in such lines as, "The boss is sure going to be riled up when he sees these typing errors." Plenty of white figured in Mr. Dalton's thoughts, too, cloaks and clouds and harps and floating things and subordinate people, too, all with such amusing comments as, "I've got to get my wings fixed."

What actually happened is that Mr. Dalton didn't get Ritchard. He didn't get E. G. Marshall either or, for that matter, anyone whose personality he could really nail down. The man did not wear a white robe, and Mr. Dalton, later on, could not recall what he wore. Something kind of vague and watery, if he wore anything at all. He certainly didn't have flip, or even impatient things to say, and he sat at something that wasn't a desk, and maybe he wasn't even sitting. He seemed to be a little lower than Mr. Dalton, and may have been sitting on a rock although Mr. Dalton could not even be sure of that. Mr. Dalton himself could not remember whether he felt light and airy or whether there were clouds around and none of the Hollywood things had happened at all. Except one. He seemed to be wearing a pair of sandals he had once purchased at Vic Tanny's Gym and Health Club so as not to get athlete's foot when working out in the gym. What else he was wearing,

he couldn't say—or even if he was wearing something.

What was most disconcerting to Mr. Dalton was that he could not remember any elevator ride. It was the one thing he counted on most of all and he was *certain* there would be one in there somewhere, a ride upward, and then, when they were finished with him, the decision as to whether to send him up or down. Mr. Dalton did not know whether to speak or wait to be spoken to, but he was so upset, he said to the man with the nebulous face and no distinctive personality,
"Look, I don't remember any elevator ride. Oh, you know what I mean. I don't really mean an elevator ride. Maybe you use a Volkswagen or a coal car, but I've got to know whether you've got a good side and a bad side here. Just tell me that and anything you say from here on in is all right with me."

"We have a good side and a bad side," the man said, and this relaxed Mr. Dalton and he felt at least there was a little something to the movie ideas he'd gotten.
"But I'll bet you don't even have it the Hollywood way," Mr. Dalton said. "Up and down is the way they do it. I'll bet you have it left side and right."

The nebulous man, if he was a man, said, "That's correct."

The reason Mr. Dalton was glad about this was that, however unsophisticated and *Reader's Digest* it may have sounded, he was quite certain that he had been a nice man during his life. He knew many people probably felt that way about themselves, but he was certain, at the very heart of himself, that he really *had* been nice and wasn't just feeling this way to buoy his spirits. If you stacked up his good deeds against his bad ones, the good ones would win ridiculously and overwhelmingly, no contest. And it wasn't that there was one sneaky thing he'd been trying to cover up and atone for by piling up millions of good deeds. There

were no sneakies at all, and even if he *had* a sneaky (he hadn't), well, by God, he was still nice. He'd say that to anyone, whether he was dead or alive or whatever the hell condition he was in now.
"Did you know I've been nice?" he asked the man. "I'm probably still nice, too, but I guess you're not concerned about me now, although by God, I'm nice now, too, even if I'm dead. I'm just always going to be nice. But did you *know* that?"
"I know," the man said.
"You probably have records and you're going to pull out a sheet on me. You have everybody's file, don't you? You have a file cabinet somewhere."
"No," the man said.

"It's not at all the way I'd imagined it," Mr. Dalton said, or thought he said. "But just so long as you know I've been nice. When do we get started?"

The man said, "We could have started a little while ago, before you started talking. Or now, later, any time."

"Do I get a say in where we get started?" Mr. Dalton asked.

The man looked through him and Mr. Dalton thought, "He isn't saying anything because a little personality was beginning to come through. He clammed up just in time. A little more and I could have nailed him down, pinned him down and found out whether he was a Ritchard or a Marshall or a goddamned Wendell Willkie. He shut up like a clam, though." And then Mr. Dalton wondered whether you were allowed to think things to yourself when you were dead. He turned off his mind for a while, just to be on the safe side. He thought of water, which was like not thinking at all to him. Maybe when you were dead, if you began thinking things they counted against you. Maybe a few interior thoughts at this moment wiped out 49 years of being nice. By God, he thought, I don't know any other way to be but nice, so I'll keep thinking. They'll be nice thoughts and

...pinpoint what kind of man he was, although Mr. Dalton himself seemed to recall once being in advertising or at least being good at packaging people.

They stopped walking, if they had been walking. Mr. Dalton knew only that they were as hell weren't standing still.

"Are we here?" Mr. Dalton asked. "I mean, where I'm going to be?" Then he added, "Forever, that is," feeling a little silly, as though he were in one of those heaven movies again.

The man nodded.

"I can't remember," Mr. Dalton asked, "whether you took me to the left or to the right. Let me get one thing straight. I hate to be a bore, but you do know I'm nice, don't you?"

The man nodded.

"And left is your nice side and right is your bad side?"

"Yes," said the man.

"Then you took me to the left, right?"

"No," said the nebulous man. "To the right." said Mr. Dalton, not without apprehension.

Mr. Dalton, rattled, and feeling he had every right to be rattled, said, "But why? You're probably not convinced that I'm nice, correct?"

"No," said the man.

"I know then," said Mr. Dalton, quite convinced he had the answer. "You have a reverse sort of logic up here. You put the nice guys on the bad side and the bad guys on the nice side. There's a perverse someone at work up here. Isn't that it? It's foolish, you know, because all us nice ones will know, even while we're on the bad side, that we're still nice. You're just being perverse for its own sake. Why do you have to knock yourselves out so much? Just to be different? Listen, do I get to punch you if I don't like something here?"

Mr. Dalton took a look at the man and for a brief second thought he could actually see him and size him up. He guessed he had 40 pounds on the man...

"Look, I mean no disrespect," said Mr. Dalton. "A week from now, if I see you again, and I suppose I do (Hollywood again), I'll probably feel silly. But you must take an awful lot of abuse."

The man said, "I've got to go now."

"Don't go," said Mr. Dalton. "I've got to get straightened out. I'm nice. You know I'm nice. Why did you put me on the bad side?"

Mr. Dalton tried to grab the man and hold on to him, looking around furiously, thinking, "Christ, I'm backed against the wall. If only I could get one of those breaks you're supposed to get when you're at an all-time low." He looked up and down the right side, where he was to be and got the break. He spotted a print he had seen once before at Bloomingdale's department store and a man he knew as Mr. Sydel. Mr. Sydel was engaged in doing something to the ground or whatever it was beneath him. "Look," said Mr. Dalton, "I know him. I don't care what in the hell he told you, and maybe this is the first un-nice thing I've ever done, but he is not a nice man. He stole paper from some kind of crazy company I used to work for with him and even if he was never caught he really was a crook. He's still a crook. And it wasn't the only bad thing he did. I can't document any others, but believe me there were others. How in the hell can we be put on the same side? You know he's bad, don't you?"

"So I understand," the man said. "That is, I don't really know, but one of my colleagues so informs me."

"He's slipping," Mr. Dalton thought. "By that statement he told me something that will enable me to package him, pin down his personality. He has 'colleagues,' which means he's classy, has studied. . . . But, still, I'll have to know more."

"If you both know he's bad, how come he's down here? Don't tell me. You've got the bad side divided up into sections. On one side you put baddies, like Mr.

...but if they're baddies, they'll be nicely motivated.

"We'll go now," the man said.

"Say some more, so I can get the hang of you," Mr. Dalton said. Mr. Dalton felt he was good at pinning personalities down, packaging people. If the man said just a little more, Mr. Dalton would have him, and perhaps be able to do a routine on him, one as good as his Jack Paar imitation. Mr. Dalton could not remember whether he himself had been in advertising or not. The only thing he could remember was that somehow, somewhere, at some time, he had been at Vic Tanny's.

They seemed to walk somewhere and, try as he might, Mr. Dalton, although he'd promised to check the man's outfit, what he looked like, his walk and mannerisms, forgot to do these things. He remembered only that the man had seemed to be a little lower than him. Mr. Dalton brought up Green Pastures as something he'd liked and then said, "I'll bet you think I'm just trying to butter you up, to say I like your racket, know about it and some of my best friends are heavenly clerks or whatever you are."

They passed a Danish modern sofa with shiny wood and Mr. Dalton thought, "Now there are two things I know. The Tanny slippers and the sofa. I wonder if there'll be any more. Maybe there are only two things you recognize in this whole trip or maybe 12. I wonder how many?" He said to the man, "I know I'm wearing Tanny slippers and I recognized a Danish modern sofa. That's all that's tangible. Will there be anything else? Anything else I can recognize or touch or sort of make reference to?"

"One more," the man said. "Air conditioning."

"I've got him now," Mr. Dalton thought. "Now I can tell what kind of person he is. And yet...

Sydel, on the other, people like me? Correct?

"No," the man said.

The air conditioning went on, and Mr. Dalton felt himself relax, in spite of himself.

"Look, for Christ's sake, what's the deal? I'll talk down to earth now, because nothing can hurt me. You have a good side and a bad side, right?"

The man nodded, but looked impatient. "I really have to go."

"Two more minutes won't kill you," said Mr. Dalton. "Who the hell do you put over on the good side? People who are nicer than me? You have some sort of score and I didn't score high enough, is that it? The place is crowded up with people who got higher scores, right?"

The man began edging away, and Mr. Dalton said, "You stay right here. I never punched people as much as I should, but by God, I'll punch you if I have to." But then Mr. Dalton felt demolished and said, "Stay with me another minute, will you? Maybe I'll never see you again and there won't be anyone to tell me what to do. How to get along here. What the hell the rules are. The machinery of the place. I mean if it's forever, I have to know, don't I?"

"I do have a schedule, Mr. Dalton," the man said kindly.

"Can you call me Philip?" Mr. Dalton asked. For a second he felt a joke coming on, like, "If I get friendly with you, can you fix traffic tickets?" but decided not to ask it. When the joke went out of his mind, the panic started again.

"What I started to ask is how in the hell I get over on the good side? I've been nice, you say you know I've been nice, but what the hell good has it done me? Can you name me one person who's over there so I can get an idea of what you've got to have, where I missed out?"

"I can't do that," the man said.

"Why, for Christ's sake? I'm a dying man. I'm dead and I'm dying all over again. I need some help."

"All right then, I'd rather not go into this, but we don't have anyone over there. There is no one on our good side."

"It's for the staff?"

"No, even the staff doesn't use it. For a while we had women, with enormous bosoms over there, for a very short while, but everyone saw the fallacy in that and so now no one gets in."

"There's no one on the good side," Mr. Dalton said. "That means we're all over here, right?"

"Yes," the man said.

"What's it like on the good side? Can anyone see it?"

"There's no point," the man said. "In an extreme case, if it will make someone feel very good, we take him or her over, but it isn't such a hot idea."

"I don't have to see it," Mr. Dalton said. "Maybe I'm a little curious, but that's all. Naturally, what bugs me—I'm talking calmly but I'm really stirred up about this —is that Mr. Sydel and all the Mr. Sydels have to be on the same side as me. I mean you say you know I was nice and you say you know he was a louse. How do you square it? Does he do another kind of thing up here? This is going to sound corny, but does he do harder work?"

"No," said the man. "Now I really have to go. I'm getting, frankly, very irritated."

"I don't care about that," Mr. Dalton said. The man looked at him sternly and Mr. Dalton said, "Of course, I care, but you've got to tell me. Do I get better food? That's silly," he added quickly. "I'm dead and I don't eat. I don't, do I?"

"If it's necessary," the man said, "we bring food in."

"Would you bring food in for Mr. Sydel if it was necessary? For all the Mr. Sydels? That's it, isn't it. You'd bring it in for me and you wouldn't for him . . .?"

"No," the man said.

"What then? There has to be something. I get to go out and have sex once a million years and he doesn't right? That's how you get him."

"No," the man said. "You both do. The figure is wrong. It's once a fortnight."

"I get prettier girls?"

"Sometimes. And sometimes he does."

"Then what—what? I've been nice. He's *been a bastard! What? What? What?*"

The man seemed to make a note on a piece of paper or something. "I'll see that you get some medication," the man said.

"I don't want any. You'd give it to Sydel, too, wouldn't you? Keep your medicine," said Mr. Dalton, weeping, demolished. Then he stopped crying and blocked what seemed to be the man's way. "The air conditioning. That's it, isn't it? I get to feel it and he doesn't. I should have known. For an eternity, Sydel sits here knowing there's air conditioning and he can't feel it and I can. That's his punishment. That's my reward."

"He feels it, too," said the man, employing a snotty tone.

"I beg you," said Mr. Dalton on his knees. "Look, I have no shame. I cry in front of you. I cry, I scream, I beg, I have no pride. Tell me, please tell me. Please." And then Mr. Dalton glanced down at his own sandals. "Tanny's," he said. "That's it. I have these slippers and he doesn't. He walks barefoot for an eternity, a million eternities, and you give me, us, slippers from Tanny's and we feel nothing in our feet and he feels every bump, every splinter, every whatever the hell you've got here. I have you now, you stubborn sonofabitch. I do, you know. I defy you to tell me Sydel has Tanny slippers on, too."

"Al Roon's Athletic Club on Eighth Avenue in New York City," said the man, and he seemed to have lost his composure the slightest bit. Mr. Dalton waited now, waited for *him* to speak.

"We, uh, couldn't get Tanny's so we got Roon's. There really isn't any difference. It's purely administrative. If we'd gotten Tanny's, we certainly wouldn't have used Roon's. You're really making a big thing out of nothing. Tanny's, Roon's, the spirit is the same, I assure you."

"But by God," *we've got the Tanny's and the Sydels have the Roon's and never mind,*the administrative stuff. That's it and you know in your black heart that's it and don't you sit there and tell me it isn't."

"No, no, no," said the man. "You've got it all wrong, Mr. Dalton."

"Philip," said Mr. Dalton, sitting on something, possibly a chair, and folding his arms. "And you can go now."

END

Every director, really any creator of any kind, has a favorite myth. Von Stroheim's was that money corrupts; Marcel Carné is always concerned with love betrayed; John Ford's myth is that the quest is everything, that actually found, nothing . . . Mizoguchi's favorite is that man's soul is saved by a woman's love.
Anderson and Richie, *The Japanese Film.*

Hitchcock's?
Truffaut's?
Jean-Luc Godard's?
Warhol's?
Kubrick's?
Buñuel's?

I would like to see more film makers trying lip sync for short sections. Even a phrase or two in a film would add a certain dimension. You just tape originally on any tape recorder, then if you work with mag striping, just keep starting the tape and pix together til they mesh. The Bank of California produced their own Super 8 in-company film, a half-hour long, with long scenes in perfect lip-sync, using this method! Zeiss-Ikon has a simple sync gadget that works with a cassette-type tape recorder, putting the sync signal on the second stereo track. Other camera makers will probably soon have similar devices. . . . I had no trouble syncing up the songs of some of the tradesmen with the film footage of *Renaissance Pleasure Faire.* I just listened for the whir of my camera in the background. Trouble is, the portion of their songs they were singing when I got my shots of them isn't the portion I want excerpted in the film. So I have a little problem. Perhaps the most unusual thing about this film will be sort of an answer to those regular 8 fans who say Super 8 is worthless because the film cannot be reversed for in-the-camera supers: The climax of the film will be supered images. (We'll run the 16mm stock through the printer twice.)
John Sunier,
Canyon Cinema News.

Sandy's Dream:
Back in Nebraska, I dreamed all my life of being Margaret O'Brien. We lived across the street from the firehouse and one day I turned in a fire—after letting it burn awhile to make sure it was a good one—and got my name in the paper. After that I thought it was so unfair that I didn't have parents like Margaret O'Brien's who would take me to Hollywood. Now that I've been there, I don't know. I hated the weather. We had a little house with a swimming pool and we could let the dogs out without having to walk them. I still have dreams of dancing through Central Park like Jane Powell, but I can't sing or dance at all. Mostly I don't like movie making.
Sandy Dennis to Rex Reed.

A Vision in Hollywood

Allen Ginsberg

Here at the atomic Crack-end of Time XX Century
History swifting past horse chariot earth wheel
So I in mid-age, finished with half desire
Tranquil in my hairy body, familiar beard face,
            Same fingers to pen
                as twenty years ago began
                scribbled Confession to fellow Beings
            Americans—
                        Heavenly creatures,

This universe a thing of dream
            substance naught & Keystone void
            vibrations of symmetry Yes   No
            Foundation of Gold Element Atom
        all the way down to the first Wave
        making opposite Nothing a mirror
which begat a wave of Ladies marrying
waves of Gentlemen till I was born in 1926
        in Newark, New Jersey under the sign
                    sweet Gemini—

Whole universes hived upon the first
            dumb Jerk
                that wasn't there—The
Only One escape from the black Not Ever
was Itself,
            a extra click of Life woke
because Nothing had no hand to switch off
the Light.
                The first dumb Jerk,
one wave, Forward! one way too many—
So forward got backward, & Sideways both
        got there simultaneous with up
            and down who got each other
Meanwhile the first Being got its non-Being
        Opposite which never had to be there before
This calamity, this accident, this Goof,
        this Imperceptible Sneak of Dimension,
            Some Move-Push tickle, Aleph or Aum

                swallowed before uttered,
    one-eyed sparkle, giant glint, any tiny fart
    or rose-whiff before roses were
                            Thought Impossible
filled every corner of Emptiness with Symmetries of
        Impossible Universe with no Idea
How Come, & Opposite Possible Kosmoses
                    assembled Doubtless—
One makes two, symmetry's infinite touch
makes Sound bounce, light sees
                    waves reproduce oceans,
            vibrations are red white & blue—

        All like a 3 dimensional TV dream
        like Science-fiction opera
            sung by inexistent Gas-brains
                in their N-dimensional bag,
        Some what a bubble, some what dewdrop
        Some what a blossom, some what
                        lightning flash,
        Some what the old Jew in the Hospital—
            snap of dying fingers.
                    "Where did it all *go*?"
Made of Ideas, waves, dots, hot projectors
mirror movie screens,
        Some what the Shadow cast at Radio City
                    Music Hall Xmas 1939
gone, gone, utterly completely gone
to a world of Snow
        White and the Seven Dwarfs—
Made up of cartoon picture clouds, paper maché
            Japanese lantern stage sets strung
        with moon lights, neon arc-flames,
                electric switches, thunder
reverberating from phonograph record tape machine
            Tin sheets of Zeus on
the Microphone jacked to gigantic Amplifiers, gauge
        needle jumping, red lights warning Other
Dimensions off the overloaded public address Sound
    Systems feedback thru blue void
        echoing the Real of Endless Film.
    Xmas 1965.

Color by DNA. (It's another trip.)

Mythology is inevitable, it is natural, it is an inherent necessity of language, if we recognize in language the outward form and manifestation of thought; it is in fact the dark shadow which language throws upon thought, and which can never disappear till language becomes entirely commensurate with thought, which it never will. Mythology, no doubt, breaks out more fiercely during the early periods of the history of human thought, but it never disappears altogether. Depend upon it, there is mythology now as there was in the time of Homer, only we do not perceive it, because we ourselves live in the very shadow of it, and because we all shrink from the full meridian light of truth. . . . Mythology, in the highest sense, is the power exercised by language on thought in every possible sphere of mental activity.
Max Müller.

When I use the word *Myth* I am referring to those great images by which man makes sense of his world.
Alan Watts.

The primary fact is that movies are shown in the darkest of theaters . . . and, with flashing light and shadow, resemble the situation of hypnosis—or sleep, with the dreams provided.
Jack C. Ellis.

Rothschild of *Popular Photography* attached an Observ-O-Scope to a series-size metal lens cap by threading a hole in the cap, and then used this on a normal lens via a filter adapter. The Observ-O-Scope is usually used to watch outsiders through a door, and when used in this way on a camera gives an inexpensive fish-eye effect.
Canyon Cinema News.

Reflections On A Sports-Page Headline.

3 Giants Back in Uniform
Giants, I have not, lo! these many years,
Heard tell of even one—now three! And suited!
I picture them, as is, I think, befitting,
Living together, in a gothic farmhouse,
Somewhere in North Dakota. Bachelors.
They keep a dog the size of a Pontiac,
Feeding him on elk and other game
Too dainty for their needs (I have not heard
Of mastodons in North Dakota, either.
But these they kill there, snapping the necks, and eat).
By the day they work, the uniforms would hint,
As public servants: not tormenting thugs
Or raiding parlors, but, as you might guess,
Moving mountains for the governor.
Nights—and here our story takes a turn
For melancholy—seven-league boots beneath
Their oaken chairs, and pipes ablaze, they sit
In monstrous silence, staring into the fire,
And dream of girls with heads to shame Mount Rushmore,
Moon-full breasts, and legs like alabaster
Buttes. The faithful pooch begins to snore,
Causing the little folk, for miles around,
To leave their beds in anger and vibration.

James Crenner.

Davy Crockett

A Star Is Born.
One actress was known to the public as "the imp girl," from the initials (IMP) of the Independent Motion-Picture Company. She became so popular that her producer, Carl Laemmle, shattered all precedent and published her rhyme-like name—Florence Lawrence—alongside the main title of her next picture. Immediately every other regularly employed performer demanded the same sort of recognition. By 1913 the cast of each picture was presented on the screen as a matter of common practice—and the "star system" was born.
Gary Jennings.

In the long lines at the box office I saw that I would never escape from the American movie. Every scene that Hollywood shoots is a shot heard round the world.
William Zinsser.

LANA TURNER HAS COLLAPSED

Lana Turner has collapsed!
I was trotting along and suddenly
it started raining and snowing
and you said it was hailing
but hailing hits you on the head
hard so it was really snowing and
raining and I was in such a hurry
to meet you but the traffic
was acting exactly like the sky
and suddenly I see a headline
LANA TURNER HAS COLLAPSED!
there is no snow in Hollywood
there is no rain in California
I have been to lots of parties
and acted perfectly disgraceful
but I never actually collapsed
oh Lana Turner we love you get up
Frank O'Hara.

Theater critic Ross Wetzsteon wrote the following description of the off-Broadway play *The Great White Hope* in a *Village Voice* review: "It begins on an Ohio farm in the early years of the century, and everything in the scene—the good-humored openness of the language, the expansive cheerfulness of the mood, the good old-fashioned, breezy, back-slapping, down-to-earth hominess, the suspenders and derbies, the stereotyped immigrant accents and melting-pot camaraderie, the frank Broadway strutting of the cast, their twangy all-American posturing, their voices on the verge of song—everything in the scene evokes our nostalgia for the wholesome rollicking, open-air musical comedy mythology of rural America. Everything, that is, except what they're talking about: how to deal with uppity niggers. In the disturbing contrasts of this striking opening . . . the playwright shows us the underside of our nostalgia, the brutality buried beneath the mythology, by utilizing and exposing the fraudulence of our methods of viewing the past . . ."
Gene Youngblood.

Robert E. Lee

106

And even before *Alphaville,* the people in *The Married Woman* were already
science fiction—so blank and affectless no mad scientist was
required to destroy their souls.
Pauline Kael.

Rilke's Words to the Young Poet:
. . . and if only we arrange our life according to that principle which counsels
us that we must always hold to the difficult then that which now seems to us the
most alien will become what we most trust and find most faithful. How
should we be able to forget those ancient myths about dragons that at the
last moment turn into princesses. **Perhaps all the dragons of our lives are
princesses** who are only waiting to see us once beautiful and brave.
Perhaps everything terrible is in its deepest being something that wants to help me.

BEOWULF
60
TV

In the darkness dwelt a demon-sprite,
Whose heart was filled with fury and hate,
When he heard each night the noise of revel
Loud in the hall, laughter and song.
To the sound of the harp the singer chanted
Lays he had learned, of long ago;
How the Almighty had made the earth,
Wonder-bright lands, washed by the ocean;
How he set, triumphant, sun and moon
To lighten all men that live on the earth.
He brightened the land with leaves and branches;
Life he created for every being,
Each in its kind, that moves upon earth.
So, happy in hall, the heroes lived,
Wanting naught, till one began
To work them woe, a wicked fiend.
The demon grim was Grendel called,
March stalker huge, the moors he roamed.
The joyless creature had kept long time
the lonely fen, the lairs of monsters,
Cast out from men, an exile accurst.
The killing of Abel, brother of Cain
Was justly avenged by the Judge Eternal.
When night had fallen, the fiend crept near
To the lofty hall, to learn how the Danes

In Heorot fared, when the feasting was done.
The athelings all within he saw
Asleep after revel, not recking of danger
And free from care. The fiend accurst;
Grim and greedy, his grip made ready;
Snatched in their sleep, with savage fury,
Thirty warriors; away he sprang
Proud of his prey, to repair to his home,
His blood-dripping booty to bring to his lair.
At early dawn, when daybreak came,
The vengeance of Grendel was revealed to all
Their wails after wassail were widely heard,
Their morning woe. The mighty ruler,
The atheling brave, sat bowed with grief.
So Grendel wrongfully ruled the hall,
One against all till empty stood
That lordly mansion, and long remained so.
For the space of twelve winters the Scyldings' Friend
Bore in his breast the brunt of this sorrow,
Measureless woe. In mournful lays
The tale became known; 'twas told abroad
In gleemen's songs, how Grendel had warred
Long against Hrothgar, and wreaked his hate
With murderous fury through many a year.
Translated by J. Duncan Spaeth.

I would suggest to [the school child] that the popular culture—as represented, for example, on television and in comic books and in movies—is based on fantasies created by very ill people, and he must be aware that these are fantasies that have nothing to do with reality.
James Baldwin.

Grendel = Florence Lawrence?

I am Myra Breckinridge whom no man will ever possess. Clad only in garter belt and one dress shield, I held off the entire elite of the Trobriand Islanders, a race who possess no words for "why" or "because." Wielding a stone axe, I broke the arms, the limbs, the balls of their finest warriors, my beauty blinding them, as it does all men, unmanning them in the way that King Kong was reduced to a mere simian whimper by beauteous Fay Wray whom I resemble left three-quarter profile if the key light is no more than five feet high during the close shot.
Gore Vidal.

Galena, Alaska
Senator George Murphy (Calif.), who appeared to lead the revolt, asserted that all of the native villages the group visited were "picked and set up" for Kennedy to gain maximum exposure from the national press, radio and television.
The former California actor recalled that it was like "sending advance men into a town to promote a picture."

Who's to blame for the loss of glamor in stars? The politicians and science—they're takin' all the headlines, they're our stars today.   Mae West.

In an argument once I told my mother it was her fault that I'm like I am. She wouldn't believe me. She's sort of crazy. She used to be a typical June Lockhart mother on the farm. It wasn't beneath her to dig ditches or milk the cows when my father was sick. She was really far out. Then we moved to Berkeley, then to Lafayette. She changed —all in three or four years—into I don't know what. She wears a wig sometimes. She wears that certain amount of makeup that makes women in their forties look sixty. She doesn't think anymore.
A student.

OH, LANA....PLEASE GET UP

One of my favorites is the detective's wife, or cop's wife. I remember her well from a picture called *The Killer Is Loose*. Rhonda Fleming played the part, but that's not important. Any number of actresses have had the identical role. Her husband, Joseph Cotten, was being hunted down by a crazy gunman, and when Rhonda couldn't stand the strain any more, she addressed her man as follows:
"I'm tired of being scared every time there's a knock on the door or the phone rings. Be sensible, Joe—give up your job so that we can start living like other people. Do you think you can bring Nails Brody in single-handed? It's suicide, and you know it. Isn't it time you gave some thought to me, especially now that there are going to be three of us . . ."
"Gee, honey," the cop replies, "you don't want me to let some other guy lay his life on the line to settle my private grudge. What kind of man do you think you married?"
"I only know that you have to choose. Either you quit the force or . . . I'm leaving, Joe."
"Madge, you can't mean it. You're joking!"
"I've never been more serious in my life."
That last line is one of my gems. I heard it many times a year, and I could always spot it in advance. When it finally came hurtling out, full of defiance, I felt the tingle that every true collector knows when he comes on an old friend.
William Zinsser.

Then they angled across the square to the picture show and bought their tickets. A few grade-school kids were going in. The picture was an Audie Murphy movie called *The Kid From Texas*, with Gale Storm.
"Why hello, Duane," Miss Mosey said. "I thought you was gone overseas. Hope you all like the show."
The boys planned to, but somehow the occasion just didn't work out. Audie Murphy was a scrapper as usual, but it didn't help. It would have taken *Winchester '73* or *Red River* or some big movie like that to have crowded out the memories the boys kept having.
Larry McMurty, *The Last Picture Show*.

Uncle Sam

108

WHAT HAVE THESE PEOPLE DONE TO YOU?
Choose the column most suited to you.

A	B
The Lone Ranger	Mrs. Robinson
Judge Hardy	Benjamin (Hoffman)
Mrs. Minniver	Bonnie Parker (Dunaway)
Ozzie and Harriet	Viva
Scarlett O'Hara	Bullitt
Marlene Dietrich	Zorba
Gene Autry	Patty Duke
Doris Day	That Girl
Walter Pidgeon	Perry Smith

WHAT HAVE YOU DONE TO THEM?

Their music was pure "bluegrass," with Lester Flatt fingerin' away on the guitar and Earl Scruggs handling the five-string banjo. For 21 years they toured the country-music circuit, had their own radio show, and were rediscovered by pop America for their background music that was very much in the foreground of *Bonnie and Clyde*. Now Flatt, 54, and Scruggs, 45, have announced they are breaking up the act. Just why, they would not say. Friends report that the two have never been close, and now that both are well off financially, they see no reason to stick together. Said one acquaintance: "They have come to hate each other's guts."
Time.

Colonel Sanders.

In the fall of 1939, Benito Mussolini condemned the Marx Brothers and ordered his subjects not to laugh at them.
Zimmerman and Goldblatt.

If Hollywood ever makes the story of my life, I want to be played by Burt Lancaster.
SS Colonel Otto Skorzy who spirited Mussolini out of Italy in September 1943.

... *blessed* celluloid upon which have been imprinted in our century all the dreams and shadows that have haunted the human race since man's harsh and turbulent origins.
Lévi-Strauss quoted by Gore Vidal.

You don't belong to any man now—you belong to Broadway.

109

She also dislikes "Cinderella" films.
"The totally unreal movie—the Doris Day kind of movie—does a tremendous amount of harm. It's a kind of brainwashing. Nobody tells what happened to Cinderella after midnight, or what happens when they *don't* live happily ever after."
Geraldine Chaplin, *On View.*

Depend upon it, there is mythology now as there was in the time of Homer, only we do not perceive it.
Max Müller.

Watching *Screen Test* starring the transvestite Mario Montez one suddenly realized that every teenage girl in America goes to the movies in order to be a better female impersonator during her next screen test—or next date!
Dan Isaac, *Drama Review.*

Movie Mystery.

I saw you in the movies once,
Starring with Tom Mix.
You were nine and twenty.
I was turning six.

You danced the Charleston when next
I saw you on the screen.
You were nine and twenty.
I was seventeen.

The talkies came, and I was thrilled
To hear you laugh and cry.
You were nine and twenty.
Funny—so was I.

I don't quite know what happened then,
But somewhere down the line
I passed you up. I'm—uh—thirty-one,
And you're still twenty-nine.

Lilyn E. Carlton.

In 1931, Thalberg was impressed by the success Universal had enjoyed with horror pictures. He told Willis Goldbeck: "I want you to give me something even more horrible than *Frankenstein.*" Starting with a story by Tod Robbins, Goldbeck produced a script about bizarre happenings among freaks of a circus sideshow. After Thalberg read the script, he placed his head in his hands. "I asked for something horrifying," he muttered to Goldbeck, "and I got it." Despite the heated opposition of Mayer and other studio officials, Thalberg allowed Tod Browning to film *Freaks* in compromising style. Browning, who had directed *Dracula* and some of Lon Chaney's best films, assembled a collection of real circus freaks and exploited their abnormalities. The result was a Grand Guignol classic, but it proved too much for movie audiences to stomach.
Bob Thomas.

QUANTRILL

Nowadays when a person lives somewhere, in a neighborhood, the place is not certified for him. More than likely he will live there sadly and the emptiness which is inside him will expand until it evacuates the entire neighborhood. But if he sees a movie which shows his very neighborhood, it becomes possible for him to live, for a time at least, as a person who is Somewhere and not Anywhere.
Walker Percy, *The Moviegoer.*

Uncle Tom

Janet wished powerfully not to be frigid. All her informal education, from Disney's *Snow White* to last week's *Life,* had taught her to place the highest value on love. Nothing but a kiss undid the wicked apple. We move from birth to death amid a crowd of others and the name of the parade is love. However unideal it was, she dreaded being left behind. Hence she could not stop flirting, could not stop reaching out, though something distrustful within her, a bitterness like a residue from her father's medicinal factory, had to be circumvented by each motion of her heart. Liquor aided the maneuver.
John Updike, *Couples.*

It was eventually Hoffman's anti-heroism that made him an anti-star. "If the hero is defined as an event-making individual who redetermines the course of history," wrote philosopher Sidney Hook, "it follows at once that a democratic community must be eternally on guard against him." Said F. Scott Fitzgerald: "Show me a hero and I will write you a tragedy." Those aphorisms were a long time catching on in America, where the legend of event makers—the cowboy and the gangster, the self-made entrepreneur and the conquering soldier—are dominant dramatic myths.
Time.

Chaplin: His name was known to savage peoples who had never heard of the world's great religions.
Gary Jennings.

Travel holds no surprises for the movie critic. Even when my wife and I visit a remote corner of the globe, I know exactly what it will be like. Hollywood has fixed in my mind an image of every faraway place . . .
One year we made plans to visit the South Seas, and again I knew exactly what the area would be like. Out of my rich Hollywood experience I told Caroline of the exotic treats that lay ahead. In Tahiti (I began), girls in grass skirts and little else will row out to meet us in outrigger canoes. One of them, a honey-skinned blonde of striking maturity, will say: "I am Noola-Noola . . . my father chief of island . . . follow me." She will take us to a clearing in the jungle surrounded by huts made of coconut shells and papaya leaves. Her father, an unimaginably old man, will look at us through eyes fogged over by time and tribal memories.
"My son," he will say, "I have waited many years for a white man I could trust with the ancient secret of the Polynesians, handed down from father to child since the sun god first climbed the sky. Go with my daughter tonight, when the moon rises, to that volcano across the lagoon, Moola Ha'i, and she will guide you to our holy cave."
. . . Well, we made the trip, and everything worked out just that way. I knew it would.
William Zinsser.

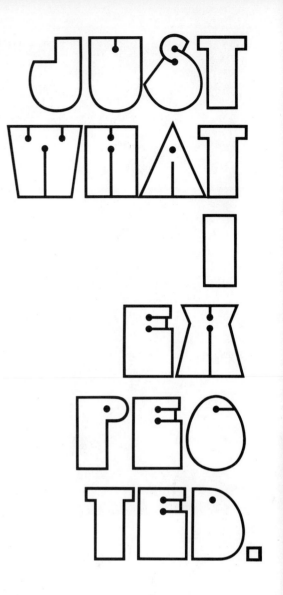

Since modern equipment was unavailable, the institute created a kind of spare-parts cinema, refurbishing the 100 commercial theaters in Havana and the 400 in the rest of the country, founding a cinematheque, and sending all films, Cuban and foreign, to villages all over the country in mobile units, which show films in fields, community centers and schoolhouses. According to an official of ICAIC, every Cuban now has access to about two films a week.
Renata Adler, *New York Times.*

Acapulco connoted deep-sea fishing, casinos, anxious rich women; and Sierra Madre meant gold, meant *Treasure of the Sierra Madre,* a movie he had seen eight times. It was Bogart's best picture, but the old guy who played the prospector, the one who reminded Perry of his father, was terrific, too. Walter Huston.
Truman Capote, *In Cold Blood.*

Perry Smith: Always, when it was too cold hardly to breathe, I'd think about Hawaii. About a movie I'd seen. With Dorothy Lamour. I wanted to go there. Where the sun was. And all you wore was grass and flowers.
Truman Capote, *In Cold Blood.*

"Remember the night we met and I lost my glass slipper?"

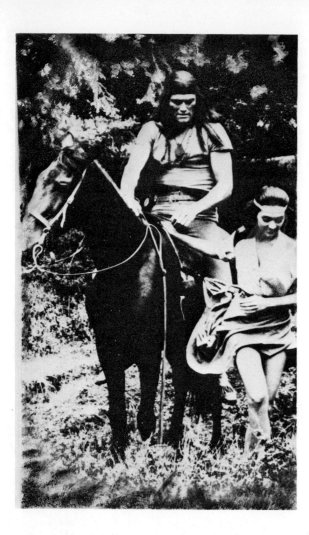

What movie conventions might the American Indian Association spot in this still?

Rioting Halts *Maya.*
Srinigar, Kashmir. Street rioting between Hindus and Moslems, now in its third week in this northern India capital, has halted production of the King Brothers, MGM-TV series, *Maya.*
The Hollywood Reporter.

Zinneman had won assent from the Studio to cast Toshiro Mifune, the Japanese star, in the role of Crazy Horse, and now suggested that another Oriental play Sitting Bull. "Jesus, Freddy," Zanuck said, "you want us ostracized by the American Indian Association? Those are the two biggest heroes in the history of Indians. And you want Japanese to play both of them?"
William Hogan.

America is the movies.
Paddy Whannel.

Film is no objective document.

Culture
The urban Japanese, knowingly or not, tends to use the foreign films as a means toward instruction. He may sit back and uncritically enjoy a Japanese film, but he also seems to feel that a foreign film demands some kind of active participation. As has already been noted, even the distribution system itself seems to place the foreign product in a special category, and upon going to foreign films the Japanese seems to feel that something special is required of him. The film is something more important than entertainment, it becomes a kind of text which he studies. The result is that the really avid Japanese movie-goer has learned from the films not everything he knows but certainly everything he remembers about Western ways and manners.
Anderson and Richie, *The Japanese Film.*

Apu?

Ikuru?

1968: Actress Faye Dunaway, the gun-toting Bonnie Parker in *Bonnie and Clyde*, has already done for the beret what Bardot did for the bikini. Now the fashion world's newest Darling is the stunning inspiration for a full-blast return to '30s styles, both here and abroad. Though revivals have cropped up before, it took the impact of the film to bring about a new synthesis that (as shown in Gayle Kirkpatrick's outfits, $100 and $125) blends the softness and droopy fit of the '30s with the swing and legginess of the '60s. *Life.*

It is by expansion of metaphor that fact becomes intelligible, the world measured, and the complexities of experience described in language. Any history of thought might begin and end with the statement that man is an analogical animal.

Ah, how complete are the uses of publicity!

Twinkle, twinkle, little Star,
Shining brightly in Show Biz,
We don't wonder what you are—
Not if we can read, that is.

Daily, in the nation's Press,
We learn something new about you:
What you eat and how you dress . . .
Who, in nightclub, tried to clout you . . .
Whether you are shy or brassy . . .
Which decor your current house is . . .
Each dimension of your chassis . . .
Who your current beau or spouse is . . .

Like Niagara flows the prose
On the Inner-Outer You!
Fascinating. And who knows?
Maybe, even, partly true.

Selma Raskin.

1968: The Bonnie & Clyde Caper.

That mythical magic of Bonnie and Clyde just will not fade. Now television is using them in a smartly satirical way.

TWA has a funny commercial that shows Bonnie, Clyde, C. W. Moss and the in-laws chugging along toward an airport in a 1931 Buick while frantic banjo music gives pace to the scene. Nobody likes to hang around an airport, says an urbane narrator—and so the bandits, every one the spit and image of the movie cast, scurry out of their car and make their way onto a TWA jet, leaving the cops behind. Flying A gasoline sponsors another Bonnie and Clyde crew. This time they roll up to a Flying A station. They're in a hurry; they've got a "withdrawal" to make. But the overfriendly attendant insists on delivering a pitch for the sponsor's latest premium offer. Finally, a gum-snapping Bonnie says: "Let's gedoutta heah awreddy!" And off they lurch. The latest addition to the literature, and perhaps the best, is three one-minute Pontiac commercials. One shows Bonnie and Clyde in the hands of an effervescent dealer. The gang has just pulled a bank job and needs "something that moves." The rest of the commercial is a hilarious takeoff on the scene from the movie in which the bandits kidnap a young couple. In this case, the unsuspecting Pontiac salesman merrily delivers his pitch—again to a banjo score—while Clyde & Co. barrel down the road with him. At length, they boot him out. Says the salesman, unperturbed: "How are you going to finance it?" Bonnie mutters sullenly: "Finance it, Clyde." Clyde tosses out a satchel of money and drives off, while the salesman, ever the honest fellow, chases them into the fadeout, protesting valiantly that he has been overpaid. The possibilities are enormous. How about a scene that depicts Clyde brandishing a .46-caliber tommy gun. It's only a silly millimeter wider. *Time.*

"Talent is not what Uncle Buck and I deal in, Miss Van Allen," I said, lightly resting my hand on Buck's clenched fist. "We deal in *myths*. At any given moment the world requires

			Optional Reader's Alternates:
___ 1.	one full-bodied blonde Aphrodite	a Melvyn Douglas	_____
___ 2.	one dark siren of flawless beauty	b Myrna Loy	_____
___ 3.	one powerful inarticulate brute of a man	c Jean Harlow	_____
___ 4.	one smooth debonair charmer	d James Cagney	_____
___ 5.	one world-weary corrupt lover past his prime	e Lon McCallister	_____
___ 6.	one eternal good-sex woman-wife	f Hedy Lamarr	_____
___ 7.	one wide-eyed chicken boy	g Susanna Foster	_____
___ 8.	one gentle girl singer	h Clark Gable	_____
___ 9.	one winning stud	i Humphrey Bogart	_____
___10.	one losing stud outside the law."	j John Wayne	_____

Like Man in *The Naked Prey* and the soldiers hitting the beach in *Beach Red*, Wilde realizes that he is working in a largely hostile universe, prey to studio and distributor. "It took me years," he admits, "to learn about distribution, about financing and the whole business end of films. It is so involved and complex, so frustrating and heartbreaking."

Max Rafferty.

OLYMPUS

Olympus supports many gods and goddesses and they are truly eternal, since whenever one fades or falls another promply takes his place, for the race requires that the pantheon be always filled. So what we are looking for—and what you, Miss Van Allen, have *found* time and again—are those mythic figures who, at the right moment, can be placed upon their proper pedestal. For instance, since the death of Marilyn Monroe, no blonde voluptuous goddess has yet appeared to take her place and so, if I were creating stars, I would look for a girl who most filled that particular bill, who could be the lost Golden Girl. In fact, as in any other business, we must begin with market research. This means carefully analyzing Olympus to find out which archetypal roles are temporarily vacant and who are the contenders. At the moment the suave male seducer is in great supply while the befuddled normal man next door, filled with ludicrous fantasies, is a drug on the market, what with at least one and a half Jack Lemmon pictures each year. But the blonde goddess, the dark goddess, the singing girl and the inarticulate hero are each currently in need of someone to make of the divine spirit living flesh as well as eternal celluloid. At this very moment, perhaps in this very room, there are unknown boys and girls destined to be—for the length of a career—like gods, if only we can find and reveal them. That is why you and I, Letitia—I may call you that?—are similar to those Tibetan priests who upon the death of the Dalai Lama must seek out his reincarnation. And so, like priestesses, despite all personal hardship, we must constantly test and analyze the young men and women of America in order to find the glittering few who are immortal, who are the old, the permanent gods of our race reborn.
Gore Vidal, *Myra Breckenridge*.

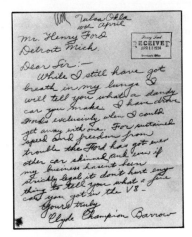

The letter.

The music.

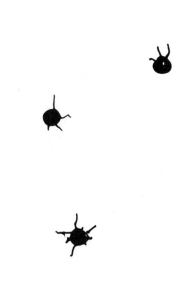

Every scene that Hollywood shoots is a shot
heard around the world.

Memo to Bonnie and Clyde: you are not welcome in
South Africa. Fashions inspired by the gangster film
can be seen on Johannesburg's Eloff Street, but its
roaring guns and racing get-away cars will not appear
in movie houses here.
South African Broadcasting Corp. has barred the film's
musical theme from its airwaves. Parliament interrupted
discussion of weightier matters to confirm the decision
banning the film hoodlum and his gun moll from the
American Thirties.
Johannesburg, South Africa (AP),
May 26, 1968.

The Conventions of the Genre:
Match column A with column B.

A

A. Science is magic.
B. Colossal disaster, inadequate response.
C. A united world, the UN fantasy, as a recurring theme.
D. The united world is achieved through technology.
E. Disaster is quantitative, ingenious, extensive; the aesthetic of universal havoc.
F. The monster from outer space affords a legitimate outlet for viewers against the ugly, the freakish, the predatory, and provides a subject for the aesthetic enjoyment of suffering.
G. Conventional clichés are reinforced and perpetuated.
H. The décor of the films is more imaginative and interesting than the people.
I. Science (technology) is the solution to danger. Dispassionate intellectual curiosity is dangerous, aberrant and abnormal.
J. Technicians are safer and more humane than excessively intellectual scientists.
K. The accidental awakening of some super-destructive monster is obviously symbolic of the Bomb.
L. Science-fiction wars are "clean" wars with no frustrating moral dilemmas.
M. "No more love, no more beauty, no more pain"— both desired and feared.
N. Our animal nature was once thought to be our greatest danger. In science-fiction films it is the threat of becoming a machine.
O. White magic is technology; black magic is the errant individual will of the lone intellectual.
P. The satisfactions for the viewer in watching historic war films are carried over intact in science-fiction films.

B

1. *King Kong*
2. Buck Rogers Serials
3. *Dr. Jekyll and Mr. Hyde*
4. Poe
5. Hawthorne
6. *The Republic*
7. Comic Books
8. Prospero
9. Grendel
10. Mary Shelly
11. Social consciousness
12. United warfare
13. *Typee*
14. Power
15. Knowledge
16. Guilt
17. The traditions of a culture
18. *Dr. Strangelove*
19. The proper use of science
20. Defoe
21. Depersonalization
22. *Dracula*
23. Security beliefs
24. *Intolerance*
25. Marlowe
26. The aesthetics of destruction
27. *Rosemary's Baby*
28. Sources of danger
29. The lone scientist
30. The technocratic team-member
31. *Wild in the Streets*
32. *Thirty Seconds over Tokyo*
33. Complexity of plot
34. Complexity of characterizations
35. Complexity of moral outlook
36. Happiness
37. Superman
38. Social criticism
39. Sets: space hardware, cities, deserts, living standards, offices, etc.
40. The collective unconscious concerns of a nation.

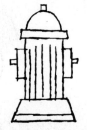

Science
Is
Magic

Which picture best matches Science-Fiction Films?

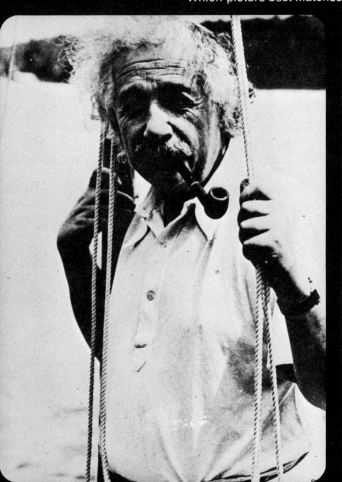

Stock & Trade.

Compile a list of cliché dialogue fragments from science-fiction movies.

1. "I hope this works."
2. "Wait, professor, there's someone on the telephone."
3. "We must do something about this."
4. "What right have we to be tampering with the laws of nature?" ✓
5. _____
6. _____
7. _____
8. etc.

I was in love with a beautiful blond once. She drove me to drink. It's the one thing I'm indebted to her for.

Mahatma Kane Jeeves.

And she was a virgin.

Faye Bainter, Andy Hardy's mother, screwed up every mother in the world. She really did, man. Dig, who can be like Faye Bainter, man? Faye Bainter was always in the kitchen sweeping with an apron. And Anglo-Saxon—and my mother was sweating and Jewish and hollering, man. Why couldn't she be like Faye Bainter? And that's what everyone wants their mother to be. And she was a virgin. Yeah, she never balled anyone because old Lewis Stone would say, "*Andrew*," and that was all, man. Unless there was some kind of pollination that way—through dates or some esoteric, mystical thing, yeah. So that's some heavy propaganda, man.
Lenny Bruce.

Stephanie.

My companion on these evening outings and weekend trips is usually my secretary. I have had three secretaries, girls named Marcia, Linda, and now Sharon. Twenty years ago, practically every other girl born in Gentilly must have been named Marcia. A year or so later it was Linda. Then Sharon. In recent years I have noticed that the name Stephanie has come into fashion. Three of my acquaintances in Gentilly have daughters named Stephanie. Last night I saw a TV play about a nuclear test explosion. Keenan Wynn played a troubled physicist who had many a bad moment with his conscience. He took solitary walks in the desert. But you could tell that in his heart of hearts he was having a good time with his soul-searching. "What right have we to do what we are doing?" he would ask his colleagues in a bitter voice. "It's my four-year-old daughter I'm really thinking of," he told another colleague and took out a snapshot. "What kind of future are we building for her?" "What is your daughter's name?" asked the colleague, looking at the picture. "Stephanie," said Keenan Wynn in a gruff voice. Hearing the name produced a sharp tingling sensation on the back of my neck. Twenty years from now I shall perhaps have a rosy young Stephanie perched at my typewriter.
Walker Percy, *The Moviegoer.*

Asteroid.

. . . middle-class and Jewish. His mother was a movie fan and named him after Dustin Farnum, the silent-screen cowboy (his older brother is Ronald, for Colman) . . .

119

The Bride of Frankenstein.

The Baron has decided to mate the
   monster,
to breed him perhaps,
in the interests of pure science, his only
   god.

So he goes up into his laboratory
which he has built in the tower of the
   castle
to be as near the interplanetary forces
   as possible,
and puts together the prettiest monster-
woman you ever saw
with a body like a pin-up girl
and hardly any stitching at all
where he sewed on the head of a raped
   and murdered beauty queen.

He sets his liquids burping, and coils
   blinking and buzzing,
and waits for an electric storm to send
   through the equipment
the spark vital for life.
The storm breaks over the castle
and the equipment really goes crazy
like a kitchen full of modern appliances
as the lightning juice starts oozing right
   into that pretty corpse.

He goes to get the monster
so he will be right there when she opens
   her eyes,
for she might fall in love with the first
   thing she sees as ducklings do.
That monster is already straining at his
   chains and slurping,
ready to go right to it:
He has been well prepared for coupling
by his pinching leering keeper who's
   been saying for weeks,
"Ya gonna get a little nookie, kid,"
or "How do you go for some poontang,
   baby?"
All the evil in him is focused on this one
   thing now
as he is led into her very presence.

She awakens slowly,
she bats her eyes,
she gets up out of the equipment,
and finally she stands in all her seamed
   glory,
a monstrous princess with a hairdo like a
   fright wig,
lightning flashing in the background
like a halo and a wedding veil,
like a photographer snapping pictures of
   great moments.
She stands and stares with her electric
   eyes,
beginning to understand that in this life
   too
she was just another body to be raped.

The monster is ready to go:

He roars with joy at the sight of her,
so they let him loose and he goes right
   for those knockers.
And she starts screaming to break your
   heart
and you realize that she was just born:
In spite of her big tits she was just a
   baby.

But her instincts are right—
rather death than that green slobber:
She jumps off the parapet.
And then the monster's sex drive goes
   wild.
Thwarted, it turns to violence,
   demonstrating sublimation crudely;
and he wrecks the lab, those burping
   acids and buzzing coils,
overturning the control panel so the
   equipment goes off like a bomb,
and the stone castle crumbles and
   crashes in the storm
destroying them all . . . perhaps.

Perhaps somehow the Baron got out of
   that wreckage of his dreams
with his evil intact, if not his good looks,
and more wicked than ever went on with
   his thrilling career.
And perhaps even the monster lived
to roam the earth, his desire still
   ungratified;
and lovers out walking in shadowy and
   deserted places
will see his shape loom up over them,
   their doom—
and children sleeping in their beds
will wake up in the dark night screaming
as his hideous body grabs them.

Edward Field.

**In the '40s the Hollywood movie
aimed to please the American wife.
What about today?**

Narrator:
Mr. Cooper, I'm a writer here. Alvah Bessie.

Cooper: Yeh, hello.

Narrator: Do you know when *For Whom the Bell Tolls* will be released?

Cooper: Purty soon, I reckon.

Narrator: I'm anxious to see it because—(significant pause) I'm one of those guys you played in the picture.

Narrator sits down without being invited.

Cooper: (chewing) That so?

Narrator: I wasn't one of the guerillas: we only had four American guerrillas. I was in the International Brigades.

Cooper: (chewing) Terrible thing, civil war. Brothers fighting each other.

Narrator: It wasn't really a civil war, Mr. Cooper.

Cooper: (mouth open) It wasn't?

Narrator: It was a war of invasion on the part of Germany and Italy—against the legal government of Spain.

Cooper: That so? (swallows) That's what's so great about this country.

Narrator: Huh?

Cooper: What I mean—a guy like you can go and fight in a war that's none of your business.

Alvah Bessie,
The Realist.

1909:
Experiments with color film begin with *The Black Pirate.*

> Reagan is trying to turn California into a 'B' movie.

Eric Hoffer.

Tom Mix, 1970.
When I was a youngster in central Montana, "us kids" spent our Saturday afternoons at the movies, watching Buck Jones or Ken Maynard or Tom Mix pursuing their eternal enemies a-horseback through Republic's boulder-strewn pastures, triumphing in the end over all evil. No doubt several million American men and women can remember this same experience out of their childhoods. The difference between my experience and theirs was that in my case much of the rest of the audience on those Saturday afternoons was made up of cowboys. Along with us smaller fry, the cowboys whooped and hollered encouragement to the hero in the final sequence, and (if memory is not playing me false) emerged from the dim auditorium of the Rialto a little more steely-eyed, their forty-dollar Stetsons a little more firmly cocked across one eyebrow, their high-heeled boots thumping a little more loudly on the sidewalk while they admired their images in the plate-glass windows of Woolworth's. Indeed, they and the manufacturers of their garb have, in the years since, succumbed more and more to the visible image of the cowboy in the Western motion picture, their shirts now grown tighter-fitting and gaudier, their Levis almost too narrow to slip over their red alligator boots; and their hats grown broader and more tightly-curled of brim (the better, one mocking story goes, to ride three in the cab of a pick-up truck). Obviously, the cowboy has come to believe in himself as the silver screen has portrayed him; not only the cowboy but the American in general has come to believe that mythic image. I suspect further that it has been this fixed belief in the reality of a West that actually never existed which has prevented even serious imaginative versions of the West from ever stepping out of it without being in some sense rejected.
John A. Barsness.

1926: The first color movie is released, starring Douglas Fairbanks Sr.

is a **well-preserved** not young man. Close-to, the painted face is webbed with delicate lines while the dyed hair, eyebrows, and eyelashes contrast oddly with the sagging muscle beneath the as yet unlifted chin, soft earnest of wattle-to-be. The effect, in repose, suggests the work of a skillful embalmer. Animated, the face is quite attractive and at a distance youthful; particularly engaging is the crooked smile full of large porcelain-capped teeth. The eyes are interesting: small, narrow, apparently dark, they glitter in the hot light, alert to every move, for this is enemy country—the liberal Eastern press who are so notoriously immune to that warm and folksy performance which

quite deliberately projects over their heads to some legendary constituency at the far end of the tube, some shining Carverville where good Lewis Stone forever lectures Andy Hardy on the virtues of thrift and the wisdom of the contract system at Metro-Goldwyn Mayer. Gore Vidal, *The Twenty-ninth Republican Convention.*

The fake Andy visited four colleges in the West, showing Andy films, giving Andy lectures and picking up Andy fees of some twenty-five hundred dollars before a sharp-eyed New York photographer spotted the hoax at the University of Oregon.

When the truth came out, the real Andy, cool and mild as always, couldn't see what the fuss was about. The "real" Andy is an image he has spent some ten years creating. Andy has no persona, no mask —image and self have, after careful development, melded to form only the image—another product of the sixties. The Andy Warhol mask is, in its way, like the image masks of LBJ or Mao Tse-tung, a part of the mythology of our time. A mask with that much social force has a life apart from the mere person represented by it—what difference does it make to the world who sees this mask, who wears it? In the case of the Andy hoax the mask worked better on Alan Midgett, an actor who enjoys getting up on a stage and talking about Andy's work more than Andy does. Andy feels he doesn't live up to his mask. "I'm not what they expect," he says ruefully, referring to the thousands of college students who have jammed auditoriums all over the country for his lecture-film showings. Elenore Lester, *Eye.*

No persona, no mask.

In the late forties the Gary Cooper Fan Club of San Antonio made a serious effort to nominate Cooper for vice-president of the United States. They argued, "He doesn't talk much; he knows what it's all about; and he gets things done." For evidence they cited any number of instances on the prairies, in Spain, in Italy, in the Himalayas.
George Bluestone.

Dorothy Malone to Ronald Reagan: **Must you always** think like a marshal? Can't you think like a human being just once?
Law and Order.

I think if I really got serious about it, I could run for Congress and probably make it—but it would be a tragedy for the nation. I just don't have the equipment— not that this has bothered some actors. Paul Newman.

Life is a movie.
RONALD REAGAN
GEORGE MURPHY
SHIRLEY TEMPLE BLACK

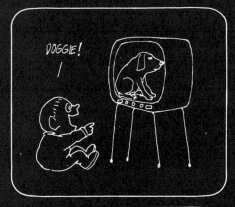

One hot afternoon last March, in a courthouse on the high wheat plains of Western Kansas, Richard Brooks turned to me, between takes of the movie he was directing, and rather reproachfully asked: "What are you laughing at?" "Oh, nothing," I said, but the truth was that I'd remembered a long-ago question by Perry Smith, one of the two murderers whose trial was being reenacted here. He had been captured a few days before, and his question was: "Were there any representatives of the cinema there?"
Truman Capote.

Near the beginning of Frank Conroy's novel *Stop-Time*, there is a scene in which a group of boys about 10 years old, at a progressive boarding school, vote—very fairly, in a child's version of due process —to beat up a disliked fat boy named Ligget. There is a trial, in which he is found guilty, on some child's pretext, of what amounts to being insufferable. The boys line up, each one entitled to land one good clean punch on Ligget's jaw. The author makes it clear that the idea of the sound, perfect "dreams-of-glory" punch is movie-inspired. But although the boys line up word-lessly to try again, and although Ligget is ultimately taken to the hospital, jaw broken in four places, the punch itself is quite unsatisfactory; "the whole complex of movements was too fast, somehow missing the exaggerated movie-punch finality."
Renata Adler.

One morning I was sitting in the Capitol Theater watching *Vera Cruz*, a film devoted largely to shooting. During one exchange of bullets, a real police-woman fired at a thief bounding down the Capitol's aisle—or so I learned later. None of the patrons noticed the event. They were so transfixed by the action on the screen that they had no ear for the live ammunition whistling around them.
William Zinsser.

The Black Pirate

GIMME A MOVIEKISS.

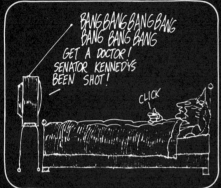

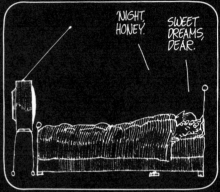

In a Movie House:
Let go of my hand.
No not you, you.

What the adult female chiefly asks of the movie is the opportunity to escape by reverie from an existence which she finds insufficiently interesting.
Margaret Farrand Thorpe.

What drives me to the movies is hunger for sensation, a tickling of the nerves (aroused) by unusual situations, fighting, impassioned clashes, love scenes, scenes of crowds, unknown worlds, the underworld . . . war, society. The film as a whole may be bad, but given the right mood, I am usually satisfied if details of the kind mentioned meet my expectations.
A student.

Seventy percent of Gary Cooper's fan mail came from women who wrote that their husbands did not appreciate them. Bluestone.

It Happened One Night.

The film is more like life than the theater. In the theater I watch a work of art which, somehow, appears to be elaborated. After a film performance I feel as if I had been in the middle of life.
A Housewife.

(My) pictures have little that happens in them and end without a conclusion—just like life.
Naruse.

One would like to get something out of life after all.
A young worker.

Steve Dwoskin divides films into those which look at life and those involved in life. "The barrier between looking at life and experiencing it can be bridged by most expressive media. But films have a natural advantage over painting or poetry as people's intellectual guard is not automatically up against films. One of the strongest ways of inducing involvement is by images and actions associated with the erotic sense because they bypass the intellectual filters which maintain the 'looking at' process." Who acts in underground films? "I usually get my friends to take part in them. The reason it takes me so long to make a film is that I have to find people who are willing to be in a film and express my ideas. I tried using stage people and actors but my films pick up so many subtleties that a dramatic smile just does not come off. It gets in the way of the naturalism I'm after."
Dick Gilbert.

It is not very likely that Siegel will ever get a spectacular to direct, partly because his movies have seldom done very good business, partly because the studio executives do not care for his bellicose, independent ways. "The brass made me put a prologue and epilogue on *Invasion of the Body Snatchers* that damned near ruined the whole thing," he recalls.

What actress put on pants and started a flourishing industry?

By adolescence, children have been programmed with a set of responses and life lessons learned almost totally from motion pictures, television and the recording industry. It is difficult to banish the notion of one's own life situations as part of a scenario, appropriately scored: "Lara's theme" for an ill-starred love, "Colonel Bogey's March" for indomitable courage, "Waltzing Mathilda" for bittersweet apocalypse. Few situations fail to evoke a cinematic response; in matters of principle we play *High Noon*, in renunciation scenes *Casablanca* . . . In pictures there is no problem without a solution: The Mafia has been cut down to size at every studio from Burbank to Culver City; Gregory Peck has personally taken on anti-Semitism, the Bomb, and Southern bigotry, licked them all, and we all feel, however spuriously, the better for it.
John Gregory Dunne.

Marilyn couldn't fight it because she wasn't strong enough. But I think I can lick it.
Raquel Welch.

Who said it?:
In Italy for 30 years under the Borgias, they had warfare, terror, murder, bloodshed—they produced Michaelangelo, Leonardo da Vinci, the Renaissance. In Switzerland they had brotherly love, 500 years of peace and what did they produce—the cuckoo clock.

That's *Clyde* Beatty!

"...and now, boys and girls, while your mother is out of the room I'll explain to you what a hunger strike is."

IMPERSONATE HUMAN BEINGS.

LEARN HOW TO

THE MOVIES TO

YOU GO TO

1934: Clark Gable took off his shirt and wasn't wearing an undershirt. The undershirt business fell off fifty per cent in one year. What movie was it?

I had some glowing dreams about what the camera could be made to do and ought to do in teaching the world things it needed to know—teaching it in a more vivid, direct way. I do not believe that any other single agency of progress has the possibilities for a great and permanent good to humanity that I can see in the motion picture.
Thomas Edison.

A good film helps me get in touch with people and with life.
A nurse.

The less interesting the people I know the more frequently do I have to go to the movies.
A businessman.

Some days a sort of "hunger for people" drives me to the cinema.
A student.

Yesterday a favorite of mine, William Holden, delivered a radio announcement on litterbugs. "Let's face it," said Holden. "Nobody can do anything about it—but you and me." This is true. I have been careful ever since.
Walker Percy, *The Moviegoer*.

At a certain stage in the development of both the individual and of society no great effort can be made without some extravagant hope of preposterous illusion. To shake a backward country out of its stagnation there is need for the illusion that what one aims at is not a prosaic step ahead but the realization of heaven on earth. Even businessmen at this stage will not exert themselves to their utmost for mere profits. They, too, must be lured by some extravagant fairy tale and made to feel that whatever they undertake is part of a momentous soul-stirring performance.
Eric Hoffer.

With a little bit of luck, Napoleon would have won through at Waterloo, Hitler at Stalingrad, John Wayne at the Alamo. Who would have won the Civil War if Tuesday Weld hadn't been lucky enough to stumble across General Lee's secret battle plans hidden in a hollow watermelon? (Or was it Shirley MacLaine?)
Art Hoppe.

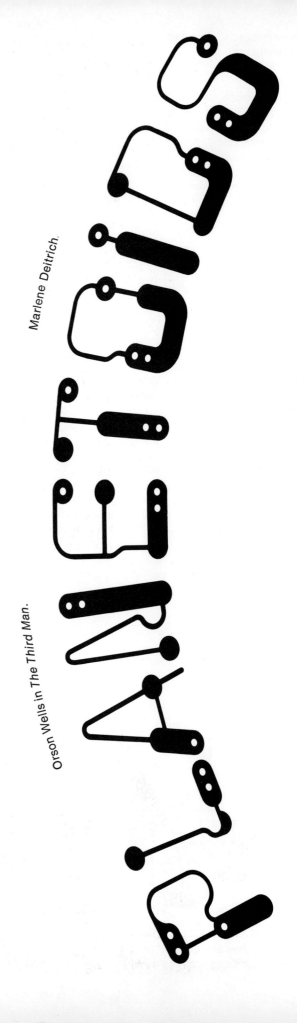

Marlene Deitrich.

Orson Wells in *The Third Man*.

Never ignore the stars, of course. But above all,
Follow the **asteroids** as well: though dark, they're more
Intense for never glittering; anyone can admire
Sparklings against a night sky, but against a bright
Background of prominence, to feel the Presences burnt
Into no fiery fame should be a more common virtue.
For, just as Vesta has no atmosphere, no verdure
Burgeons on barren Ceres, bit-players never surge
Into the rhythms of expansion and collapse, such
As all the flaming bodies live and move among.
But there, more steadfast than stars are, loved for their being,
Not for their burning, move the great Characters: see
Thin Donald Meek, that shuffling essence ever so
Affronting to Eros and to Pride; the pair of bloated
Capitalists, Walter Connolly and Eugene Pallette, seated
High in their offices above New York; the evil,
Blackening eyes of Sheldon Leonard, and the awful
Stare of Eduardo Cianelli. Remember those who have gone—
(Where's bat-squeaking Butterfly McQueen? Will we see again
That ever-anonymous drunk, waxed-moustached, rubber-legged
Caught in revolving doors?) and think of the light-years logged
Up in those humbly noble orbits, where no hot
Spotlight of solar grace consumes some blazing hearts,
Bestowing the flimsy immortality of stars
For some great distant instant. Out of the darkness stares
Venus, who seems to be what once we were, the fair
Form of emerging love, her nitrous atmosphere
Hiding her prizes. Into the black expanses peers
Mars, whom we in time will come to resemble: parched,
Xanthlne desolations, dead Cimmerian seas, the far
Distant past preserved in the blood-colored crusts; fire
And water both remembered only. Having shined
Means having died. But having been real only, and shunned
Stardom, the planetoids are what we now are, humming
With us, above us, ever into the future, seeming
Ever to take the shapes of the world we wake to from dreams.
John Hollander, *Movie-going.*

The Way It Reelly Was

(title printed upside-down)

___	1. The telephone	a. Cornel Wilde
___	2. "Your Cheatin' Heart"	b. Gary Cooper
___	3. The greatest first baseman in history	c. Ralph Bellamy
___	4. "We have nothing to fear but fear itself."	d. Don Ameche
___	5. "Polanaise"	e. Kirk Douglas
___	6. Painter who fled to the South Seas, friend of Kirk Douglas	f. Anthony Quinn
___	7. Radium	g. George Hamilton
___	8. Van Gogh	h. Paul Muni
___	9. Liberated Patty Duke from a world of darkness and silence.	i. Anne Bancroft
___	10. The Emancipation Proclamation	j. Raymond Massey

I played a stinker in the movie *The Apartment*, and it was fun to do. But I got letters from mothers saying, 'I took the children to see *The Apartment* because *you* were in it . . .!' And so you start thinking that you owe something to the producers of the shows and to Disney and to the TV series and you think, well, you have a certain image and you have to be careful what you do.

Inside the three-car garage sits Raquel's Silver Cloud Rolls-Royce with license plate RWC. "The Rolls-Royce is good for prestige," she feels. "And Patrick looks like a great manager when he's sitting in the back seat."

For your "Only in America" file: Last January, the big Peter Paul Candy Co. of Salinas stopped making Walnettos (born in 1926) because the demand had just plain petered-and-pauled out. Then came those hilarious *Laugh-In* TV scenes during which the Dirty Old Man (Arte Johnson) mumbles to Ruth Buzzi: "You want a Walnetto?" Now EVERY-BODY wants a Walnetto. Result: They are back on the assembly line at the Peter Paul Candy Co.
Herb Caen.

To think that after Hud *and* Cool Hand Luke, *and all the other pictures I've done and all the parts I've dug into, I come off as the guy women would most like to go to bed with—it's frightening.*
Paul Newman.

MAE WEST

LEG OF LAMB

UNCLE SAM

Norman Mailer

Satyajit Ray is dedicated to putting the nature and truth of his country on film. This gives his work a rooted, authentic quality that most films lack. The attendant risk is the touch of the illustrated lecture on folkways.
Arthur Knight.

Rick Marshall manages a theater, called the Avenue, which specializes in showing classic films of the 20s and 30s. The idea is to present them in their original setting—a technique no one has ever tried before—complete with slide shows, organ accompaniment and a singing MC in a tuxedo. . . . Marshall's pride and joy . . . is the theater's mighty 10-ton Wur-litzer organ. The instrument is 40 years old, and came from the now defunct State Lake Theater in Chicago . . . Performances at the Avenue are like nothing you've ever seen. Dressed in his $11 Goodwill tux, which looks at least three sizes too small, Rick waddles onstage, seizes the old circular mike, and introduces a program that may include a vocalist, a sing-along and an organ recital in addition to Buster Keaton, Jean Harlow and the best of D. W. Griffith.
Walter Blum.

Horatio Alger.

Every seat is the best seat.

128

Huston's third and final Army documentary was never seen by the public. Entitled *Let There Be Light*, it was filmed entirely at the Mason General Hospital on Long Island, and commissioned by the War Department.

"They told me they wanted a film to show to industry, to prove that nervous and emotional veterans were not lunatics," says Huston. "At that time these men just weren't getting jobs. Our purpose was to help them."

It was necessary to obtain footage on actual interviews and psychiatric treatment at the hospital. Huston set up several hidden cameras to record the emotionally disturbed veterans as they discussed their problems and, later, as they were put under hypnosis and given drugs and medicine. No written script was used; each foot of film was genuine, unplanned. (Later Huston added the narration, which his father read onto the soundtrack.)

"This was the most joyous, hopeful thing I ever had a hand in," says Huston. "I felt as though I were going to church every day I went out there to that hospital." At one point in the film a young soldier, who had developed a terrible stutter in battle due to the hiss of high-explosive shells, suddenly found that he had regained the power of clear speech: "I can talk, I can talk! Listen, I can talk! Oh God, Listen! I can talk!"

To get moments such as this, Huston often had three cameras operating at once, but he repeatedly declared: "I take no credit for this. What happened there in front of us was a wonder and a miracle."

The *Nation* called *Let There Be Light* "noble and fiercely moving," and film critic Archer Winston said (in the *New York Post*): "It's so great a picture, so inspiring medically and humanly, so tremendously graphic . . . of basic fears and joys . . . that seeing it I felt as if I had never before witnessed emotion on the screen so stripped of self-consciousness . . . it is a visible ascent from Hell . . . an experience to remember for years."

When the War Department restricted the film, refusing to release it, Huston was shocked and outraged.

"I never dreamed they'd ban it," he said. "I guess they didn't want the public to see what war can do to a man's emotions and nerves—so they claimed that it would be an invasion of privacy to let the film be shown. Yet we had obtained signed releases from each of the patients.

"Years later, some friends of mine who wanted very much to see this film asked me to arrange a showing at the Museum of Modern Art in New York. So I did. The Army Public Relations Office gave me their okay to screen it. Well, just before it was shown, minutes before, a bunch of MPs arrived and seized the print and took it right back to Washington. The PRO people had reversed their decision."

Let There Be Light was never taken off the restricted list, notwithstanding the concerted efforts of Huston and several influential critics and film notables. In 1947 a re-make called *Shades of Gray* was produced as a "commercial" version of the original in which the psychoneurotic veterans were replaced by professional actors.

As John Huston sadly remarked: "It was hardly the same thing."

William F. Nolan.

I identified him in the morgue. Identified him! I couldn't even identify him. It was just—like a skeleton with some stuff on it. [*Willie Rupoli, a bookie, talks about his brother Ernie, who had been a Mafia gunman and professional killer before his body was found on the beach.*] I told them, "To tell you it's my brother, I can't. Not the way he looks. Not what you're showing me." When I saw him he had the cinder blocks on him. And the rope around. That's an awful thing. That's what I can't see, why they had to do it like that. It's not even a clean knock-off. It's, I don't know, savages. Shot him, stabbed him, I can't understand it. To kill him, that's one thing. But not like that. Not only me, but even the others in the underworld, his own friends, they can't figure it. If you live by the gun, you die by the gun. But do it right. Wait outside his home or something and hit him when he comes out, but not like they did it. If you want to get rid of him, hit him clean. Like get him in a car, hit him, and throw him out of the car. What's all this here rigamajig? I don't know if they saw television, or what.
Life.

Over 230 Hollywood movie titles begin with 'love,' 'loving,' or 'loveable.' Hundreds of others have 'love' somewhere in the title.

"TV: chewing gum for the eyes."
Anne Baxter's grandfather.

Our whole trouble in Japan is that, despite a surface affection, Japanese just don't like new things. . . . Another problem is the Japanese respect for authority resulting in blind mother-love, blind respect for the male. Such things are thoroughly Japanese. In films such themes are always sure to win for the picture the special endorsement of the Education Ministry.
Yoshimura.

It's Only a Movie:

Engulfed in this domed
    structure,
A movie flicks, punctur-
    ing the mind.
In their seats the people
    gaze, still and silent;
With neither threat nor
    violence
The falling darkness
    stifles thought.

Light streaks; minds fall
At its·glowing feat.
Bounding from glazed
    faces
It takes something with
    it . . .

Such a bother to think
    What's the ruin?
        Movies are enter-
            taining, too;
Who the hell is
    McLuhan?

Jay Marchus.

From 1956 to 1966 the National Communications Laboratories conducted a unique study of the mass media. We reached some startling conclusions. We discovered evidence of what we call "ghost teaching"—effective academic three-Rs teaching—in operation in some of the least likely places on TV. Efficient ghost teachers were found lurking on cereal box tops, in commercials produced by unsuspecting advertisers, in comedians' frivolous gags— all over the television channels.

In a TV spy series there was a gymnasium door with the word "KARATE" printed on it in large capital letters. If a word is prominently displayed and shown repeatedly over a period of time, it becomes an automatic spelling drill. The more often a child sees a difficult word in print, the more likely he is to learn its spelling. I know of a high school student who, perfectly innocently— and logically—once spelled the word "CA-ROTTY." We can be almost certain that she had not been exposed to that film-set door.

If, every weekday, Mom tunes in the soap opera *Love Is a Many Splendored Thing*, it is likely that 5-year-old Junior will find it easier to spell "splendored" than "cat" by the time he is 6, if the title is printed in letters sufficiently large on his TV screen.

Bill Cullen may not look like Janie's private reading tutor, but he may be. Television's quiz-show hosts are among the most valuable members of the medium's ghost faculty. *Eye Guess, Concentration* and other lightweight games teach spelling, reading and arithmetic.

We need less than a 500-word vocabulary to get along in the world on a normal day. A single episode of the game-show *Jeopardy* drilled us in more than 400 sight-reading words. As the program's host, Art Fleming, called out words which appeared in prop windows or on signs, he became an effective reading teacher for an audience of millions.

If you doubt that TV could program a child's reading from the start, just pay attention to the station-identification announcements and the network blurbs. You can start with ABC, then go on to NBC, then CBS, as the letters flash by. Along with *P.D.Q., N.Y.P.D.* and other alphabeticals, these are automatic, first-step reading lessons that radio could never have produced for us. As for vocabulary building, you have to look no further than those scary Saturday morning cartoons.

In one cartoon a hero is told by the villain, "You are powerful," rather than just "strong." In a fight scene, you hear, in rapid sequence, "You are an able foe," about to become "food for the serpents of the sea." The adversary is warned to "yield to the mighty fighter." We are then told that the "time regressor" will take us back to "the 12th Century and earlier"—back to the days of the Vikings. And it does. We see the Vikings, dressed in authentic garb, complete with horned helmets, sailing their beautiful ships.

Yet schoolteachers still believe that a child has to wait to get a film strip in class to learn about Leif Ericson's bold voyages. The fact is, teachers are hopelessly outclassed by those ghost educators who work around the clock without pay and who can transform even the most difficult information into

1896: Georges Méliès, cartoonist, painter, magician, owner of a music hall begins making movies. He subsequently invents double exposure, stop motion, slow and fast motion, dissolves, fade ins and fade outs and sharp juxtapositions for magical effects.

Time-Life doesn't own a controlling interest in MGM. True or False.

Of course I was influenced by films. Who wasn't?
Joseph von Sternberg.

child's play.
Math? Televised baseball games give a 7-year-old child excellent and continuous practice in adding. For nine innings he is doing real math homework, just by keeping score in his head.
His 9-year-old brother watching a football game does more sophisticated kinds of arithmetic, by adding up touchdowns by sixes and tacking on extra points by ones, then varying the mental number drill by adding on field goals three points at a time. And in the daytime game shows, where scores can mount by tens or twenties or fifties or hundreds, schoolchildren can learn to add large sums painlessly.
Languages? Doris Day joined the ghost faculty when, in the televised movie *The Man Who Knew Too Much* she taught us that "Que Sera, Sera" means "Whatever Will Be, Will Be." And

once Dean Martin informs us that "amore" means "love" in Italian, we are not likely to forget it.
Even ethics, a subject taught in college, is part of television's ghost curriculum. Along with Anthony Perkins in the movie *Tall Story*, which has been rerun many times on TV, millions of viewers have taken a 10-question quiz in ethics. This is not bad homework.
One more example: The average person will never, in his whole lifetime, read one of Freud's books. He may, however, have learned some useful things about psychoanalysis from *Dr. Kildare* or *Ben Casey*— or even from a Bob Hope quip.
One of the things that prompted us to take a close look at the play pedagogues on television was an opinion poll we conducted. We were looking for the

most important or influential science teacher in the United States. We polled average citizens, educators, community leaders and students. The winner? Walt Disney! Nobody even ran a close second. There are many people who think this is just awful. Perhaps it is a hangover from our Puritan ancestry, but there is strong opposition to any form of learning that is not disciplined and formal. If we enjoy it or if we come by it quickly and painlessly—even joyfully—then it is to be condemned. If it ain't book larnin', it's good-for-nothing.
But think: If we can acquire our facts painlessly, during our leisure hours, we have that much more time for the tougher tasks of using the information wisely for more efficient problem-solving. What seems to the formal educator to be an addiction, if not an afflic-

tion, turns out to be an unexpected but powerful ally.
The thought of giving a cap and gown to Soupy Sales or the Flintstones or the Munsters and punsters and duncesters who fill so many of television's hours may not sit well with some people. But the facts of educational life do demand such symbolic recognition. Formal education owes much to the informal medium of television.

Rosalyn L. Switzen.

Resplendent Reality.

Elysian Fields is not the shortest route to my aunt's house. But I have my reasons for going through the Quarter. William Holden, I read in the paper this morning, is in New Orleans shooting a few scenes in the Place d'Armes. It would be interesting to catch a glimpse of him.

It is a gloomy March day. The swamps are still burning at Chef Menteur and the sky over Gentilly is the color of ashes. The bus is crowded with shoppers, nearly all women. The windows are steamed. I sit on the lengthwise seat in front. Women sit beside me and stand above me. On the long back seat are five Negresses so black that the whole rear of the bus seems darkened. Directly next to me, on the first cross seat, is a very fine-looking girl. She is a strapping girl but by no means too big, done up head to toe in cellophane, the hood pushed back to show a helmet of glossy black hair. She is magnificent with her split tooth and her Prince Val bangs split on her forehead. Gray eyes and wide black brows, a good arm and a fine swell of calf above the cellophane boot. One of those solitary Amazons one sees on Fifty-seventh Street in New York or in Nieman Marcus in Dallas. Our eyes meet. Am I mistaken or does the corner of her mouth tuck in ever so slightly and the petal of her lower lip curl out ever so richly? She is smiling—at me! My mind hits upon half a dozen schemes to circumvent the terrible moment of separation. No doubt she is a Texan. They are nearly always bad judges of men, these splendid Amazons. Most men are afraid of them and so they fall victim to the first little Mickey Rooney that comes along. In a better world I should be able to speak to her: come, darling, you can see that I love you. If you are planning to meet some little Mickey, think better of it. What a tragedy it is that I do not know her, will probably never see her again. What good times we could have! This very afternoon we could go spinning along the Gulf Coast. What consideration and tenderness I could show her! If it were a movie, I would have only to wait. The bus would get lost or the city would be bombed and she and I would tend the wounded. As it is, I may as well stop thinking about her. . . .

Today I am in luck. Who should come out of Pirate's Alley half a block ahead of me but William Holden! Holden crosses Royal and turns toward Canal. As yet he is unnoticed. The tourists are either browsing along antique shops or snapping pictures of balconies. No doubt he is on his way to Galatoire's for lunch. He is an attractive fellow with his ordinary good looks, very sun-tanned, walking along hands in pockets, raincoat slung over one shoulder. Presently he passes a young couple, who are now between me and him. Now we go along the four of us, not twenty feet apart. It takes two seconds to size up the couple. They are twenty, twenty-one, and on their honeymoon. Not Southern. Probably Northeast. He wears a jacket with leather elbow patches, pipestem pants, dirty white shoes, and affects the kind of rolling seafaring gait you see in Northern college boys. Both are plain. He has thick lips, cropped reddish hair

and skin to match. She is mousy. They are not really happy. He is afraid their honeymoon is too conventional, that they are just another honeymoon couple. No doubt he figured it would be fun to drive down the Shenandoah Valley to New Orleans and escape the honeymooners at Niagara Falls and Saratoga. Now fifteen hundred miles from home they find themselves surrounded by couples from Memphis and Chicago. He is anxious; he is threatened from every side. Each stranger he passes is a reproach to him, every doorway a threat. What is wrong? he wonders. She is unhappy but for a different reason, because he is unhappy and she knows it but doesn't know why. Now they spot Holden. The girl nudges her companion. The boy perks up for a second, but seeing Holden doesn't really help him. On the contrary. He can only contrast Holden's resplendent reality with his own shadowy and precarious existence. Obviously he is more miserable than ever. What a deal, he must be thinking, trailing along behind a movie star—we might just as well be rubbernecking in Hollywood.

Holden slaps his pockets for a match. He has stopped behind some ladies looking at iron furniture on the sidewalk. They look like housewives from Hattiesburg come down for a day of shopping. He asks for a match; they shake their heads and then recognize him. There follows much blushing and confusion. But nobody can find a match for Holden. By now the couple have caught up with him. The boy holds out a light, nods briefly to Holden's thanks, then passes on without a flicker of recognition. Holden walks along between them for a second; he and the boy talk briefly, look up at the sky, shake their heads. Holden gives them a pat on the shoulder and moves on ahead. The boy has done it! He has won title to his own existence, as plenary an existence now as Holden's, by refusing to be stampeded like the ladies from Hattiesburg. He is a citizen like Holden; two men of the world they are. All at once the world is open to him. Nobody threatens from patio and alley. His girl is open to him too. He puts his arm around her neck, noodles her head. She feels the difference too. She had not known what was wrong nor how it was righted but she knows now that all is well.

Holden has turned down Toulouse shedding light as he goes. An aura of heightened reality moves with him and all who fall within it feel it. Now everyone is aware of him. He creates a regular eddy among the tourists and barkeeps and B-girls who come running to the doors of the joints. I am attracted to movie stars but not for the usual reasons. I have no desire to speak to Holden or get his autograph. It is their peculiar reality which astounds me. The Yankee boy is well aware of it, even though he pretends to ignore Holden. Clearly he would like nothing better than to take Holden over to his fraternity house in the most casual way. "Bill, I want you to meet Phil. Phil, Bill Holden," he would say and go sauntering off in the best seafaring style.

Walker Percy, *The Moviegoer.*

Name and Essence.

The notion that name and essence bear a necessary and internal relation to each other, that the name does not merely denote but actually is the essence of its object, that the potency of the real thing is contained in the name—that is one of the fundamental assumptions of the myth-making consciousness itself.
Ernst Cassirer.

Essence

___1. Kirk Douglas
___2. Greta Garbo
___3. William Holden
___4. Cary Grant
___5. Joan Crawford
___6. John Wayne
___7. Hedda Hopper

a. Archibald Leach
b. Issur Danielovich
c. Bill Beedle
d. Marion Morrison
e. Elda Furry
f. Greta Gustafson
g. Lucille Le Sueur

Asteriods

___1. Loveable old codger
___2. Best friend (M)
___3. Best friend (F)
___4. Wise-cracking maid
___5. Dignified grandfather
___6. Wise-cracking waitress
___7. Small time gambler

a. Thelma Ritter
b. Eddie Albert
c. Cedric Hardwicke
d. Walter Brennan
e. Gloria Grahame
f. Keenan Wynn
g. Ann Sothern

Harpo customarily brought the teacher an orange, which he kept in a clean place, under his hat. But one night in Waukegan, he tossed it at the piano player, and the rest of the family, moved by the same demonic spirit, dumped everything from books to stilettos into the pit. Later, when Chico launched into an extended Italian-American ad lib, the violin player split into howling convulsions, nearly stopping the show. His name was Benny Kubelsky . . .
Zimmerman and Goldblatt.

In myth precision is sacrificed for a greater degree of suggestion. It is the mode of simultaneous awareness of a complex group of causes and effects.

Shirley [Temple] had a most remarkable capacity to study and remember, not only her own, but also the lines of the actor or actress with whom she would be playing scenes. On these occasions when an actor blew his lines, Shirley would innocently say, "You're supposed to say . . ." but that's as far as she got before Mother, on the sidelines, would call "Shirley," and that stopped any further prompting. Arthur C. Miller, *One Reel a Week.*

The Sidney Greenstreet Blues

I think something beautiful
and amusing is gained
by remembering Sidney Greenstreet,
but it is a fragile thing.

The hand picks up a glass.
The eye looks at the glass
and then hand, glass and eye
fall away.

Richard Brautigan.

. . . the star is ideally beautiful . . . the star is pure . . . the star is profoundly good . . . beauty and spirituality combine to form a mythic superpersonality . . . worshipped as heroes, divinized, the stars are more than objects of admiration. A religion in embryo has formed round them . . . the star is like a patron saint to whom the faithful dedicate themselves. . . .

Edgar Morin, *The Stars.*

Jack Lemmon, for instance.

One of the European delegates asked the cost of *Tony Rome*, and when told, he mused that *Alfie*, *Georgie Girl*, *Morgan*, and *Blow-up* combined had not cost so much, and all were enormously successful. As if talking to himself, he wondered if it weren't sometimes better to make a small picture and hope for a large return. "Sure, *Alfie* was successful," said James Denton, . . . "But think what it could have done if it had stars. Jack Lemmon, for instance, and Shirley MacLaine." John Gregory Dunne, *The Studio.*

IRVING FISHMAN CARRIES A BIG STICK AND HE SWINGS IT TOO

"I read a great deal of material officially. On my own time, I prefer to stay away from anything that might be in any way controversial. I get enough to see officially." (Irving Fishman, director of the imports compliance division, office of the Regional Commissioner of Customs, New York.)

Washington, 1968. OFFICIALLY Irving Fishman, with a bachelor's degree in business administration, tries to keep you and me from reading dirty books and seeing dirty movies brought into New York from abroad.

A movie he doesn't want us to see is called *I Am Curious—Yellow*. The film arrived from Sweden December 30, 1967, Fishman saw it January 4, 1968, and seized it to prevent its distribution by Grove Press, Inc. (U.S. release in April, 1968.)

In legal terminology the movie was "arrested" but unlike people who are arrested it can't go free on bail until after the moral policeman's judgment is tested in court.

Irving Fishman swings a big stick.

He seized the movie in accordance with Section 1305, Title 19, of the United States Code, which deals with the importation of pornographic or seditious material. Fishman looks at movies and if he thinks they are obscene we don't see them unless the courts decide he is wrong.

So the question is what is legally obscene.

In the 1967 Supreme Court case of Redrup v. New York, three tests for obscenity were determined: 1) The dominant theme of the material taken as a whole must appeal to a prurient interest in sex; 2) the material must be shown to be patently offensive by affronting community standards relating to the description or representation of sexual material; 3) The material must be utterly without redeeming social value, these three elements must coalesce and no material can be proscribed unless it is found to be utterly without redeeming social value.

I saw *I Am Curious* at the Treasury Department. Edward de Grazia, a local poet, playwright and lawyer who has defended many books in censorship cases, arranged with the Customs Bureau and the Justice Department to let a handful of people see the movie so they could judge its merits, as critics and private citizens.

Before the screening a statement was read by John Murphy of the Justice Department. The statement, prepared by Lawrence Schilling, an assistant U.S. attorney in New York who is prosecuting the film concluded:

"The film is being shown solely for purposes of pending litigation and persons viewing the film at this showing should not publicize the contents of the film or publish any comment on the film, except in the course of proceedings in this action, unless and until a final judicial determination is made that the film can be imported into the United States."

In other words, not only are you not to see the movie, you aren't supposed to know about it either. But, as Murphy later said, the request was only that; it hasn't the force of law.

I Am Curious—Yellow is the first of a two-part film, the other called *I Am Curious—Blue.* It is extremely complicated, a movie about its own making, about itself. The director, Vilgot Sjöman, appears as an actor-director. Lena Nyman, the leading actress, appears both as herself and in the role of a radical apostle of non-violence and social equality.

Parts of the film consist of documentary footage of interviews with Martin Luther King, poetry readings by Yevteshenko, and Swedish opinion polls about the welfare state.

Interspersed throughout are scenes of extraordinarily explicit sexual activity. Lena and Borje Ahlstedt, the leading actor, are shown naked, often front-on. They make love perched on a balustrade in front of the Swedish royal palace, on a lawn, in a tree. Everything that happens is shown: there are no delicate fade-outs, there is no disguising behind sheets. Sexual violence is also explored, presumably to enlighten the contemplation of political non-violence. Sjoman has said in an interview that part of his intention, in a film aspiring to be a "Portrait of

Sweden,'' was to parody sexual obsessions.

Grove Press has assembled an impressive number of effusive reviews from abroad testifying to its brilliance. The film censorship council of Sweden approved it unanimously for uncut screenings to all Swedes over 15. Ingmar Bergman called it a "masterpiece." I think it is far from that; rather, it seems an ambitious, serious, now and again comic examination of the state of Sweden's moral, political and social climate. It is too long.

What I think of it makes no difference.

What Irving Fishman thinks of it, under present practice, makes all the difference in the world. It is this fact that a book or movie is restrained before the public can approve or condemn it in the marketplace of public judgment that is so reprehensible.

De Grazia, to win the release of the film, recently questioned Fishman on the reasons he seized it.

De Grazia: "Did you feel the film was utterly without social importance?"

Fishman: "No."

De Grazia: "Would you please state the respects in which you felt this film had some social importance."

Fishman: "I thought that the film dealt with social problems in Sweden . . . but I can't honestly say that to me the film carried a tremendous message."

Given the law of the land, determined by our highest court, it would appear that

Fishman, and other enemies of sexual candor, are running out of legal resources since there is hardly any work imaginable that is "utterly" without public relevance. Accordingly, de Grazia asked whether, having admitted that the film is not utterly without social importance, the Bureau of Customs is "reluctant to follow the mandate of the majority of the Supreme Court in this area?"

Fishman replied: "I find no clear mandate of the Supreme Court here. I find, instead, some discussions about social significance, or redeeming social value . . . I feel that a motion picture film is in a separate category from every other utterance, a public utterance. I think a book, a magazine, can perhaps be judged differently from a motion picture film. I personally am looking for some law on motion picture films.

And it is no doubt a good thing such law be sought. For, as the area of legal obscenity is honed down to an ever finer point, it becomes increasingly clear that we may sense obscenity for ourselves but can never define it for others. But whether or not obscenity rulings are amended, or discarded, Irving Fishman should no longer have the right to determine what you and I can see and read.
Geoffrey Wolff,
Times Post Service.

If one decides to abandon the pajamas and sheets

convention and to present people as naked as they usually are while making love, what is one to do about the male organ? Is one to show an erection too? Suddenly I discover that I have never thought realism to its conclusion. Oh, this business of consistency! If you have said A, do you have to say B too?
Vilgot Sjöman.

The open portrayal of intercourse destroyed the ancient Roman theater, Welles said, and it may be doing the same today. "First of all, it doesn't work," he declared. "The two things you cannot do effectively on stage is pray and copulate. Audiences never believe God is up there in the spotlight or that the guy is really making love."
New York Times.

Get sex out of the movies and back into the bathroom where it belongs.

— **Portnoy.**

The Charade principle.
From the outset I took film conventions so much for granted that Max von Sydow in *The Mistress* got out of the girl's bed fully dressed right after a passionate and intimate embrace. I was acting on the very principle I had mocked in my book on Hollywood: "Why, everybody knows that this stands for something else."
Vilgot Sjöman.

M OVEMEN T.

The most exciting thing in film is movement. The rhythmic, pulsing, changing progression of images on the screen of a darkened room can be endowed with all the power and magic or delicacy that one can imagine. Out of our eyes all things move and express themselves in their movement. The action of shapes in reality or the abstract can have a wonderful range and depth of communication, from the flick of a cat's tail to the majesty of the earth's rotation. When you begin to think about it every mood, character, animal or place has its kind of movement and, conversely, every movement expresses something.
Hilary Harris.

♀LD-FASHIONED?

Getting undressed before going to bed with someone—this seems painfully
trivial. The filmmakers evidently don't believe either the public or the actors
capable of getting tenderness, joy, or any other effect out of that process. No,
first there must be a kiss while the actors are dressed. Then a dissolve to bodies
hidden in sheets. Undressing—that is something to be smuggled out of sight
in a dissolve. Oh, sacred conventions!
Vilgot Sjöman.

Nafkeh?

ONCE UPON A time there was a young
lad named Horatio Alger, who was determined to struggle and persevere and
somehow get himself a good education.
A good sex education.
But the little lad faced many hurdles. The
first was the local school board, which
voted 5–4 against showing Horatio any
sex education films. The second was
Horatio's parents, who voted 2–0 against
allowing Horatio to attend any Adult
Movies.
"Adult movies," thundered Horatio's
father, "are corrupting the morals of
our youth and destroying our American
way of life."
So Horatio was 18 and on his own before
he saw his first Adult Movie. He didn't,
of course, understand it. But he thrust
forth his chin and vowed to persevere.
FOR TWO YEARS, Horatio persevered.
He saw Adult Movies thrice weekly and
twice on Saturdays. "It was a hard
struggle," he said proudly on reaching
20, "but at last I have won myself a good
sex education."
It was then that he met Miss Penelope
Trueheart and fell in love.
"All I desire on this earth," he said,
falling to his knees one night in her apartment, "is to be the father of your child
and spend the rest of my life as your
husband."
"Oh, dearest," said Miss Trueheart
ecstatically, "when will we be married?"
"As soon as we have a child," said
Horatio, drawing on his good sex education. "For we can't have one afterward,
you know. People never do."
AND HOW DO we have a child?" she

asked, blushing modestly.
"There are several ways," said Horatio.
"The easiest, I believe, is for you to
smoke a cigarette on the couch. I will
pounce on you. Your hand will go limp
and the cigarette will fall on the carpet.
(We can use an ashtray, I suppose, if
you worry about fire.) And then you
will cry."
"I don't smoke," said Miss Trueheart.
"Then we'll have to throw our clothes on
the floor," said Horatio, "though it isn't
very tidy. But please turn up the heat first
as we have to lie under just a sheet and
talk. Then I will go for a drive and you
will cry."
"Will you take me in your arms, dearest?"
she asked hesitantly.
"Yes," said Horatio. "In the shower."
"I don't have a shower," said Miss
Trueheart, close to tears.
"Well, I guess we can skip that," said
Horatio dubiously, as he threw his tie on
the floor. "Come, my love, I can hardly
wait."
So they threw their clothes on the floor,
got under the sheet, talked, and then
Horatio dressed and went for a drive
while Miss Trueheart cried.
But, oddly enough, though they faithfully
repeated this routine every night for
seven years, they never did have a child.
With his good sex education, Horatio
privately blamed Miss Trueheart for
neither smoking nor having a shower.
But he was too gallant to say so.
MORAL: Adult Movies may, indeed,
destroy our way of life. And the human
race along with it.
Art Hoppe.

I was surprised to discover that even running theaters which show girlie films is not all that simple. When I was with another company, we had about seven theaters. We had a house right downtown, a choice piece of property. But it hadn't been making any money for three or four years. They tried a policy of fifty cents, three features, everything, everything you could imagine. And it just didn't go over. So a fellow in another city who specializes in sex pictures and nudies, said, "Why don't you put in the sex pictures? Try it." Our company was hesitant; they weren't sure the town had enough of an audience for that sort of film. They didn't particularly want to get into that end of the business. But he said, "It'll make money for you." They had to tear the place down, sell the property, do something with it, so they decided they would try it. They took some of his films and went into it. Matinees every day, and—nothing. They called Pete and said, "It's not going to go here. The people won't buy it." You're showing the same thing you're showing in your city, and they're not buying it."

"We're showing it."

"How much are you charging?"

"A dollar and a quarter."

"Well, no wonder."

"We can't go any lower than going lower."

"I'm not talking about that."

"Well, what do you mean?"

"Charge three dollars."

"Three dollars! They won't come in for one twenty-five, what makes you think they're going to buy for three dollars?"

"Try it for two weeks. If you don't make money, I'll pay your overhead."

They went to three dollars. They haven't had a red week in the house since. They're a better matinee house than Cinerama! No overhead, no maintenance, all adults, one person operates the whole theater. Monday through Thursday, it will out-gross any house in the circuit. It's a funny business.

Robert Reeves, a theater manager.

Always go in the morning if you can; it will
Be something more than habit if you do. Keep well
Away from most French farces.
Try to see a set
Of old blue movies every so often, that the sight
Of animal doings out of the clothes of 'thirty-five
May remind you that even the natural act is phrased
In the terms and shapes of particular times and places.

John Hollander, Movie Going.

hypocrisy: nudity in films
... is always female nudity;
Never male.

Vilgot Sjöman.

Warhol's —— is, to my knowledge, the first full-length film which includes an instance of clear, plain, unmistakeable sexual intercourse. Many films have feigned this, but in —— it's right there ... bingo. Yet it's about as sexy as any given segment of The Beverly Hillbillies. I suspect that the, uh, plot evolved only after the camera was running, the film appears spontaneous and includes giggling looks at the camera (professional heavy breathers never, ever look at the camera).

The most interesting thing about —— and I Am Curious—Yellow is that neither is sexy and neither is intended to be sexy.

San Francisco Chronicle.

In July 1969 Denmark abolished all laws against pornography for adults. Any Dane over 16 became free to indulge his taste for pornography to the limit through photographs, books, films. Sales of all forms of pornography have markedly declined. One publisher was stuck with 500,000 copies of *I, a Woman*. Price reductions did not halt the diminished interest. Beaver films formerly selling for $40 went begging at $8.50. Said one dealer, "Legalization has killed the business. You have to be content with what you can sell of decent magazines."
Sex crimes reportedly dropped slightly, and officials could find no evidence that school children had more contact with obscene material. One headmaster observed that the new freedom simply proved that children are not interested in pornography. "This so-called altruism about protecting the children is often just a false way adults have of saving themselves from embarrassment." "When they are freely available," said Minister of Justice Knud Thestrup, "pornographic books and pictures very quickly become boring and distasteful to adults with a normal sexual life. The public's interest in pornography is mostly the result of curiosity about what is forbidden."

God made sex for a joke, but when He found out people were taking it seriously, He made it a sin.
The L Shaped Room.

Start from Skid Row: no sound of cars or trucks;
Only, at times, a shout—high without tone.
And these gaunt wanderers are its only flux:
In dusty pinstriped jackets, men of bone,

Their eyes lit with an untenable glow, they stray
—Vaguely, but not with drink—from here to there,
Dark in the dark. Now I, as stiff as they,
Return along the quiet street to where

I am halted by a compact diadem,
Beneath which sit the dreaming, faces white:
Marine and hunchback without ruling them
Gaze at the fluent vehicles of light.

Nipples like hubcaps tilt across the screen;
A great thigh heaves by, thirty times the size
A thigh should be; it is toward us they lean,
Vast forms which make it only to our eyes.

And though her chin is sharp, and her eyes beady,
We sit here hour by hour, with mouths gone dry,
Greyly remote from the complex and less heady
Commitments of the flesh, yet transfixed by

Her curved and tense verisimilitude,
The shaped intangibles are no dream, but
The familiar matter of obsession, crude,
Contrived, we have always to sit out.
Thom Gunn.

1903: Edwin S. Porter's *The Great Train Robbery* develops narrative technique through cutting and contrasting scenes.

Cartoon

"They're all going to the movies now."

Finally, remember always to
  honor the martyred dead.
The forces of darkness spread
  everywhere now, and the best
And brightest screens fade out,
  while many-antennaed beasts
Perch on the housetops, and
  along the grandest streets
Palaces crumble, one by one.
  The dimming starts
Slowly at first; the signs are few,
  as "Movies are
Better Than Ever," "Get More
  out of Life. See a Movie" Or
Else there's no warning at all
  and, Whoosh! the theater falls,
Alas, transmogrified: no double-
  feature fills
A gleaming marquee with
  promises, now only lit
With "Pike and Whitefish Fresh
  Today" "Drano" and "Light
Or Dark Brown Sugar, Special"
  Try never to patronize
Such places (or pass them by
  one day a year). The noise

Of movie mansions changing
  form, caught in the toils
Of our lives' withering, rumbles,
  resounds and tolls
The knell of neighborhoods. Do
  not forget the old
Places, for everyone's home has
  been a battlefield.
John Hollander, *Movie Going.*

We go to the movies
because we want to.

Pauline Kael.

One cannot write without a public
and without a myth—without a
certain public which historical
circumstances have made, without a certain myth of literature
which depends to a very great
extent upon the demand of this
public.
Jean Paul Sartre.

When I saw *The Dirty Dozen*, I had thought that it was a good representative of a new kind of war movie, which seems to be replacing the kind that people were making five or ten years ago. In the old war films—films such as *The Bridge on the River Kwai and Beachhead*—the writers and directors were careful to show the enemy in a poor light, usually as machinelike, brutal professional soldiers who practiced torture and were power-mad, and to show our soldiers in a good light, usually as informal, friendly civilian types who somehow managed to humanely and charmingly overcome superior enemy forces by turning their skills as ballplayers to the throwing of hand grenades. In the old war films, when the time came to have the enemy soldiers killed, the moral gap between the enemy robots and our citizen-soldiers was so well established that few in the audience could feel anything but righteous satisfaction at the enemy deaths. But in the new kind of war film the enemy is depicted as quite neutral morally and our own soldiers turn out to be unspeakably brutal, as though this were some-thing to admire. Although the directors of the new kind of film apparently want the audience to root for our soldiers, their grip on the old stratagems for winning our sympathy seems to be slipping. . . .
The New Yorker.

Then it is that the idea of the search occurs to me. I
become absorbed and for a minute or so forget about the girl.
What is the nature of the search? you ask.
Really it is very simple, at least for a fellow like me;
so simple that it is easily overlooked.
The search is what anyone would undertake if he were
not sunk in the everydayness of his own life. This morning, for example, I felt as if I had come to myself on a
strange island. And what does such a castaway do? Why,
he pokes around the neighborhood and he doesn't miss a trick.
To become aware of the possibility of the search is to
be onto something. Not to be onto something is to be in despair.
The movies are onto the search, but they screw it up.
The search always ends in despair. They like to show a
fellow coming to himself in a strange place—but what
does he do? He takes up with the local librarian, sets
about proving to the local children what a nice fellow
he is, and settles down with a vengeance. In two weeks
time he is so sunk in everydayness that he might just as well be dead.
Walker Percy, *The Moviegoers.*

Our revels now are ended. These our actors,
As I foretold you, were all spirits, and
are melted into air, into thin air;
And, like the baseless fabric of this vision,
The cloud-capped towers, the gorgeous palaces,
The solemn temples, the great globe itself,
Yea, all which it inherit, shall dissolve
And, like this insubstantial pageant faded,
Leave not a rack behind. We are such stuff
As dreams are made on, and our little life
Is rounded with a sleep.
The Tempest.

The experience of each age demands a
new confession, and the world seems always
waiting for its poet.
Emerson.

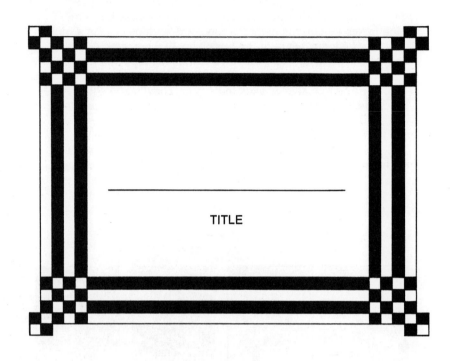

TITLE

**The Scene Pope John
Wouldn't Let Fellini Film.**
Tape   collage   sound   bursts
conducted   by   Karl   Heinz   Weissner
in stolid old Heidelberg
where the student prince drowned
in the gigantic wein stube
only a German would be gross
enough to perpetuate with dwarfs
locked arm in dunklewald singing
because *ja-ja* they are always wanting
to liberate their subliminal demons
and if just once they'd shape their genius,
refine that fantastic myth capacity
we would hear the glorious 9th pouring
from every beer hall until that exalting
silence . . . and the piping bum-ta-ta
of a three-piece Bavarian tanz band
with all the clowns, burghers, lovers
fathers of the ecumenical council
parading round & round the space ship
up the iron scaffold like a stupendous
circus Noah act of two by holy two
until safely locked in the capsule—
they blast off for the stars!
Dan Georgakas.

Ev-'ry-thing that hap-pens in life can hap-pen in a show.

144

Story Time Games

Each person must supply a story ending in the manner of a famous film director that the others toss to him. Then discuss each solution.

Aspersia, or the Sad Story of an Unhappy Little Girl.

Aspersia was an unhappy little girl. No one liked her. At school the other kids made a circle and danced around her yelling, Asper*in*, asper*in*, be*cause* you *are* a *pill!*" over and over again. Then Miss Buckminster made them stop. But Aspersia was pretty sure that Miss Buckminster didn't like her either, the way she kept saying mean things.

Once when Aspersia was two years old she had had a friend, but the friend died in a cholera epidemic. Now she couldn't find one anywhere. She tried the postman but he ran away. The boy who delivered the groceries turned out to be a deaf mute. Aspersia was very unlucky as well as unhappy.

When she was seven years old she had a birthday party and invited everybody in her class and said she would give *them* presents. They were all going to come but the afternoon of her party there was a blizzard and nobody showed up. Aspersia felt more unlucky than ever, since it was July when it rarely snows in New Jersey.

One day on the way home from school she saw a little dog that was obviously lost. She thought, "If I take him home and give him a hamburger maybe he will be my friend!" But when she reached down to pet him he bit her.

It didn't hurt much but it made her even unhappier.

Two months later she still didn't have a friend. She was walking home and it was snowing and very cold. She saw a little kitten shivering in a snow drift. "He'll *freeze!*" thought Aspersia who was very kind. She reached down and picked up the kitten to warm him inside her jacket, but instead of purring the kitten hissed and scratched Aspersia right through her mittens.

Aspersia decided she would never touch anything again. All winter she moped around, pretending to like television because television pretended to like her. One day she tried loving her mother's African violet in the kitchen window, but it wasn't satisfying. So she stopped caring about anything.

Then in the spring things seemed a little better. She couldn't help but be hopeful, with everything growing again. She even started to think about having a friend again.

One day coming home from school she saw a toad in the middle of the sidewalk, looking up at her.

Continued on page 146.

Al Jolson had 150 overcoats in his closet when he died.

Ed Castle, *Mickey One.*

Today's Movies are full of yesterdays.

"Hello, toad," she said without thinking. Right away she was sure he would give her a wart or something. But he just breathed deeply and looked up at her. She bent down to look at him a little closer and she heard a soft, continuous, grateful sound, like purring. His eyes looked right into hers and they almost seemed affectionate. Cautiously Aspersia petted the toad with an index finger. Nothing bad happened. Then the toad hopped even closer and nuzzled against her sneaker. Aspersia's eyes filled with tears of joy. "Oh, toady," she said, "at last I have a friend!" She was so excited that she kissed the toad on the top of its head. . . . All at once there was a flash of purple light and the toad changed into a handsome Prince! He was dressed in velvet with gold buckles and had curly hair with a crown on top of it. He was older than Aspersia, but not *too* much older. He seemed very tall. He looked down at Aspersia and smiled, and then he laughed and walked away. Aspersia tried to run after the Prince.

But she could only hop!

Poor Aspersia had turned into a toad!

Donald Hall.

It's either a stag film, an underground movie or a cigarette commercial!

Kitsch:
Borrows from a fully developed cultural tradition, devices, tricks, stratagems, rules of thumb, themes. Mechanical, operates by formula. Vicarious experience, faked sensations. Predigests art for the spectator and spares him effort. Appears to be a short cut to the pleasures of art but is in fact a detour of what is necessarily difficult in genuine art. It is synthetic art.

They butchered the book.

Note for academic art criticism: What the artist *gives* (not what he hopes to take from you). Like Krishna's idea of it being the labor (path) itself not the fruits of labor (goal):

        Discovery (going)
      seems to begin
     . . . when it starts
        when what you have or are disappears
        when
        when . . . (from my notes . . . still thinking about film festivals: one could deliberately make film festival films. Which becomes—like in any commercial art—a process of taking from others.)

Bruce Baillie.

At the moment, the most exciting thing for me in the development of mechanics in media is that people will be able to control the speed with which they can be exposed to a movie. You're going to be able to buy movies or rent them from a library the way you can rent books, and you're going to be able to look at them just the way you read a book. You'll be able to say: "I want to see that again." You're going to see a picture like *8½*, which is, you know, difficult to assimilate the first time around, or let's say a movie like *Mickey One*, which does not completely successfully do what it intends the first time around, and you're going to be able to look at it again. Now it fascinates me that a filmmaker won't have to worry whether people get it, understand it the first time around. They can come back and try it again. And once that can be thrown away—once the worry whether they are going to get it right the first time can be thrown away—something really personal is going to be able to happen to film. When anyone—this girl photographer with you—can go out and make a personal account of something on film and not have to take 40 teamsters with her, something special is going to happen, something fascinating. A little girl is going to be able to go out and make a film the same way David Lean makes it and there are not going to be all those conferences with Sam Spiegel and Colum-

bia Pictures. I'm not saying something negative about them, but she's going to be able to go out and say, "I want that; I want 25 feet of film of that; and I want to cut over to here." Then there are going to

be no boundaries, and all the promoting and selling, which I must confess to at the moment, all that's not going to count much, and that's what I look forward to.
Warren Beatty.

I guess when it comes to the quality of a film, people have to rely on their own judgment, but they also have to learn to question that judgment. They should trust what they first see, but they should be ready to examine it when they make their final criticism. In *The Sound of Music* I felt as though the film makers were relying on our stock responses —and not very imaginatively either. There was no special treatment of the photography, the music, the situations. Wooden characters. The appeal of little children, animals, death.

It was straight out of the thirties. They used an old stock form. People bought it because it was wide screen, good, clear photography, picture postcard.

Do we have a right to criticize it on these grounds, since the film makers knew what they were doing, and that's exactly what the audiences wanted?

I think they got exactly what they wanted, and the ones who said they didn't like it had no business going in the first place. It was all cutesy fluffsy in the ads.

There was no artificiality about it.

It was frankly pornographic.

When I came out of Antonioni's *Blow Up*, I enjoyed standing in the lobby and watching people's faces as they came out of the theater. I saw all those bewildered looks. They seemed right at that moment trying to decide whether they should like it or they shouldn't, trying to get clues from their friends. Was it a masterpiece or trash? I do think that most successful films are those which are ambiguous; they leave a lot of things unanswered, and you go home and think about it.
John Korty.

VIOLENCE

PRACTICE

① Run a short film, but do not show the title.
② Then have a group select a perfect title.

Match number list with letter list:

___ 1. "Oh, gosh, what a marvelous guide to motels!"

___ 2. ". . . entirely occupied with mamas and priests."

___ 3. "A gigantic real estate venture blessed by the Lord."

___ 4. "This dramatic self-love affair."

___ 5. "Bad picture postcard art."

___ 6. "A Mustang commercial."

___ 7. "A Salem commercial."

___ 8. "The *Silas Marner* of high school study groups."

___ 9. "How did you like it?" "By whom, God or John Huston?"

___10. "The best picture of 1956."

a. *The Song of Bernadette* (cited by Oscar Levant).

b. *Guess Who's Coming to Dinner.*

c. The cycle of imported Italian pictures (attributed to Virgil Thomson by Oscar Levant).

d. *Dr. Zhivago* (Pauline Kael).

e. *The Loneliness of the Long Distance Runner* (John Culkins).

f. *The Bible.*

g. *Elvira Madigan.*

h. *Lolita* (attributed to Christopher Isherwood by Oscar Levant).

i. *After the Fall* (Oscar Levant).

j. *A Man and A Woman* (Ernest Callenbach).

Answers: HCAIDJGEFB.

Film Festival Flophouses.

Film festivals . . . Film flophouses!
What happened to the San Francisco Film Festival?
Did it ever really exist?
Film as Art was shown in someone's garage.
Or was it the back room of the church
Which God had vacated . . .
Why pay ten dollars to show in someone's bathroom?
Fuck that!
What's more, like all festivals,
You have to carry a credit card in the Elite group
Whatever that is . . . .
But look at the articles
And the things that appear in all of the film-makers news mags . . .
They're written by the same people
About the Same things
In the Same way.
Is anybody out there?
Are there any real people?
The film festivals are the same way.
No difference.
No face.
Same. Same.
Don't think for yourself.
How did all the judges get so close to God?
Must have taken one hell of a space ship to get there.
Many of the films they select are beautiful.
And I watch them over and over.
But others make me puke and retch,
And audiences say, "What IS this?"
A lot of cast-iron shit . . .
Cast down from the Ivory Tower to the "*Cul*ture-hungry masses" below.
But the hungry throngs don't know it's shit . . .
It lost its color on the way down.
That's where film's at right now.
So what about film festivals?
I wish there were some.
Oh, there is one!
It's the best I know of in the whole country (even though the people who run
it are schmucks, taking film-makers for a ride on their
"tour," a banana boat sinking slowly in the west)
But nonetheless, the Foothill Film Festival is a groove
Because it's fun.
Everybody grooves behind it.
And that's where life is at.
It's grooving behind what you dig.
And digging it with others.
And digging others digging it.
But it isn't sitting up in some Ivory Tower "leading the way."
Leading what way?
They don't know the direction,
And they never had a map to begin with.
That's some sort of public masturbation.
Did we forget all about communication?
Or is there nothing left to be said?
Larry Booth.

Medium Cool.

In [Carl Linder's] *Skin*, flowers are seen in all their lush, feminine beauty—glowing inwardly and outwardly; bees, pollen, stamens—all the reproductive beauties of flowers are shown, with quick subliminal flashes of their human counterparts . . . Skin becomes/is the outerleaf of the body—the exposed. Skin is the porous, delicate sense of touch. And as the flower thief is seen in the end escaping with his carpetbag through green botanical gardens we realize all this must not be stolen or allowed to wither away.
Gregg Barrios.

JACK SMITH
CARL LINDER
ANDY WARHOL
HARRY SMITH
JOHN KEATS

No man lives in external truth among salts and acids, but in the warm phantasmagoric chamber of his brain, with the painted windows and the storied walls.
William James.

The fact is that, whether or not Andy is a genius, he has brought something very new and exciting into films in a period when mannered, slick film-making by fine American and foreign directors has been just about exhausted. Andy, despite his reputation as a put-on, is a superbly honest film-maker. Using improvisation and crude camera technique—in fact, almost no technique at all, except to keep his hand-held camera trained on the subject until the film runs out—he manages to create his characters with more insight than directors with a whole battery of technical equipment.
Elenore Lester, *Eye.*

Forever piping songs forever new.

Most of his pieces find the same sore spot and rub; flowers take on the paralysis of graveyard bouquets; girlie photos make the viewer feel like a corpse remembering former pleasures; lace associates directly with arsenic; flickering votive lamps desecrate instead of sanctify. The detritus and debris of old nylons, comic strips, wrappers, beads, cigarette butts, are accumulated in a sort of inspired excess that becomes a curious digestive process in which fire seems catalytic —everything burned and singed so it looks as if one puff of air would disperse the whole flimsy structure . . . Brian O'Doherty about Bruce Conner.

Bruce Baillie is one of the true poets of the New American Cinema. He is sensitive to the form, texture, color, line, pattern, and movement of both the world of nature and of the material, industrial world created by man. His work is marked by two salient characteristics: the first is the use of the conflict between the world of nature, which Baillie sees as poetic and lyric, and the world man has made, which is often barbaric, ugly, coarse, and mechanical; the second is tension inherent in each work, a tension that comes from a conflict between the lyric and poetic style of the film, and the horrors of modern Western civilization. John Bragin.

My first film was made by imprinting the cork off an ink bottle and all that sort of thing, as I said before. The second one was made with come-clean gum dots, automatic adhesive dots that Dick Foster got for me. It's like a paper dot with gum on the back. The film was painted over with a brush to make it wet, then with a mouth-type spray gun dye was sprayed onto the film. When that dried the whole film was greased with Vaseline. Of course this was in short sections—maybe six-foot-long sections. Anyway they would be tacked down. With a tweezers the dots were pulled off. That's where those colored balls drop and that sort of stuff. Being as it was pulled off, it was naturally dry where the dot had been and that part which had been colored was protected by the Vaseline coating at this point. Then color was sprayed into where the dot had been. After that dried, the whole film was cleaned with carbon tetrachloride.
The next one was made by putting masking tape onto the film and slitting the tape lightly with a razor blade and a ruler, and then picking off all those little squares that are revolving around. I worked off and on on that film for about five years pretty consistently; I worked on it every day at least. I may have abandoned it at one point for three months at the most. . . .
I developed certain really complicated hand painting techniques of which I made only short versions. For example, painting the whole film a certain color and then smearing Vaseline on it; and then taking a stylus and scraping designs off. It is possible to get a lot of spirals and curvilinear designs which I was never able to get by cutting off the masking tape; then spraying bleach into the place that had been scraped off, I think Clorox, which would then remove the background material where it had been scraped off; washing the Clorox out; and then spraying another color into the place where the groove was.
Harry Smith to P. Adams Sitney.

I don't think I'll make any more animated films. They're too laborious and bad for the health. Sitting under those lights for hours is terrible. I've made enough of those; just like I've made enough hand-drawn films. I would like to make an "underground" movie that could be shown everywhere in little towns, because it was seeing art films, or whatever they used to call them, that first got me interested in these things. Now there must be lots of kids all over the world that would make films if they saw some of the things that are being made now.
Harry Smith to P. Adams Sitney.

In *Empire* Warhol has clearly dismissed the idea that "movement" is an essential characteristic of movies . . . Sound is dispensed with . . ., and its absence is consistent with the object photographed (the camera was focused on the Empire State Building for several hours) . . .
Black and white and everything in between is one subject of this film. Another, even more important, is time.
Gregory Battcock, *The New American Cinema.*

Notes on a Male Character for *The Devil Is Dead.*
The boy is hard, full of nails.
He hears the excitement of tearing. Meaning that he should tear, cloth perhaps, perhaps panties, perhaps.
He needs protection, seeking shelter under a mattress.
All of his life is devoted to fools, he takes to dolls, and then knives.
What he has in his head is a gut string, wearing the end of a whip around his head, tightening, he loathes on his face, the tightening of fidelity, for isn't this against the grain, sawing.
Perhaps he finds himself sawing, grinding a thing of beauty in half, a thing of contempt like a child's potty, or perhaps beautiful in the way of a penis, grinding a penis against stone. And this represents his poverty to hold onto life respectably.
He looks out of openings, through holes, in paper, and he applies these holes to himself, around his foot.
The boy wears gloves, protection against being caught, and then being able to handle the situation. This is a real gloved boy, and he places his hands in stickiness . . .
Carl Linder.

Making
this
book
into
a
real
live
thing.

June, 1896: Last night I was in the Kingdom of Shadows. . . . I was at Aumont's and saw Lumiére's cinematograph—moving photography. The extraordinary impression it creates is so unique and complex that I doubt my ability to describe it with all its nuances. . . . It seems as though it carries a warning, fraught with a vague but sinister meaning that makes your heart grow faint. You are forgetting where you are. Strange imaginings invade your mind and your consciousness begins to wane and grow dim. But suddenly, alongside of you the gay chatter and provoking laughter of a woman is heard . . . and you remember that you are at Aumont's, Charles Aumont's. But why of all places should this remarkable invention which affirms once again that energy and the curiosity of the human mind, forever striving to solve and grasp all, and . . . while on the way to the solution of the mystery of life, incidentally builds Aumont's fortune? . . . I am convinced that these pictures will soon be replaced by others of a genre more suited to the general tone of the "Concert Parisien." For example, they will show a picture titled: *As She Undresses* or *Madame at Her Bath* or *A Woman in Stockings*.
Maxim Gorky.

Distortion of some kind is present in all art.
Herbert Read.

Bill — what do you think about letting our readers see us actually making this book — like when Truffaut lets the screen go dark as though a the projector ~~light~~ light turned out or when he lets the leader show (5, 4, 3, 2, 1 etc.)? I think we have to join in this movement to break the illusionists hypnotic spell. I don't want people reading this to be mere audience. I think they should realize that ~~so~~ they have to come right out and share in the making of the concepts.
Clark

Absolutely, Clark. I think that ~~if those~~ who are really reading this book are also participating in creating it. They can begin with what we have suggested and use that as a point of departure for their own direction of movement.
Bill.

a view of the boys

Robert Nelson
War is Hell

Stan Brakhage
Anticipation of Night

Gunvor Nelson
Schmeerguntz

Will Hindle
Billabong
Chinese Firedrill
FFFTCM
Merci, Merci

Carl Linder
Closed Mondays
Overflow
Womancock
Skin

Bruce Baillie
Quick Billy
Mass for the
Dakota Sioux
To Parsifal
All My Life

It is the function of
true genius to disturb all
settled ideas.
Goethe.

But the men who made Hollywood were poets—even gang-
sters, who took it by force
to dictate their poetic law.
Jean-Luc Godard.

Larry Jordan
The Old House, Pass-
ing
Gymnopedies
Duo Concertantes
Portrait of Sharon

Bruce Conner
Report
A Movie
Easter Morning Raga
Cosmic Ray

Scorpio Rising made
$80,000 for Kenneth
Anger. He went to Paris.

Robert Downey
The Sweet Smell of Sex

John Schofill
X-Film

Lenny Lipton
Show and Tell

155

Editor. I have adjusted this page some, but I do want it retained in the book. It's an important educational element of the book. I would also like it typewritten or in some other way identified as different for the rest of the book. C∿

THIS BOOK IS MADE OF CELLULOID

Okay. Now, that Bonnie and Clyde material is pretty solid. What about these quotes we were going to use?

Well, you know, this question that you raise about how you get readers to see how this book is put together--I think that's pretty important. I'm wondering if there's some way we could tie in the question, "Is this book like a movie; is it made like a movie?" Something which would get them to think about the way it's been done.

I would like them to see the similarity to movies: strips of celluloid put together in a certain way according to someone's perception of the way life would go, something of that sort.

Well, we'll think about it.

Of course, you could just take some of this "footage" and put one piece after another and say, "How about making up three pages or so for us of the book?" Maybe just put an envelope of stuff in there. And ask them to make a meaningful montage of that, like you might make a movie.

Why don't we do it?

I don't think I'd like it.

No, not the envelope, but we have several useful quotes. Why structure them in any way?

Put two or three pages in?

Yes, and say, "Arrange these in some meaningful way." They could cut them out. This could follow those notes you and I just wrote up. That would be an introduction to these three or four pages of random material.

Anything could go on those pages, handwritten things, notes, reminders. They could suggest stills or drawings to go with them. I think that would be fascinating to do. They could go back through the book and take out visuals for this.

I'm not interested in film. I'm interested in getting my opinions and feeling about people expressed.
John Cassavettes.

Marxism:
Harpo, Chico, Groucho, Zeppo & ————.

Critic: But don't all films have to have a beginning, a middle and an end?
Godard: Yes, but not necessarily in that order.
Jean-Luc Godard.

This is a movie.
This is an actor.
This is fake.
Only you are real.
You are real aren't you?

I remember with one movie I said, "Patricia Neal is one of the finest actresses around and Samantha Eggar is certainly one of the most attractive sexpots we have seen in years, and what either of them is doing in *Psyche 68* (or whatever that movie was) I cannot for one venture to guess." What do you think came out? "Patricia Neal is one of the finest actresses around and Samantha Eggar is the most luscious sexpot we have seen in years." You can't say I didn't say that. The most recent example was *Grand Prix*. I had said on the *Today* show that every year at this time we get a great big luscious Cinerama special. This year it is *Grand Prix*. Well, they had an enormous ad with a seven-column headline that said. "This year it is *Grand Prix*- Judith Crist, *World Tribune*."
Judith Crist.

LIKE REVIEWS, IT IS NOT ONLY THE CRITIC OR THE COLUMNIST, IT IS THE PAPER THAT PRINTS THE STUFF WHICH MAKES THE DIFFERENCE.
Oscar Levant.

THE DIRECTOR IS
THE SUBJECT OF FILMS.

Who's playing in it?

8½ :
a movie about a movie about a movie within a movie.

Ugliness in art occurs when the artist is unsure of what he wants to do.
Rudolf Arnheim.

Nobody has been able to say definitely whether picture making is really a business or an art . . .

It should be conducted with budgets and cost sheets, but it cannot be conducted with blueprints and graphs.
Irving Thalberg

My God, I'm standing here in the middle of a revolution.

157

Billy Wilder
to Otto Preminger:
I gotta be nice to you.
I still have family in Germany.

When one is an artist, all mediums open up.
Henry Miller.

The most remarkable thing about *The Cocoanuts* is that it is terrifically funny. Generally a stage show literally transcribed onto the screen is as captivating as a filibuster. It doesn't work, foiled by the aesthetic law that tells us to expect one set of conventions from the stage and another from the screen. But the Marx Brothers, who violated all laws, logical and social, found this last one no barrier at all, mainly because they were perfect screen comedians before talkies even began. Their wild sight gags profit little from the confines of the stage. But film captures, energizes and magnifies their rapid-fire, kinetic humor. Film editing, with its quick and crazy cutting, complements perfectly the helter-skelter movements of the Marxes themselves. Someone located in the back of the theater might miss the subtle, second-to-second emotional changes that play across Harpo's face. But film closeups turn the Marxes' mugs into visual playgrounds filled with comic events. *The Cocoanuts* is one of those happy accidents of art and technology in which cinema found sound just in time to give full voice to Groucho's wit, Chico's verbal tenacity and Harpo's silence.
Zimmerman and Goldblatt.

Most American films released in France are considered to have done well if they bring $300,000 or $400,000 to the distributor. Lewis's films do at least twice that. While it is not much of a surprise that Lewis should appeal to the mass movie audience in France, it is rather remarkable that French intellectuals, of all people, have an immense admiration for him.
Hollis Alpert.

Cinema, even where fantasy is introduced, is much more realistic than the stage. Especially in an historical picture, the setting, the costume, and the way of life represented have to be accurate. Even a minor anachronism is intolerable. On the stage much more can be overlooked or forgiven; and indeed, an excessive care for accuracy of historical detail can become burdensome and distracting. In watching a stage performance, the member of the audience is in direct contact with the actor playing a part. In looking at a film, we are much more passive; as audience, we contribute less. We are seized with the illusion that we are observing an actual event, or at least a series of photographs of the actual event; and nothing must be allowed to break this illusion. Hence the precise attention to detail.
T. S. Eliot.

I was in London during the Second World War when a picture by John Van Druten opened. It was called *Old Acquaintance*, and it co-starred Bette Davis and Miriam Hopkins. The critics of two London Sunday papers both used the same tag line at the end of their reviews. What do you think it was? "Auld acquaintances should be forgot." In other words, even if the picture had been good, they just couldn't resist that line.
Alfred Hitchcock.

Unless there is encouragement to reflect on film experience, its impact can be minimal and fleeting.
Anthony Schillaci.

Faces would never have been finished if everyone had gotten interested in the directing problems rather than in the human problems. Films are not very important to me. People are more important.
John Cassavetes.

Jacqueline Bisset took her place at the railing of the sundeck. The camera was behind her, looking down over her at the figures on the beach.
Pasternak shook his head sadly. "How can you tell a director that this shot isn't worth shooting?" he said. "He should do a reverse and show her standing on the porch. You get her face that way." He started back up the steps for his car. "And I'm selling a face, not an ass."
John Gregory Dunne, *The Studio.*

Griffith was the first to photograph thought.
Cecil B. DeMille.

MUTATIONS ARE PROBABLE THE MOMENT ONE GOES FROM ONE SET OF CONVENTIONS TO ANOTHER.

This is a cliché.
This is Art.
The difference is obvious.
What is the difference?

Instead of putting a lot of pock-marked faces on the screen—big horrible head, eye—I just don't like it—if I can play a scene in a two-shot, where you can see both faces very well, I prefer it that way.
John Ford.

Are you one of these talkers, or would you like to see a little criticism?

Lights and shades react not only on the objects but also on each other.
Pierre Leprohon.

What such films as *Hour of the Wolf*, *Belle de Jour*, *La Chinoise*, *2001* and even *The Young Girls of Rochefort*, have in common is something that might be called the inward camera —the camera turned upon the mind of an author, or of characters, so that what reality there is is interior; the world on screen is personal, a fantasy or a convergence of fantasies.
Renata Adler.

You have to be in love with the movies. Or the movies will not be in love with you.

story at every instant. The visual tempo must change to stay in harmony with the slow tempo. Short strips, fast tempo. Visual tempo must change to stay in harmony with the story at every instant.

Montage:
The very length of the strips of film cemented together causes a rhythm or lack of it. Long strips, slow tempo. Short strips, fast tempo. Visual

F.T. The stabbing of Janet Leigh was very well done also.
A.H. It took us seven days to shoot that scene, and there were seventy camera setups for forty-five seconds of footage. We had a torso specially made up for that scene, with the blood that was supposed to spurt away from the knife, but I didn't use it. I used a live girl instead, a naked model who stood in for Miss Leigh. We only showed Miss Leigh's hands, shoulders, and head. All the rest was the stand-in. Naturally, the knife never touched the body; it was all done in the montage. I shot some of it in slow motion so as to cover the breasts. The slow shots were not accelerated later on because they were inserted in the montage so as to give an impression of normal speed.
F.T. It's an exceptionally violent scene.
A.H. This is the most violent scene of the picture. As the film unfolds, there is less violence because the harrowing memory of this initial killing carries over to the suspenseful passages that come later.
François Truffaut, *Hitchcock*.

"Watching a Buñuel film," as Jean Cocteau once put it, "is like watching a bullfight in which you are the bull."
Brad Darrach.

Oscar Levant.

reaction but not the one he expected.
"*Relax!*" It got quite a bull elephant from ambush and roared: then fluffed them again. Preminger sprang out of his director's chair like vously fluffed his lines, pictures, an actor nervously fluffed his lines, then fluffed them again. Preminger sprang out of his director's chair like a bull elephant from ambush and roared: "*Relax!*" It got quite a reaction but not the one he expected.
Oscar Levant.

If the spectator has let slip some vital parts of the film, his apprehension of the whole will be correspondingly less rich than was the artist's.

Margo Channing (Goddess).
night.
It's going to be a bumpy
Fasten your seatbelts,

Art is bumpy.
Kitsch is slick.

THE OSCAR

___ 1. In reference to her appearance at the 1967 Academy Awards show, "a gentile Molly Berg."

a. Judy Garland

___ 2. "a gifted amateur."

b. Elizabeth Taylor

___ 3. "She just married the first prince who asked her."

c. Barbara Streisand

___ 4. "She can only sing for nothing."

d. Lauren Bacall.

___ 5. "A wonderful woman, kind, warm, charitable; she possesses generous instincts; she is a good mother and a great success in life."

e. Arlene Francis or Rosalind Russell.

___ 6. "She's a vibrato in search of a voice."

f. Grace Kelly.

___ 7. Shah of Iran: "You dance beautifully." Her answer: "You bet your ass, Shah."

g. Judy Garland.

___ 8. Her reference to the Academy Awards: "I lost to a tracheotomy."

h. Kim Stanley.

___ 9. "Her conversation is faster than her mind. I don't believe she could be analyzed—she doesn't seem to have a subconscious. Her face is inscrutable, but I can't vouch for the rest of her."

i. Olivia de Havilland.

___10. "My candidate to play the life of Jimmy Durante."

j. Zsa Zsa Gabor.

(All cited in Oscar Levant, *The Unimportance of Being Oscar.*)

Answers: IHFAEGDBJC.

'Bonnie and Clyde' Gang Robs Bank

Newark. N. J.
A "Bonnie and Clyde" style gang of gun toting bandits held up a bank yesterday and fled with $151.000 in a getaway car driven by a woman.

To come to the point: the cinema is quite simply becoming a means of expression, just as all the other arts have been before it, and in particular painting and the novel. After having been successively a fairground attraction, an amusement analogous to boulevard theatre, or a means of preserving the images of an era, it is gradually becoming a language. By language, I mean a form in which and by which an artist can express his thoughts, however abstract they may be, or translate his obsessions exactly as he does in the contemporary essay and novel.
Alexandre Astruc, *The New Wave.*

TRUE/FALSE

The critical principles underlying the following are valid or invalid, both, neither, some of each? What are your critical principles? Are they any good?

1.
The tired businessman might be thought to have sufficient means of relaxation without the cinema; but if he must be further catered for, it should be made perfectly clear that the films which satisfy him are of an inferior nature. It is not that they transfer him to a world of fantasy, rather than fact; much of the greatest art, and nearly all music, is a resolution of spiritual conflicts rather than a remedy for social ills. It is that his transport to an unreal world is conducted by the simplest appeal to the senses; there is no call upon his imagination, nor upon his thought or deeper emotions.

2.
The critic should judge a film against other films or a comparable genre and not according to his moral preferences or prejudices.

3.
The storm over style and content will rage forever.

4.
There is no justification for using clichés in a film.

5.
The young look at film as potential or actual film-makers, and this fact raises participation to an unprecedented critical level.

6.
Movement is a unique quality of film. Time is a unique characteristic of film.

7.
Even among serious film critics, good Westerns are liable to be judged on mythic rather than aesthetic values. The result is that such pictures as *Stagecoach* (1939), *Red River* (1947) and *High Noon* (1952) can hardly be talked about in terms of literary merit or the historical realities which such standards imply.

8.
Movies are so contemporary. But it is true only to a very limited extent. Though people care very deeply about the form, the product has lately not been much.
Basically, there are not many lines or scenes or behaviors on the screen just now that a generation would want to imitate or even remember. And though people go to the movies all the time, it could be argued that hardly anyone's sensibility is affected by them.

9.
It is discontinuity, not continuity, in which resides most of the cinema's special powers.

10.
First identify the genre. What is it trying to do?

11.
Judge films not with your ears but with your eyes.

12.
The interesting thing about the cinema is not . . . the similarity between the image on the screen and the real world but . . . the difference between the two.

13.

After you have read the script, the biggest problem is not how you are going to direct individual scenes, but in what style are you going to make the entire film? It is always bad to consider a scene by itself. The worst directors are those who mix styles.

14.

Criticism means taking a stand on the basis of who you are.

15.

It's sometimes said that a critic, by the very nature of his work, is unimaginative, and in a way, that makes sense, since imagination may be a deterrent to his objectivity. Anyway, that lack of imagination might account for a predilection for films that are close to real life. On seeing *The Bicycle Thief*, for instance, he's likely to think this is just the sort of thing he might have written himself, but that thought couldn't possibly occur to him in connection with *North by Northwest*. This being so, he's bound to attribute all kinds of merit to *The Bicycle Thief* and none whatever to *North by Northwest*.

16.

One goes to see a movie to review it in exactly the way you go to a movie. You know, kids say "What should I look for?" when they are going to review a movie. And I say, you don't look for a thing and you are not supposed to notice, to see anything in fact, if it is a good movie. You don't hear the sound track. You don't see the performers. You don't see the camera technique. You see the movie. You walk out and say "This is fantastic." Why was it fantastic? The critic's function is to articulate—put that "fantastic" or "echch" into 800 words. That is the tough part with good or great movies because you know when a movie is bad from the minute it hits you while you are watching it, you sit there and you start picking out everything that is bad for the duration. But when a movie is good, all you really want to say is "Wonderful, beautiful." Everything that gets quoted in the ads. That is all you want to say and you don't want that great labor of saying "why" and it is hard to do it right afterwards because you are still caught up with it.

17.

The procedure of appreciation . . . begins as follows. The spectator, inexpert at first, watches the film with as much intelligence and sensibility as he can bring to it. In the passages where the theme, or intellectual and emotional narrative, is most intensive, he will be at least able to mark the technique and technicalities by which parts of the effect are produced. But when the theme weakens, he will find that he has a surplus of attention which he can profitably direct to these matters. As he continues to watch films in this way, his powers of insight and discrimination will increase. . . .

He is now able to take in the full import of the three channels of communication: sight, sound and rhythm of cutting. Within the shot, he weighs up the interrelated differentiating factors, noting that in one place composition has been marred by misplaced lighting, and in another that the camera has tracked or panned an unnecessary distance. Thus, even in a bad film, the spectator's attention need never wander; he can mentally reconstruct a shot or sequence in order to bring it closer to what he conceives to be the mood or instruction it seeks to convey. At the same time, his mind must be alert to seize the implications of different related passages, and to guard against such ideological montages as arise from unthinking prejudice or predilection. Finally, if the film is acted, he must judge the quality of the acting, and criticize the speech accompaniment, just as he questioned the value of each example of simultaneous montage in the other type of film.

All these processes need not take place at the same seeing. By successive doses, the tyro can gradually assimilate nearly as much as the connoisseur; but to successive applications of the film there will accrue successively smaller rewards, until finally the dissatisfaction of going to see it, and looking at what was already known, exactly balances the satisfaction of completing the remaining montages and observing the remaining relations between the differentiating factors . . . at the first seeing attention may be concentrated on the theme; at the second, on the technical ability of the acting; at the third, on the various montages, and so on; or, on the other hand, it may be distributed in varying proportions over all these at each seeing.

18.
The film itself dictates the critical approach to be used:
Goethe's rules:
1. What was the creator trying to do?
2. How well did he do it?
3. Was it worth doing in the first place?

19.
Reflecting on one's experience is an integral part of making that
experience part of one's self.

20.
In their own work, young people can celebrate bad film-making as "honest"
and voyeuristic films as "mature."

21.
The Auteur Theory.

22.
First, to what extent does the particular film take advantage of the strengths
and limitations of film form and communicate ideas and emotions that
can best (or only) be communicated within it? Second, assuming a subject
congenial to film, to what extent is the purpose accomplished? Third, if the
intention is the creation of an art work, to what extent is a complete and
unique artistic experience offered? Finally, to what extent does the work contain
the qualities of brilliance, profundity and universality?

23.
Schickel never takes notes or sees a film twice. "The audience can't," he says.
"Why should I?"

24.
Metz, too; he's a peculiar case. He's the easiest to like of them all [the critics]:
because he actually goes to movies; he really likes movies. But I can't understand
what he wants to do. He begins with film, all right. But then he goes off on a
tangent. He comes back to film from time to time; he'll poke around in it for a
bit. But then he's off again on another track. What bothers me is that
he seems not to have noticed; it's unconscious.

25.
Beautiful, symmetrical shots are not the essence of cinematography.

"But how will I know what wheat
is unless I look at the chaff?"

Antonioni appears mostly amused by the
comments of critics. "Even the ones who approve
my work give reasons I don't understand."

I am . . . willing to state flat out that the film is the best of its genre ever made, the realest evocation of the rural American 1930's screened to date (all the movies made in the 1930's included), and one of the most trenchant commentaries on the senseless drift of American life into violence. . . .

Jay Jacobs, *The Reporter.*

Merriment, murder, and mayhem . . . a tale of bullets and blood in a strange and purposeless mingling of fact and claptrap that teeters uneasily on the brink of burlesque.

A.H. To insist that a storyteller stick to the facts is just as ridiculous as to demand of a representative painter that he show objects accurately. What's the ultimate in representative painting? Color photography. Don't you agree?

A raw and unmitigated campaign of sheer pressagentry has been trying to put across the notion that *Bonnie and Clyde* is a faithful representation of the desperado careers of Clyde Barrow and Bonnie Parker. It is nothing of the sort. It is a cheap piece of baldfaced slapstick comedy that treats the hideous depredations of that sleazy, moronic pair as though they were as full of fun and frolic as the jazz-age cut-ups in *Thoroughly Modern Millie.* And it puts forth Warren Beatty and Faye Dunaway in the leading roles, and Michael J. Pollard as their sidekick, a simpering, nose-picking rube, as though they were striving mightily to be the Beverly Hillbillies of next year. It has Mr. Beatty clowning broadly as the killer who fondles various types of guns with as much nonchalance and dispassion as he airly twirls a big cigar, and it has Miss Dunaway squirming grossly as his thrill-seeking, sex-starved moll. It is loaded with farcical hold-ups, screaming chases in stolen getaway cars that have the antique appearance and speeded-up movement of the clumsy vehicles of the Keystone Cops, and indications of the impotence of Barrow, until Bonnie writes a poem about him to extol his prowess, that are as ludicrous as they are crude. Such ridiculous, camp-tinctured travesties of the kind of people these desperados were and of the way people lived in the dusty Southwest back in those barren years might be passed off as candidly commercial movie comedy, nothing more, if the film weren't reddened with blotches of violence of the most grisly sort. Arthur Penn, the aggressive director, has evidently gone out of his way to splash the comedy holdups with smears of vivid blood as astonished people are machine-gunned. And he has staged the terminal scene of the ambuscading and killing of Barrow and Bonnie by a posse of policemen with as much noise and gore as is in the climax of *The St. Valentine's Day Massacre.* This blending of farce with brutal killings is as pointless as it is lacking in taste, since it makes no valid commentary upon the already travestied truth. And it leaves an astonished critic wondering just what purpose Mr. Penn and Mr. Beatty think they serve with this strangely antique, sentimental claptrap.

Bosley Crowther, *The New York Times.*

Legend or Life?

It's such a nice film.

. . . an imaginative work that is interested in something other than historical "truth."

Richard Gilman, *New Republic.*

Banners:

Criticism isn't mechanical.

Kitsch is mechanical.

Any form is allowable.

Any style is allowable.

Any topic is allowable.

Close-ups aren't essential.

Criticism isn't absolute.

Historical inaccuracy is allowable.

Nostalgia for the thirties?

We had heard people saying that our movie was really about: 1) Lee Harvey Oswald; 2) the riots in Watts; 3) police brutality (anti, of course); 4) the Hippie movement and 5) Vietnam. And sometimes people got mad when we said, or director Arthur Penn said, that it really wasn't about any of those things, it was about Bonnie and Clyde and a lot of other ideas and theories and themes that we had.

This got us thinking about the way we "read" movies and books ten years ago when we, too, indulged in no doubt fanciful interpretations. But with this difference: ten years ago we came out of the precepts, concepts and practices of The New Criticism, and so we hungrily searched for hidden meanings and symbols everywhere just so long as we could justify them by finding them in the work itself. We saw a word "dog" on page 13 of a novel and later on page 458 "dog" again and we attempted to make a connection and put forward a dog-symbol theory. We saw a TV aerial in the shape of a cross in *On the Waterfront* and a walk by Brando at the end that looked like Christ carrying the cross up the hill, and we came up with a Christ-story parable.

But now, the students are responding with real fervor to works of art (and movies most often) only when they can somehow relate the movies to their own outside experiences, ideas, life. They bring outside interpretations to films or force films to correspond with preconceived notions, and then, if it seems to work, they dig the movie. The advantage of this to the film maker is that he can't do anything about it (if he does, it will probably look forced) and so must just be as good and inventive as he can, send the picture out into the world and *see* what the reverberations are.
Benton and Newman.

Usually after two nights I can tell how well the picture will do for the whole run.
And often you can't even pay off the guarantee and pull the picture; you have to run it the full time anyway. But there have been two pictures that fouled the theater people completely. The first was *The Pink Panther* which did nothing the first two weeks and all of a sudden caught on, grossing and grossing and building and building. Probably the most fantastic picture was *Bonnie and Clyde.*
It opened on a multiple run, they went for wide distribution. First week nothing, second week nothing. They were pulling it out. Then it started to get hot, they started bringing it back, doing more on a Friday night than in the whole two weeks before.
Robert Reeves, a theater manager.

Art is whatever you can get away with.

WHY BONNIE AND CLYDE?

Why not *Birth of a Nation* or *M*A*S*H*?
Why not *Citizen Kane*?
It's certainly not a classic. Is it?

Historical inaccuracy? Moral turpitude? Excessive violence? Childish? Childlike? Tasteless?

motor courts, in robberies and bloodshed? It could just as easily have happened on The African Queen. Or on a dustbowl farm. She is her mother's daughter; she accepts. All paths are foolish; it is only the struggle which gives them meaning.

Both Bonnie and Clyde come to accept their lives and each other. Which gives them the definition they have been stumbling about hunting for. When one looks at his possibilities and sees himself on a path and then follows through with the knowledge of the inevitable failure, that is a coming of age. They recognize their lot and deal with it within the limits of their intelligence and knowledge. They play out the hand. It is not only reasonable but likely that psychological impotence would diminish with the growth of sensibility and character. Clyde has finally entered puberty at least. The ordeal by fire and love has educated his sensorium if not his mind—which is characteristically slower. He never quite grasps what it's all about, but through accepting a crappy destiny (self-imposed, certainly) he becomes not noble, but human.

In the amalgam of laughter and horror, American films turned a corner with *Bonnie and Clyde*. (*Catch 22* went beyond juxtaposi-tion; it created scenes in which the two reactions actually merged). The film makes death real, but it also makes it acceptable—if we have learned to live life. Is it real? Is it a myth? The only reality we have is our myths. *Bonnie and Clyde* has entered our minds and is now a part of our reality. It is a folk-myth, though possibly not more accurate in its version of life than those Andy Hardy days which influenced us more (and less) than is believed. *Bonnie and Clyde* seems to reflect life more accurately, but as the culture enters our post-pubescent stage, perhaps *Bonnie and Clyde's* conception will seem as humorous as the naive, cruel, ignorant, provincial thirties this film so accurately delineates. Thirties seen with distance and love. Not camp, the sport of cynics, nor kitsch, the sop of dullards. An existential film, which shows life both as we thought it was and as it is at the same time. It makes us both participants and observers. Both the country bumpkin and the (somewhat) mature perceiver. Double vision. Remember, too, this is fiction. Made up. Like Shakespeare's *Richard III*. So forget those other characters with the same names. The film Bonnie and Clyde are two other people, just as real (more real) even if they didn't happen, to para-phrase Ken Kesey.

But we have to see the story kaleidoscopically if we are to see it at all. Dreams and the real mingle together to produce what we are. We are such stuff. Our schizophrenia divides us up into realists and romantics. But we are both and everything else, too. Penn won't let us slide over to one side or the other. *Bonnie and Clyde* is a third view which can entertain a more complete version of our lives and even make it refreshing—like cleared sinuses. It is an old-fashioned plot. It's a gangster flick, a chase, doomed lovers on the lam. But whose side should we be on? Those who expected the film to tell us how we should feel about Bonnie and Clyde were left scratching their heads.

Ain't life grand! A film like this comes along every ten years or so and destroys our ways of seeing, and if we're willing to go with it, we get a chance to restructure our picture of reality a bit less sentimental, a lot more satisfying. A quest to be. Bonnie and Clyde don't quite know what they're really up to, but they finally begin to feel their lives and to snuggle down into being.

Welty Hanna

TOWARD BECOMING A PERSON.

Start on page 169.

Wouldn't it have been nice if not one critic had challenged the right of a movie to have that much blood in it? They could have devoted the space to considering the artistic effectiveness of the violence, not the morality of having it there. There would have been no need to trot out in defense all the blood and corpses in *Richard III*, and *Hamlet* and *Oedipus* and *Antigone*. It might have been useful to explore how those scenes were set up—for reflection, for enriching something a moviegoer has already enjoyed—the way analyses of certain baseball plays allow a fan to run the taste of it over his tongue again. Bonnie and Clyde's death scene was beautiful. How did the filmmakers accomplish this? Don't lecture me about violence. If you're a specialist in these matters, tell me how the conjuror manages to make it such a satisfying ending, that ballet of death. That long death. The accelerated and slow motion. The intercuts and closeups. The action repeated from different angles. One instant closeup of Bonnie and Clyde's flash of realization. Terrible and quiet. Almost a suspension of time-space. A feeling of stillness. Musical.

The comedy is strong, fully equal to the pathos. (Tragedy is too strong a word. That's always romantic—as though anything men do could ever be that significant.) Bitter and sweet. Naive and ordinary. It's more the way things are: neither good nor bad. The script and direction dare to present a story which isn't only serious. More like the way things are. Like a good, rollicking wake. The mourners know goddamned well what they're doing. Only cousin Frank's moronic wife is dull-witted enough (and unrelated enough) to babble, ''How can you sit there and laugh at a time like this?'' We weren't ''put on,'' as some would have it, with *Bonnie and Clyde*. We were taken out of the Andy Hardy reality we had been living (and not living) and brought back to the feel of life and death as our genes remember them. One and the same, utterly interdependent. We have so many screwed up preachers among us. What a relief to get it all together. To laugh whether we ''should'' or not and come alive to the fullness of the whole thing.

Yet this was accomplished through theatrical tricks. Of course; what else! Through distortion, to come closer to the way things are. Bonnie's hairdo is psychological. Both for her and for the audience. You have Blanche in the mode. Bonnie in the mode would not work. By the end, though, Bonnie's makeup and garb have softened. isn't that neat: to take us through our misremembered past, to use those collective unconscious myths (they never really were the way we remember them), nostalgic half-truths. To present them distorted (just as we like to remember them) and actually make us break through to the wholeness of our minds and senses. No platitudes or moral dictums. To see, to hear. ''To make you, to make you feel.''

The film is two overlapping cones. It goes from broad, farcical humor to straight drama with what's left of the comedy only strengthening the stark denouement. As when C. W. smiles knowingly at Bonnie and Clyde's ''escape'' from the cops and their last buggy ride. C. W. still thinks he's in the Keystone cops part of the picture. But we know better. His puckish smile only deepens the inevitability of their execution. We have known from the first blast in the first bank clerk's face what is going to happen (it is classic. Greek.) The humor and pathos reach a balance at this point. From then on, the humor becomes more and more ''informed'' until for us it becomes sympathetic and knowing. ''I was not young long,'' says the poet. ''I met the soul early.'' This is an American story, our coming of age. Losing our taste for pulling wings off butterflies, but not regretting having done it either. Accepting our insensitivity and growing into oneness with life. Yes, it's a story about Bonnie and Clyde, but it reminds us of us. Some say Bonnie and Clyde never learn, but they do—as much as they're capable of. Which, being unheatrical and undramatic, is not enough for those accustomed to theatrical transformations. Bonnie learns. She matures. She doesn't get smarter—did we expect miracles? She gains that pioneer-woman stoicism which sometimes comes out of the fire of living. So what if she developed it in shoddy

In 1967 Bonnie and Clyde seemed like a watershed picture. Three years later that still seems true. American theatrical films turned a corner at that point, and things haven't been the same since. It was the first film of this era, a television movie, incorporating the Late-Late Show, the news from Viet Nam, and the heartbreak of psoriasis: the asymmetrical montage, the abrupt cuts, the loose ends (from brutally cut movies where it was discovered we didn't need everything spelled out), the full color, naivety and sophistication, comic strip fantasy and real blood, frank and open flaunting of camera techniques like slow and accelerated motion, mixing of styles like stark documentaries and soft-focus daydreams. All these were here already, just lying around in the culture, but *Bonnie and Clyde* put them all together and made them work.

In its wake have come a number of good films that make you feel almost adult for a change, but inevitably none so far with anything near the impact and startling freshness. It is not likely that another departure of this magnitude will occur within the decade. Other films will still be mastering and working out the lessons of *Bonnie and Clyde* for several more years. Good American films since 1967 are in some way or another the children of *Bonnie and Clyde. The Graduate:* freedom of technique. *The Wild Bunch:* artistic handling of gore. *M*A*S*H:* irreverent treatment of our favorite war clichés.

Patton: existential characterization of an American war hero. And of course all the really rotten movies that imitate the surface of these departures but never touch their heart. (As others have pointed out, most movies went on their dreary way despite monumental breakthroughs like *Birth of a Nation, Stagecoach,* and *Citizen Kane.* Because the reason for making the film in the first place is weak, even when they imitate techniques and attitudes they don't have the power.)

Three years later, just reminiscing a little, these come readily to mind:

Blanche comes barreling out of the kitchen, wildly waving the spatula, into the middle of shots and cops and cars and chaos, screeching hysterically as the getaway chariot makes a return sweep, bumps, jerks, jumps a curb, flings out a door and hauls her in and away.

Clyde holds up a grocery store ("Are you sure you don't have any peach pie back there?"): the butcher just misses splitting him down the middle with a cleaver. "That sombitch tried to kill me!" reports the shaken and bewildered shopper as they lurch away.

"Foggy Mountain Breakdown." The reunion with Buck, the two brothers rasslin' and pounding each other. "Whoooee!" says Buck. "Are we going to have a time!" Pause. Then, quizzically, "What'll we do?" A quiet clearing, dark, night sounds. Gradual dawning. Birds, trees, grass. A sudden pandemonium of gunfire and shattered glass. The relentless, systematic demolition of the car. Buck, a slaughtered animal, his last agonized screams piercing the fresh morning air.

"I love to spend each Sunday with you."

"This isn't mine! I ordered catsup."

Burma Shave signs flashing by.
The Grapes of Wrath squatters' encampment in dull, muted colors.
Sending out for fried chicken.
Front porches, swings, hot summer nights.
Dr. Pepper.
Old Man Moss betting C. W. for getting a tattoo.
Clyde eating an eskimo pie.
Old Man Moss carrying a little pail of hand-dipped ice cream.
Bonnie making herself a necklace of coins and singing snatches of "We're in The Money."

Like baseball—which can be enjoyed on several levels by the same person—*Bonnie and Clyde* is an American movie. In this sense: It's not something you have to do (un*ess you're really bad off). You don't have to study for it; it's home grown. Or practice. Or say polite things. You go in and you have a ball. Drink beer, if you want to. Scream and yell, if you want to. Really notice the subtlety of the game and the art of it—if you're capable of it, and if you want to. You could do that with *Bonnie and Clyde.* The audience went mad when Blanche got rescued by that rickety thirties car. They came out of the theater damned quiet. Purged. The way *Macbeth* is supposed to do, and almost never does for Americans.

The day *Time* magazine decided to criticize itself.
Time's review made the mistake of comparing the
fictional and real Bonnie and Clyde, a totally irrelevant exercise.

Drawing by Robert Schulenberg, after the style of the late Gluyas Williams

Gangster flick.

Comedy.

**The hippies inherit
the thirties.**

**Commentary
on violence.**

I am curious to discover why
a film that purportedly deals with a pair
of hayseed hold-up artists of the Thirties
has evoked such immediate and over-
whelming emotional response in 1967. Is
it merely another instance of Camp, of
going ga-ga over the garments, vehicles
and gimcracks of the Thirties, or does it
represent something more profound? *Bonnie and Clyde* has pushed all varieties of
subliminal buttons, and as a psychological
phenomenon, it cannot be explained away
simply as a well-made gangster film. The
impact of *Bonnie and Clyde* is incalculable
and the controversy it has unleashed will
be with us for years to come.
San Francisco.

Folk saga.

Western.

Keystone Kops.

Camp.

BORSALINO.

Predecessors:

1937 You Only Live Once

1948 They Live By Night

1948 Gun Crazy

1958 The Bonnie Parker Story

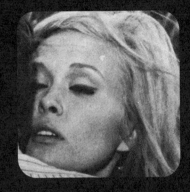

Ain't Life Grand?
Birth of a Nation (1915)
Deep Night
Shadow Waltz
Singin' in the Rain (1952).
Stage Coach (1939).
Gene Wilder?

Clyde makes his characteristic fake charmer's noises to the old mother, saying that he and Bonnie want to come and live near her; the blessedly anti-sentimental woman merely says they had better keep running. The shot of her American face is one of the best things in the picture. So is the line.
Penelope Gilliatt,
New Yorker.

A tale of bullets and blood in a strange and purposeless mingling of fact and claptrap that teeters uneasily on the brink of burlesque.
Time.

And it leaves an astonished critic wondering just what purpose Mr. Penn and Mr. Beatty think they serve with this strangely antique, sentimental claptrap.
Bosley Crowther,
New York Times.

. . . refusal fully to identify with [the protagonists] or to be merely the vehicle of their perversely romantic story.
Richard Gilman.

Eskimo Pie
Dub Taylor?
Citizen Kane (1940)

Someday they'll go down together;
They'll bury them side by side;
To few it'll be grief—
To the law a relief—
But it's death for Bonnie and Clyde.
Bonnie Parker.

The characters in *Bonnie and Clyde* are
not the stereotypes of Hollywood
gangsterism, but believable little people with believable little vanities and
ambitions—and with an abiding
faith in the traditional American
system of values as advertised from
the pulpit and the speaker's platform, in the inspirational novel and
on the silver screen.
Jay Jacobs, *The Reporter*.

At times one seems to be
entirely on the outside, wit-
nessing a clinical demon-
stration; then the filter shifts
and we are enveloped in
sudsy sentiment. Passages
are offered in an estrang-
ing, mocking slapstick, only
to merge into old-fashioned
chase melodrama and then
into the pain of real emotion and real laceration
from real bullets. The effect
is morally queasy; it leads
to charges of exploitation,
sensationalism and irre-
sponsibility. This was perhaps bound to happen, but
it may be unfair. I think Penn
wanted to make a picture
that, through poetic re-
move from the extravagance
of its incidents, would
both gratify as entertainment and instruct as fable.
It is not easy to drive that
tandem vehicle, but *Bonnie
and Clyde* comes near
enough success to make its
intention clear.
Robert Hatch, *The Nation*.

One time Bonnie's leg
was burned real bad in
a car wreck. It took $9-a-
day worth of Unguen-
tine to put on her leg.
Clyde *had* to rob places.
Besides we used to take
Bonnie pretty clothes.
They didn't go around
like a bunch of tramps.
Billie Jean Parker.

I wanted the film to
have a certain rhythm, a nervous
montage. Also, my memory of
Bonnie and Clyde was from snapshots; I didn't want a moving camera that would stay on a scene for a
long time. I wanted something more
kaleidoscopic.
Arthur Penn.

In *Bonnie and Clyde*, we don't
have a story of very strong characters. They're relatively shallow,
rather empty people as far as we
know. Nice enough, and with certain problems, but we don't have a
moral dilemma which would help us
to understand what the characters
are going through in their interior
lives. Consequently, we had to deal
more at the level of the outer side,
like the cartoon, more the outline. I
thought in terms of cartoons—each
frame changing. Here we laugh,
here we cry, here we laugh again,
and so we cut the film like that and
the images were made up like that
instead of long, fluid ones.
Arthur Penn.

Praise:
Penn's rendering
of the aridity and
emptiness of
the countryside.

The script, for
its emphasis on
Bonnie and Clyde's
urge for
recognition as
well as money.

The casual, child-
like, mindless
violence is
esthetically
correct: "carries
none of the sado-
sexual overtones
of today's repre-
sentation of
violence."

Blame:
"cute" period decor,
costumes, and music,
dull the cutting
edge of the satire.

often degenerates
into an arch attempt
to get us to giggle
along with
the gang.

What might have been
a breakthrough for
the American screen
falls back in con-
fusion at the final
barriers of self-
realization.
Richard Schickel
Life.

The Camp attitude is only possible in a person inoculated
against popular culture by education. It is spurious tolerance
based on condescension.
David Kerr, *Screen Education.*

On the edge of campiness, but
saved from full sneering superi-
ority to its material by the camera's own inventive humility, the
first half-hour proceeds with as
much visual pleasure as anything I've ever seen this year.
Richard Gilman.

Hackman, Parsons,
Pollard—marvelous.

Beatty and Dunaway: 'A'
for effort . . . They
remain movie stars.

Are you sure you don't have
any peach pie back there?
Clyde.

Psycho (1960).

Dreamsicle.

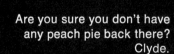

Lolita (1962).

ART HAS
NO RULES

NO R

Jules Furthman?

The Manchurian Candidate

Your advertisement's
just dandy.

. . . comic and wittily lyric moments, framed widely and moving slowly . . ., they are . . . set-pieces around a central act of intelligent imagining.

CRITICISM HAS NO RULES

ULES

We're gonna have a great old time. What'll we do?

I was up in Stockbridge, Mass., working with Arthur Penn, and he told me that he had a perfect part for me and not to take anything that fall. Estelle Parsons.

Furthman

Morocco
Shanghai Express
Only Angels Have Wings
To Have and Have Not
The Big Sleep
Rio Bravo

In *The Battleship Potemkin* (1925) Eisenstein deliberately expanded the screen time for the Odessa steps sequence. As the Cossacks march down the steps, the film cuts back and forth from the soldiers to the screaming victims, blood spilling on the steps, a woman being shot in the face, a runaway baby carriage bounding down the stairs. In reality this action would have taken only a few seconds, but Eisenstein drew it out for several minutes to a peak of horror.

It is loaded with farcical hold-ups, screaming chases in stolen getaway cars that have the antique appearance and speeded-up movement of the clumsy vehicles of the Keystone Kops.
Bosley Crowther.

The death of these two people is a foregone conclusion. It's not as if it just happened. Since you know it's going to happen, I figure you should do an abstraction of it rather than a replica of it.
Arthur Penn.

. . . a series of . . . rides in which the mad, self-generating life of the automobile in America is given a fertile choreography, Mack Sennett turned half-serious. . .
Richard Gilman.

I wanted to get the spasm of death, and so I used four cameras, each one at a different speed, 24, 48, 72 and 96, I think, and different lenses, so that I could cut to get the shock and at the same time the ballet of death. There's a moment in death when the body no longer functions, when it becomes an object and has a certain kind of detached ugly beauty. It was that aspect that I was trying to get.
Arthur Penn.

1. Criticism and creation cannot be programmed or replaced by a set of principles to be mechanically applied.

2. We should analyze our reasons for disliking a particular film and see how far we agree in reasoning; and we should see whether we dislike other films for the same reasons.

3. Film criticism should make clear-cut statements about the way the film works and the effects it has. The reader should be able to test these for himself when he sees the film.

4. Principles must be tentative canons subject to revision in the light of criticism.
Ian Jarrie, *Film Quarterly.*

I never thought about being well-known . . . I'd never been interviewed before I was nominated for Blanche . . . I always thought of being part of a company . . . maybe doing ensemble work. Now it's a little frightening. I do feel uncomfortable.
Estelle Parsons.

After he turned in a brilliant performance in the movie *Five Card Stud*, the veteran director Henry Hathaway called him aside. "Denver," he said, "where have you been all these years?" Pyle shrugged. "Around," he replied. "I've been around."

If *Bonnie and Clyde* had been handled cinematically as tragedy, it might have been a great film. The movie's changing color values and camera speeds would have given the audience the catharsis that is derived from great dramatic works. But the director took a tragic stance without giving us a tragedy. The film slams the audience around until one walks out of the theater feeling bashed in. It is a torture-some emotional experience that leaves one stunned and dissatisfied —some young people have gone back to see it as many as twenty times. But if these same young people met a bona fide tragedy they would be satisfied with less exposure. They would want to analyze and reflect upon rather than re-experience the film. It seems, then, that the director's problem was the same as that encountered when characters in a Broadway musical comedy-drama striving for success have to die or be killed. The "unpleasantness" is rushed by quickly, more production values— lights, costumes, sets—are marshaled on the stage, and a comic character comes immediately to insure that the audience will not have to linger over feelings that might blemish the evening. Thus, Arthur Penn's use of fine artistic devices become, in the context in which he places them, cinematic shenanigans. When used to bail him out of a reality that might be unpleasant, they "put the lie" to his film and expose it as a bag of tawdry tricks.
Robert Steele, *The Catholic World.*

"I would have done Bonnie for nothing. For my picture with Jerry, I'm getting a low salary and a percentage. For *Bonnie and Clyde* I was paid $35,000." It was more for her next film. *The Thomas Crown Affair* with Steve McQueen. But unless she is participating in the profits, all future films have a price tag of between $400,000 and $500,000.

Henry Hathaway?

ROBERT WISE WILLIAM WYLER CESARE ZAVATTINI RENÉ CLAIR
RICHARD LESTER JOSEPH LOSEY ERNST LUBITSCH BILLY WILDER
ROBERT BRESSON LUIS BUÑUEL GRIGORI CHUKRAI DAVID LEAN
CAROL REED KAREL REISZ JEAN RENOIR BERNARDO BERTOLUCCI
FELLINI ROBERT FLAHERTY VSEVOLOD PUDOVKIN SATYAJIT RAY
ERIC VON STROHEIM BLAKE EDWARDS SERGEI EISENSTEIN FEDERICO
JOHN HUSTON HIROSHI INAGAKI ELIA KAZAN GEORGE STEVENS
VITTORIO DE SICA JOSEF VON STERNBERG ALFRED HITCHCOCK
DAVID WARK GRIFFITH HOWARD HAWKS JOHN SCHLESINGER

1. For myself, the theme is and remains the fundamental in all film-making. The form must submit to it . . . Another thing that I admire so much in *The Lady with the Little Dog* is that not an ounce of sentimentality is to be found in the film.

2. The Names to conjure with are Ovid, Rabelais and Dickens rather than useless comparisons with other directors, such as Antonioni or De Sica, who are only interested in domestic drama.

3. You get the feeling that _____ can 'play' film the way Bach must have played the organ at the end of his life.
Jean–Luc Godard.

4. _____, claustrophobia of the spirit.
Philip Crick.

5. His most frequently recurring theme is the tragedy and peculiar glory of defeat.
Peter Bogdanovich.

6. His moral universe rests on the assumption that guilt is universal.
John Howard Lawson.

7. The rewards of life are gained in the process of seeking a goal, not in actual attainment.

8. When he looks through a camera lens he sees like nobody else in the world . . . He paints on celluloid.
Jose Ferrer.

9. Trained as a painter, he treats the motion picture medium with as much importance as poetry or painting. But instead of placing an intensely personal viewpoint upon life and contemporary problems he utilized the

precept of his instructor Nandalai Bose. "Draw a tree, but not in Western fashion. Not from the top downwards. A tree grows up not down." He states that this is basic to his belief—"reverence for life, for organic growth."

10. The William Blake of cinema.
Daniel Millar.

11. Harry Carey tutored me in the early years, sort of brought me along, and the only thing I always had was an eye for composition—I don't know where I got it—and that's all I did have.

12. I make movies in the same way that I talk to people whether it's a friend, a girl, a priest or anyone: to seek some clarification.

13. The truth of our daily lives is neither mechanical, conventional nor artificial, as stories generally are, and if films are made that way they will show it. The rhythm of life is not made up of one steady beat; it is, instead, a rhythm that is sometimes fast, sometimes slow: it remains motionless for a while, then at the next moment it starts spinning around. . . . The important thing is this: that our acts, our gestures, our words are nothing more than the consequences of our own personal situation in relation to the world around us.

Asked which American directors appealed to him most, Orson Welles replied, ". . . the old masters. By which I mean John Ford, John Ford and John Ford. . . . With Ford at his best you feel that the movie has lived and breathed the real world."

Answers:

1. Ingmar Bergman.
2. Federico Fellini.
3. Luis Buñuel.
4. Ingmar Bergman.
5. John Ford.
6. Alfred Hitchcock.
7. John Huston.
8. John Huston.
9. Satyajit Ray.
10. Luis Buñuel.
11. John Ford.
12. Federico Fellini.
13. Michelangelo Antonioni.

TEN

The moments I remember best are these:
Grey soldiers, lightning-writ, on vast retreats
Roofs, lurching bridges, maid in maddened hands
Relentless boots on steps, screams, sabres, fright
The judge's lips, the saint's tear falling true
Bleak Aran's rocks lashed by cascading spray
Prince-wakened princess, once upon a day
Marmorial clutching, clanging Xanadu
On Crispin's feast, bows' twang and arrows' flight
Black rider imaged in reflecting sands
Remembered childhood, scrubbed and swathed in sheets.
At such times eye leaps, pulse stops, senses freeze.
Owen Lee.

> If you want
> anything just whistle.

The Cocoanuts
The Graduate
Potemkin
Riverrun
African Queen

> Some like
> it hot.

Name That Flick:
Bogie was visibly shaken. "You're not gonna really put those damn things on me, are you, John?"
"Absolutely," said Huston. "I want you to shudder as you burn each of them off with the tip of your cigarette. Now, kid, you just wouldn't shudder if the leeches were phony."
Bogart shuddered—and this scene was among the most memorable in the film.

. . .a film should leave you not only with a story which had its beginning, middle and ending, but it should leave you with some tactile sensations. In this new film, I would like people to go out remembering the color of water, the texture of rocks and all those things. John Korty.

Question: Do you feel that the addition of motion to photography made the task of the artist any easier?
Von Sternberg: Actually, motion multiplies the hazards that attend and impede creative effort. Let me give you a somewhat crass example, Da Vinci's "Mona Lisa" would become ridiculous were she so made that she could raise or lower an eyebrow.

THAT IS, AFTER ALL
WHAT REMAINS OF ALL
FILMS—THESE SEPARATE
IMAGES, ALIVE IN THE
MIND LONG AFTER THE
FILM ITSELF MAY BE
FORGOTTEN.
Donald Richie

Stella.

Name That Flick:

1.

If this scene is trying once, imagine what it must have been for the Marx Brothers, who not only performed it nightly for two years, but who had to repeat it twenty-seven times in the filming because the crackling of the blueprints drowned out the dialogue. Finally the director hit on the idea of soaking the blueprints in water. The twenty-eighth take was quiet and kept.
The Marx Brothers at the Movies.

2.

John Gilbert is maddened when Dane ventures into no-man's land and is killed. "They got him! They got him, God damn their souls!" he cries, stalking forth to battle. He wounds an advancing German and crawls into a shell hole with him, holding a bayonet to the enemy's neck. But Gilbert is overcome with compassion and cannot kill him. He lights a cigarette for the German, who then dies. Gilbert then smokes the cigarette himself.
Bob Thomas.

Playing dangerously precipitates positions with richer possibilities of invention.

Frankly my dear,
I don't give a damn.

You skinny old maid.

Cool Hand Luke
A Streetcar Named Desire
Bonnie and Clyde
Gone With the Wind

These images have remained alive in *your* mind:

1.
2.
3.
4.
5.
6.
7.

I too once met a girl in Central Park, but it is not much to remember. What I remember is the time John Wayne killed three men with a carbine as he was falling to the dusty street in *Stage Coach*, and the time the kitten found Orson Welles in the doorway in *The Third Man.*
Walker Percy,
The Moviegoer.

Bogart: I came to Casablanca to take the waters.
Claude Rains: There are no waters in Casablanca.
Bogart: I was misinformed.

What are the 70's clichés?
1. Youth cult?
2. Your own thing?
3. jump cut?
4.
5.
6.
7.
8.
9.
10.

"Just think, Ellen. Soon we'll be
seeing this in three dimensions."

Ed Emshwiller: *Body Works*, images
flashed on live dancers.

Stan Vanderbeek: *The Movie-Drone*,
spectator lies on floor while stored
images flash over hemispheric dome.

John Whitney and Sons: Automated and
computerized camera and animation
stand; quick and precise geometric
animated designs.

You are in your offiice. The setting bores
you. You dial a number on your desk console
and spend the rest of the day working in
Tahiti or Madrid or Paris, everything
authentic to the minutest detail. What a
movie!

Expo 67

Don Levy: *Sources of Energy*,
Multiple images on three
screens.

National Film Board of Canada:
Five screens, 12 x 16, arranged in a cross, different
images on one or all of the five screens.

The Province of Ontario: *A Place
to Stand,*
A screen three stories high
by six stories wide. Multiple
images of all shapes and sizes
printed on one 70mm film for
single-projector screening.

Multiple screens force the
viewer to be selective and
thus increase his involvement.

The Sound of Music

Truly three-dimensional movies are already
demonstrable through holograms made possible
by laser beams. Holograms store visual
information in a manner analogous to the
storing of music on a phonograph disc.
The laser beams feel their way in and about
an object and the light-wave information is
recorded on film. It is now possible to
project ordinary white light through the
film and duplicate the recorded object or
setting visually. One can look under it,
over it, even inside it.
What's more, any portion of a hologram contains all of the code information needed
to reproduce the complete image. Any piece
will show the whole scene. Instead of
thousands of feet of celluloid, one could
store a whole movie in a matchbox.

The Big Parade (1925).
In 1969 Roger Ferragallo described plans for development of a Total Environ-
ment Learning Laboratory (TELL) or "Sensorium" at Laney College in Oakland,
California. The console has three main groups of functions:

1. Atmospheres: involves the aromatic scale (the seven primary odors); tactile-
floor resonation; wind and temperature controls; chromatic light, allowing for
color saturation within the TELL space; strobe control, which will allow for pulsing
effects to be automatically or manually articulated with sound.

2. Aural: vortex sound involving variable speed, radially directed sound; line and
sector control, providing for point-reference sound as well as moving fields of sound.

3. Visual: multiple slide and cinematic images in a 360 degree field; panoramic
two-dimensional and stereo projected imagery; hemispheric projection.

The environment is housed inside a sixty-foot geodesic dome. This dome encloses
a student space platform that hydraulically lifts, turns, tilts and vibrates.
Around this platform are arranged sixteen nine-foot rear-projection screens.
And above will be hung a forty-five foot planetarium-screen umbrella.

Drugs or LSD are sense-impressive,

and so is electronic stimulus to the brain, but until it is possible to control them they will remain ouside art (except conceivably as a stimulus to the imagination). We might imagine, however, drugs packaged as pills whose successive layers dissolve in our stomach and cause predetermined hallucinatory experiences, or prerecorded stimulus tracks which can be played directly into our brains. "Feelies" are fantastic, but we cannot rule them out as potential art experiences. Robert E. Mueller.

Ray Craig, a 28 year old engineer-filmmaker, devoted a year and one-half to transforming a school bus into the dynamic flagship of MOVIMOBILES, INC.

This versatile facility is equipped for light shows, slide projections, small band concerts and one man shows such as folk-singers and poets.

1. Air-cooled 4,000 watt generator
2. Generator controls
3. Alternating set of 8mm, Super 8mm or 16mm projectors
4. Stereo sound system and indoor-outdoor public address system
5. Two-way radio

6. Special light show equipment and controls
7. Seating for 5 across; total of 34–40 passengers
8. Pillow-floor seating
9. Air vents
10. Exit
11. Roll-down screen

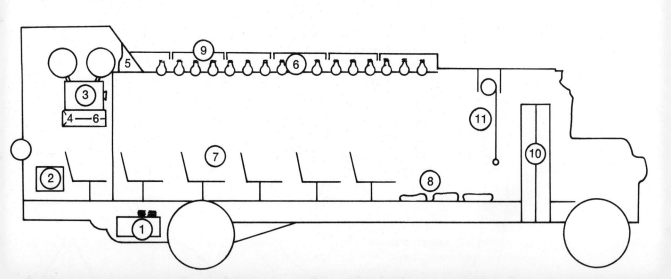

It is for the heart to suggest our problems; it is for the intellect to solve them. . . . The position for which the intellect is primarily adapted is to be the servant of the social sympathies. Comte.

moon-full breasts
Potemkin
pattern recognition
triptych
the sound envelope
a cinematic *Tristram Shandy*
film as environment
the frame effect
McLuhan
the shape of a landscape painting
an old whore
close-ups
John Korty
bird song
persistence of vision
artistic instrument
Sjöman
filmic time
a lens is soulless
Warhol
Andy Hardy
filmic space
count the cuts
earlids
episodic structure
like a party
mosaic structure
culture shock
censorship
film as literature
emotionless distance from subject
film as theater
pretending to be fake
W. C. Fields
Jockey shorts
un-clichéd
it's only a movie
language of the eye?
film as labyrinth
the right illusion
Olympus
Eisenstein
Einstein

asteroids
Dub Taylor
cutting tone
like a sonata
a coolly neutral eye
multiple perspective
camera angle
no cinema vérité
allowable forms
to see a perfume
Griffith
Clyde Beatty
Flatt and Scruggs
Truffaut
Egyptian serial painting
"Madam, do not flatter yourself; it is hanging out."
Lana Turner Has Collapsed
American Indian Association
the sound of sound
Norman Mailer
compilation
like circus or variety
Mae West
the sound of silence
like architecture
tones of grey
"Nude on a Cushion"
close-ups reveal soul
Bruce Conner
establishing shots
'The Feelies'
Orson Welles
David
shot heard round the world
chewing gum for the eyes
whorehouse décor
theatrical films
temple of shades
Mother
Intolerance
painting
psychological
metaphor
theory
Art is anything you can get away with
blue movies
charge $3.00
frankly pornographic
censorship
criticism
It's Only a Movie

Lenny Bruce
The Independent Filmmaker's Handbook
Nafkeh
A pyramid to sight the stars by
Lenny Lipton
observ-o-scope
most daring
the feel of film
film and the other arts
film in the cultural setting
film criticism
Thalberg
Marx Brothers
familiar strangers
Jules Furthman
Sonnet—To Science
Pudovkin
Like a private diary
blue movies
the frame effect
independent filmmakers
underground films
experimentalists
Sidney Greenstreet Blues
haiku
John Cassavetes
John Howard Lawson
the interior landscape
dissolves
fades
cutting tone
Ingmar Bergman
Stella!
don't blink
Dick 'n Pat
Bosley Crowther
movimobile
nudity
Titian in black and white
George Bernard Shaw
It's Only a Movie
George Arliss
Montage is conflict
Reel name game
pattern recognition
Chester Snavely
Film Quarterly
Mary Pohland

Richard Schickel
Renata Adler
The Unicorn in the Garden
Antonioni
It's Only a Movie
tracking
panning
splicing
Don Siegel
cinema vérité
Jean Renoir
great movie clichés
yin and yang
It's Only a Movie
Greer Garson with fur
Chaplin
To discover the obvious reality
Gone With the Wind
Like writing history with lightning
Judith Crist
I'm only interested in the superficial
Louis Malle
Sex
Art Hoppe
Dr. Pepper
Louis B. Mayer
Robert Bresson
Tanny slippers
Grendel
Cinderella
It's Only a Movie
no objective document
Stephanie
Give us a moviekiss
Let go of my hand
No, not you, you!
Anne Baxter's grandfather
Flicker
We are such stuff as dreams are made on . . .
Aspersia
Anything, anything can go
How can I get to Carnegie Hall?
Oh, gosh, what a marvelous guide to motels
practice
Black and white are colors, too
You bet your ass, Shah!
Ain't life grand?
It's Only a Movie

Literary Permissions.

3, from *The Aging Ghost* by James Crenner, reprinted by permission of The Golden Quill Press, Francestown, New Hampshire, 1964.

5, 8, 22, 54, 55, 63, 72, 82, 89, 93, 158 and 159, from *Hitchcock* by François Truffaut, copyright © 1967 by François Truffaut, reprinted by permission of Simon & Schuster, Inc., and A. D. Peters & Company.

6, 8, 24, 38, 48, 61, 93, 137, 139 and 140, from John Lahr's interview with Vilgot Sjöman in *Evergreen Review*, July, 1968, copyright © 1968 by Grove Press, Inc., published by Grove Press, Inc.

9, 82, 84 and 122, from *Novels into Film* by George Bluestone, copyright © 1957 by The Johns Hopkins Press, reprinted by permission of the publishers.

12, 22, 29 and 106, from Gene Youngblood in the *Los Angeles Free Press*, October 25, 1968, reprinted by permission of the author.

15, from Terrence O'Flaherty in *The San Francisco Chronicle*, 1968, reprinted by permission of the author.

18, 36, 63, 74, 76 and 85, from "Looking Backward" by Ernest Callenbach, copyright © 1968 by The Regents of the University of California, reprinted from *Film Quarterly*, Vol. XXII, No. 1, pp. 1–10, by permission of The Regents.

25, 37, 51, 60, 64, 71, 76, 77, 93, 94–95, 103 and 112, from *The Japanese Film* by Donald Richie, reprinted by permission of the publisher, Charles E. Tuttle Co., Inc.

25, 119, 126, 133 and 143, from *The Moviegoer* by Walker Percy, copyright © 1960, 1961 by Walker Percy, reprinted by permission of Alfred A. Knopf, Inc., and McIntosh and Otis, Inc.

25, from "Woman Shoots Andy" in *The San Francisco Chronicle*, June 4, 1968, reprinted by permission of The Associated Press.

30–32, 58, 89, 90 and 148, from "An Interview with John Korty," reprinted by permission of John Korty.

33, from "The Critic's Table" in "Stanton Delaplane's Postcard from San Francisco," *The San Francisco Chronicle*, March, 1968, reprinted by permission of the author.

34, poem from *An Untitled Book of Mandalas and Poems* by Michael McClure and Bruce Conner, copyright © 1966 by Michael McClure, reprinted by permission of The Sterling Lord Agency and the poet, Michael McClure.

36 and 67, from an article by Stephen Farber in *Film Quarterly*, copyright © 1968 by The Regents of the University of California, reprinted from *Film Quarterly*, Vol. XXII, No. 1, pp. 67–70, by permission of The Regents and the author.

40, 88 and 159, from *The Unimportance of Being Oscar* by Oscar Levant, copyright © 1968 by Oscar Levant, reprinted by permission of G. P. Putnam's Sons.

41, "The Movie House" by John Updike, from *Telephone Poles and Other Poems*, reprinted by permission of Alfred A. Knopf, Inc., and Andre Deutsch Limited.

49 and 128, from *The Liveliest Art* by Arthur Knight, copyright © 1959 by Ment. NAL, reprinted by permission of The Macmillan Company.

48 and 61, from *I Am Curious (Yellow)* by Vilgot Sjöman, copyright © 1968 by Grove Press, Inc., published by Grove Press, Inc., reprinted by permission of the publisher.

53, 97, 127, 140 and 142, from "Movie-Going" in *Movie-Going* by John Hollander, copyright © 1960 by John Hollander, reprinted by permission of Atheneum Publishers.

55, "Pierrot le Foux" by Adrienne Rich, reprinted by permission of the poet.

58, "Readings of History (I), The Evil Eye" from *Snapshots of a Daughter-in-Law*, by Adrienne Rich, copyright © 1956, 1957, 1958, 1959, 1960, 1961, 1962, 1963 and 1967, by Adrienne Rich, reprinted by permission of W. W. Norton & Company and Chatto & Windus Ltd.

62, from *Brave New World* by Aldous Huxley, pp. 198–201 (hardbound edition), copyright 1932 and 1960 by Aldous Huxley, reprinted by permission of Harper & Row, Publishers, Chatto & Windus Ltd. and Mrs. Laura Huxley.

63, 64, 65 and 68, from *A Grammar of the Film* by Raymond Spottiswoode, reprinted by permission of Faber and Faber Ltd.

65 and 78, "In the Middle" and "To My Friends" by Stephen Berg, from *The Queen's Triangle and Other Poems*, copyright © 1970 by Stephen Berg, reprinted by permission of Bobbs-Merrill Co., Inc., Publishers, and the poet.

66, coyright © 1940 James Thurber and copyright © 1968 Helen Thurber, from *Fables for Our Time*, published by Harper and Row, New York, originally printed in *The New Yorker*, also appeared in *Vintage Thurber* by James Thurber, copyright © 1963 by Hamish Hamilton, Ltd., London, reprinted by permission of Helen Thurber and Hamish Hamilton, Ltd.

70, "Flicker" by Fred Moeller, reprinted by permission of the poet.

75, "Cartoon" by John Stevens Wade, copyright © 1961 by The Regents of the University of California, reprinted from *Film Quarterly*, Vol. XIV, No. 4, p. 4, by permission of The Regents and the artist.

76, haiku by Kyokusui from *Japanese Haiku*, translated by Peter Beilenson, reprinted by permission of The Peter Pauper Press.

77, haiku by Buson from *An Introduction to Haiku* by Harold G. Henderson, copyright © 1958 by Harold G. Henderson, reprinted by permission of Doubleday & Company, Inc.

77, haiku by Basho from *An Introduction to Haiku* by Harold G. Henderson, copyright © 1958 by Harold G. Henderson, reprinted by permission of Doubleday & Company, Inc.

85, from "The Pathetics" by Florence Keady, copyright © 1924 by Harper's Magazine, Inc., reprinted from the September, 1924 issue of *Harper's Magazine*.

87, 106 and 123, from *Seen Any Good Movies Lately?* by William K. Zinsser, copyright © 1958 by William K. Zinsser, reprinted by permission of Doubleday & Company, Inc., and the author.

91–92, from *Little Me* by Patrick Dennis, with photographs by Chris Alexander, copyright © 1961 by Lancelot Leopard, Ltd., used by permission of E. P. Dutton & Co., Inc.

93, from an interview with Judith Crist by David Paletz in *Film Quarterly*, copyright © 1969 by The Regents of the University of California, reprinted from *Film Quarterly*, Vol. XXII, No. 3, pp. 27–36, by permission of The Regents and the author.

100–103, from "Yes, We Have No Ritchard" by Bruce Jay Friedman in *Fantasy and Science Fiction*, copyright © 1960 by Bruce Jay Friedman, reprinted by permission of Robert Lantz-Candida Donadio Literary Agency, Inc.

103, reprinted by permission of The World Publishing Company and

W. H. Allen & Company from *Do You Sleep in the Nude?* by Rex Reed, an NAL Book, copyright © 1968 by Rex Reed.

103, from an article by John Sunier in *Canyon Cinema News*, by permission of the author.

106, "Lana Turner Has collapsed!" by Frank O'Hara in *Lunch Poems*, copyright © 1964 by Frank O'Hara, reprinted by permission of City Lights Books.

107, from "Beowulf" in *Old English Poetry* by J. Duncan Spaeth, copyright 1921 by Princeton University Press, reprinted by permission of Princeton University Press.

79, from *Time*, March 21, 1969, reprinted by permission of *Time*, copyright © 1969, Time, Inc.

113, from *Time*, November 15, 1968, reprinted by permission of *Time*, copyright © 1968, Time, Inc.

113, "Ah, How Complete Are the Uses of Publicity" by Selma Raskin, copyright © 1964 by The Regents of the University of California, reprinted from *Film Quarterly*, Vol. XVII, No. 2, p. 2, by permission of The Regents.

114, from *Myra Breckenridge* by Gore Vidal, copyright © 1968 by Gore Vidal, reprinted by permission of Little, Brown and Co. and Anthony Blond Ltd., London.

120, "The Bride of Frankenstein" by Edward Field, from *Variety Photoplays*, copyright © 1967 by Edward Field, reprinted by permission of Grove Press, Inc.

121, from an article by John A. Barsness, copyright © 1967 by The Regents of the University of California, reprinted from *Film Quarterly*, Vol. 21, No. 1, by permission of The Regents and the author.

122 and 151, from "Andy Warhol" by Elenore Lester, copyright © 1968 by The Hearst Corporation, all rights reserved.

121 and 126, from "Sunday Thoughts" by Eric Hoffer, reprinted by permission of Eric Hoffer from *The San Francisco Chronicle*, April 14, 1968.

125, 135 and 158, from *The Studio* by John Gregory Dunne, copyright © 1969 by Farrar, Straus, & Giroux, Inc. reprinted by permission of Farrar, Straus & Giroux, Inc., and W. H. Allen & Co., Ltd.

129, from *John Huston, King Rebel* by William F. Nolan, copyright © 1965 by William F. Nolan, used by permission of the publisher, Sherbourne Press, Inc.

130-31, from "Ghost Teachers of TV" by Rosalyn L. Switzen, copyright © 1968 by Triangle Publications, Inc., reprinted from *TV Guide* ® with permission.

130, from "For 36.31 at Century 21" by Jay Marchus, reprinted by permission of the poet.

136-37, from "Irving Fishman Carries a Big Stick and He Swings It Too" by Geoffrey Wolff in *The San Francisco Chronicle*, copyright © 1968 by the Times-Post Service, reprinted by permission of the Times-Post Service.

126 and 139, from "Is Sex Old-Fashioned?" by Art Hoppe in *The San Francisco Chronicle*, September 15, 1968, copyright © 1968 by Art Hoppe, reprinted by permission of the author.

134, 158 and 183, from *The Marx Brothers at the Movies* by Paul D. Zimmerman and Burt Goldblatt, copyright © 1968 by Paul D. Zimmerman and Burt Goldblatt, reprinted by permission of G. P. Putnam's Sons and Robert P. Mills.

141, "All Night Burlesque" by Thom Gunn, copyright © 1960 by The Regents of the University of California, reprinted from *Film Quarterly*, Vol. XIII, No. 3, p. 35, by permis-

sion of The Regents and the author.

142, from *The New Yorker*, August 31, 1968, copyright © 1968 by The New Yorker Magazine, Inc., reprinted by permission.

144, "The Scene Pope John Wouldn't Let Fellini Film" by Dan Georgakas, reprinted by permission of the poet.

145-46, from "Aspersia, or The Sad Story of an Unhappy Little Girl" by Donald Hall, in the *Carleton Miscellany*, copyright by Carleton College, reprinted by permission of Carleton College.

146-47, from "Note for Academic Art Criticism" by Bruce Baillie in *Canyon Cinema News*, May, 1967, reprinted by permission of the author.

65 and 148, from "Beatty Raps" by an *Eye* Magazine interviewer, copyright © 1968 by The Hearst Corporation, all rights reserved.

150, "Film-Festival-Film-Flophouses" by Larry Booth, copyright © 1969 by Larry Booth, reprinted by permission of the poet.

152, from an interview with P. Adams Sitney by Harry Smith in *Film Culture*, Summer, 1965, reprinted by permission of *Film Culture*.

152, from "Notes for The Devil is Dead" in *The New American Cinema* by Gregory Battcock, reprinted by permission of Carl Linder.

"Statement" by Carl Linder, reprinted by permission of Carl Linder.

164, from *The Reporter*, October 5, 1967 by Jay Jacobs, reprinted by permission of the author.

164 and 178, from an article by Bosley Crowther in *The New York Times*, August 14, 1967, copyright © 1967 by The New York Times Company, reprinted by permission.

166, from "The Movies Will Save Themselves" by David Newman and Robert Benton in *Esquire Magazine*, October, 1968, copyright © 1968 by Esquire, Inc., reprinted by permission of *Esquire Magazine*.

182, "Ten" by Owen Lee, copyright © 1968 by The Regents of the University of California, reprinted from *Film Quarterly*, Vol. XXI, No. 4, p. 13, by permission of The Regents and the author.

Photo and Art Permissions.

i–iii, Maurice Chevalier: "Paramount on Parade," courtesy of Universal Pictures.

6, Orson Welles: a scene from the motion picture "The Lady from Shanghai," a Columbia Picture copyright © 1948 Columbia Pictures Industries, Inc.

12, Marilyn Monroe: Dennis Stock, Magnum Photos, Inc.

13, Alfred Hitchcock: Elliott Erwitt, Magnum Photos, Inc.

16, George Raft: "It Had to Happen," courtesy of Twentieth Century Fox Film Corporation, copyright © 1936 by Twentieth Century Fox Film Corporation, all rights reserved.

20, Spider and fly: "The Living Desert," copyright © 1953 Walt Disney Productions.

21, Female nude: Ruth Bernhard.

22 and 132, Jackie Curtis: copyright © Jack Mitchell.

25, Andy Warhol: Bill Cogan.

26, Cartoon: drawing by Chas. Addams, copyright © 1946 The New Yorker Magazine, Inc.

28, Movie schedule: *San Francisco Chronicle*.

29, Soup label: courtesy of Campbell Soup Company.

29, The Hardy family: "The Hardys Ride High," Metro–Goldwin–Mayer Inc.

30, Scenes being shot: "Riverrun,"

Columbia Pictures Industries, Inc.

31, Peter Bonerz: "Funnyman," Korty Films.

32, Scenes being shot: "Crazy Quilt," Korty Films.

34, Bruce Connor: printed by permission of Bruce Connor.

37, Scene from: "Ugetsu," distributed by Janus Films.

40, 109 and 143, The Marx Brothers: "Duck Soup," courtesy of Universal Pictures.

43, Eternal Idol: Rodin, permission S.P.A.D.E.M. 1970 by French Reproduction Rights, Inc.

44 and 45, Nude on a cushion: Amadeo Modigliani, Collection Gianni Mattioli, Milan, Italy.

47 and 83 David: Michelangelo, Art Reference Bureau Inc.

48, Xeroxed nude: Titian, Soprintendenza Alle Gallerie, Cabinetto Fotografico, Florence, Italy.

49, "I Am Curious (Yellow)": Grove Press Evergreen Films, copyright © 1968 by Grove Press, Inc., published by Grove Press, Inc.

50, Will Hindle: printed by permission of Will Hindle; Larry Jordan: Printed by permission of Larry Jordan; Carl Linder: printed by permission of Carl Linder; Bruce Baillie: printed by permission of Bruce Baillie.

54, Female nude: Ruth Bernhard.

57, Carl Linder: printed by permission of Carl Linder, "Overflow:" Carl Linder Films; "Vampira: The Passion of:" Carl Linder Films.

58, Laurel and Hardy: "Four Clowns," Twentieth Century Fox Film Corporation.

59 and 77, Michael Caine: "Deadfall," courtesy of Twentieth Century Fox Film Corporation, copyright © 1968 by Salamander Film Productions Ltd., all rights reserved.

61, Female nude: Ruth Bernhard.

63, François Truffaut: Epoque Ltd. of London.

66, Drawing: copyright © 1940 James Thurber, copyright © 1968 Helen Thurber, from *Fables For Our Time*, published by Harper and Row, New York, and from *Vintage Thurber* by James Thurber, copyright © 1963 Hamish Hamilton, London, originally printed in *The New Yorker*.

72 and 75, Cartoon: Atlas, copyright © Punch, London.

86, D. W. Griffith: Culver Pictures Inc.

88, W. C. Fields: "The Man on the Flying Trapeze," courtesy of Universal Pictures.

90, Sergei Eisenstein: The Bettmann Archive Inc.

92, W. C. Fields: "The Man on the Flying Trapeze," courtesy of Universal Pictures.

95, Samurai: "Seven Samurai," The Museum of Modern Art film stills archive, copyright © Toho Productions.

96, Female nude: Ruth Bernhard.

98, Gene Wilder: "The Producers," from the motion picture "The Producers" copyright © 1967 by Avco Embassy Pictures Corp.

99 and 127, Rex Reason, Faith Domerque, "This Island Earth," courtesy of Universal Pictures.

100, 101 and 143, "Ebb Tide:" courtesy of Universal Pictures.

106 and 107, "Birth of a Nation:" Culver Pictures Inc.

110, Bela Lugosi: "Murders in the Rue Morgue," courtesy of Universal Pictures.

111, Cartoon: Edward Frascino, copyright © 1969 Saturday Review, Inc.

112, 121 and 143, Chuck Connors, Kamala Devi: "Geronimo," a Levy-Gardner-Laven production released through United Artists Corporation, permission Chuck Connors and Kamala Devi.

113, Cover: printed by permission of Mad Magazine, copyright © 1968 E. C. Publications, Inc.

115, Letter: owned by The Henry Ford Museum, Dearborn, Michigan.

115 and 143, Advertisement: *Music Box*.

117 and 143, Albert Einstein: The Bettmann Archive Inc.

117 and 143, "Birth of a Nation:" Culver Pictures Inc.

118, "The Deadly Mantis:" courtesy of Universal Pictures.

119, W. C. Fields: "The Man on the Flying Trapeze," courtesy of Universal Pictures.

120 and 143, Doris Day: "Midnight Lace," courtesy of Universal Pictures.

123 and 124, Cartoon: copyright © Jules Feiffer, courtesy Publishers-Hall Syndicate.

125, Cartoon: Scott Taber, reprinted from *TV Guide* ® with permission, copyright © 1968 by Triangle Publications, Inc.

127, Walter Brennan, Jack Gilford, Jim Hutton: a scene from the motion picture "Who's Minding the Mint?," a Columbia picture, copyright © 1967 Columbia Pictures Industries, Inc.; Richard Lane, Rudy Vallee, Alan Jenkins: a scene from the motion picture "Time Out for Rhythm," a Columbia picture, copyright © 1941 Columbia Pictures Industries, Inc.

134, "The Man from the Alamo:" courtesy of Universal Pictures.

135, Jack Benny: The Bettmann Archive Inc.

137, Cartoon: Miss Peach, by Mell Lazarus, courtesy Publishers-Hall Syndicate.

138, Joe Dallesandro: copyright © Jack Mitchell.

146, Cartoon: reproduced by special permission of *Playboy Magazine*, copyright © 1968 by HMH Publishing Co., Inc.

147, Cartoon: copyright © Jules Feiffer, courtesy Publishers-Hall Syndicate.

155, Allen Danian: production of "Daisy Chain," Carl Linder Films.

155, Carl Linder: production of "Daisy Chain," Carl Linder Films.

155, Hand: "FFFTCM," Will Hindle.

155, Face: "Chinese Firedrill," Will Hindle.

155, Larry Jordan: permission of Larry Jordan.

155, Bruce Baillie: "Quick Billy," Bruce Baillie.

155, Head and butterflies: "Duo Concertantes," Larry Jordan.

157, Bruce Connor: permission of Bruce Connor.

163, Cartoon: Claude Smith, reprinted from *TV Guide* ® with permission, copyright © 1968 by Triangle Publications, Inc.

170, Drawing: Robert Schulenberg, reprinted by permission of *Esquire Magazine*, copyright © 1968 by Esquire, Inc.

171, Faye Dunaway, Warren Beatty: "Bonnie & Clyde," from the motion picture "Bonnie & Clyde," copyright © 1967 by Warner Bros.-Seven Arts, Inc.

172, Feet: Gene Hackman, Estelle Parsons, Warren Beatty, Faye Dunaway

175, Michael Pollard: "Bonnie and Clyde," from the motion picture "Bonnie & Clyde," copyright © 1967 by Warner Bros.-Seven Arts, Inc.

178, Auto and policeman: "Bonnie and Clyde," from the motion picture "Bonnie & Clyde," copyright © 1967 by Warner Bros.-Seven Arts, Inc.

184, Cartoon: Lee Lorenz, reprinted from *TV Guide* ® with permission, copyright © 1968 by Triangle Publications, Inc.

185, Movimobile: used by permission of Ray Craig, Movimobiles, Inc.